Moving Bodies
Nonverbal Communication
in Social Relationships

Moving Bodies
Nonverbal Communication in Social Relationships

Marianne LaFrance
Boston College

Clara Mayo
Boston University

Brooks/Cole Publishing Company
Monterey, California
A Division of Wadsworth Publishing Company, Inc.

Consulting Editor: Lawrence S. Wrightsman, University of Kansas

Printed in the United States of America

10 9 8 7 6 5 4 3 2 1

Library of Congress Cataloging in Publication Data

LaFrance, Marianne, 1947–
    Moving bodies.

    Bibliography: p. 195
    Includes index.
    1. Nonverbal communication.   I. Mayo, Clara Alexandra Weiss, 1931–
joint author. II. Title.
BF637.C45L33   152.3′84   77-13569
ISBN 0-8185-0259-2

Acquisition Editor: *William H. Hicks*
Production Editor: *Fiorella Ljunggren*
Interior Design: *Jamie Brooks*
Cover Design: *Alan May*
Photographs: *Mikki Ehrenfeld*
Typesetting: *Central Graphics, San Diego, California*

For our very "verbal" friends

Preface

Our instincts tell us that there's more to human communication than words. We know that people use their whole bodies and the full range of their voices to communicate. This book is designed to articulate this knowledge and to review the growing field known as nonverbal communication—a field that, especially in the last 15 years, has seen an enormous amount of research.

A little less than a decade ago, the first author came to the second author to propose doing research in nonverbal communication. Initially unconvinced, the second author argued for the priority of the verbal means of expression. That discussion marked the beginning of an ongoing series of lively—verbal and nonverbal—debates between the two of us. What in the long run proved convincing to the second author was not just *what* points the first author was making but *how* she was making them. Communication is a two-way process, so the influence worked both ways. It became clearer to us that we wanted not only to do our own research in nonverbal communication but also to survey the research done by others in this emerging field. So we began to collaborate on research, teaching, and consulting in nonverbal communication. This book synthesizes what we've learned from our efforts.

The organization of *Moving Bodies* differs markedly from that of other books on this topic. Instead of being primarily descriptive, this text develops a conceptual framework that allows for explanation and interpretation. Instead of taking the nonverbal channels one at a time and treating each in separate chapters, the book brings the various channels together and integrates them to provide a more realistic assessment of the ways in which communication processes naturally operate. Instead of being selective with respect to the research literature, we present a thorough account of the relevant work from many disciplines.

After two introductory chapters that set the stage and provide a conceptual framework, the book is organized into three major sections. The first deals with what nonverbal cues tell us about the psychology of the individual and includes chapters on emotional expression, personality, and psychopathology. The second section addresses the question of what information nonverbal behavior provides about the relationships between and among people. Included here are chapters on attraction, aggression, status, and influence. And the last section looks at the role that nonverbal processes play in larger systems of communication. The chapters in this section deal with the integration of verbal and nonverbal modes and with the ways in which our nonverbal behavior cues our social memberships—those of age, sex, and culture.

This text can serve as primary reading for courses in nonverbal communication or as supplementary reading for courses in interpersonal and group communication, social psychology, and linguistics. Because of its orientation, the book can also be a useful tool for courses focusing on applied communication in education, business, law, and the helping professions.

A number of colleagues and friends have come to share our interest in nonverbal communication and have contributed significantly to our efforts that culminated in this book. Specifically, we wish to thank the reviewers of the manuscript, Irwin Altman of the University of Utah, Starkey Duncan, Jr., of the University of Chicago, and Walter G. Stephan of the University of Texas at Austin. We are also indebted to our colleagues Barry Dym, Len Saxe, and Abby Stewart, who commented on parts of the manuscript. That the book exists here and now is thanks to Bill Hicks, Managing Editor at Brooks/Cole, who encouraged, persuaded, and even pushed a little to get the project moving, and to Larry Wrightsman, Consulting Editor, who kept the project on track once it was rolling. It gives us special pleasure to thank Fiorella Ljunggren, Production Editor, who brought to the editing task an unusually sensitive appreciation of what we were trying to put into words and who helped those words to flow. To Mikki Ehrenfeld, skilled photographer and warm friend, go our gratitude and affection for her creativity in turning our words back into images that capture the very essence of "moving bodies." If authors in general owe a debt to those who render handwriting into typescript, our own indebtedness is especially great; thanks to our colleague Gina Abeles, who typed the final manuscript, and to our secretaries, Sue Thompson and Nancy Sieron, who worked on earlier drafts and deciphered not one but two illegible handwritings that, often alternating from sentence to sentence, reflected our struggle to fix the words on the page.

Marianne LaFrance
Clara Mayo

Contents

Chapter 1

Moving into a Context

Nonverbal Behavior Is Report and Command

Nonverbal Communication Is between People

Context in Nonverbal Communication

Meaning of Nonverbal Behavior

Summary

The scene is a classroom. It could be located anywhere. The school might be a large, sprawling complex in an urban area or a small one-room building in the country. The time could be today or yesterday or years back. The class could be a fourth-grade reading class or an advanced graduate seminar in the philosophy of science. The situation is a familiar one. You're the student. You're sitting somewhere near the back of the room, surrounded by others—in front, behind, beside you—all sitting at the same sort of desks and wearing much the same clothes. But right at this moment it is as though you were the only one. And you know why. The teacher is looking in your direction. A question is being asked, and you don't have the answer. The urge is to simply disappear. Given the impossibility of physically disappearing, you do the next best thing. Your glance drops to the desk, your hands are stuffed into your pockets, you scrunch down in the chair, and all movement ceases. You hold your breath—and then you hear your name!

Although your behavior shows that you don't know today's lesson, it is in itself a valuable lesson in communication. What your behavior so clearly shows is the impossibility of *not* communicating. In silence as well as in speech, we are constantly communicating with one another. Through gesture and posture, sound and distance, glance and blush, we are in a perpetual process of communication. Communication does not stop when words do. Human communication is more than speech or sound.

A paradox is created any time you announce with determination to a friend or enemy "I'm just not going to talk about it anymore." You intend to stop communicating, but silence, stillness, and withdrawal are all communication nonetheless. This principle has been articulated by Watzlawick and his associates (Watzlawick, Beavin, & Jackson, 1967, p. 51) as "one cannot *not* communicate." Specifically, as soon as someone is there responding—even if the response is also silence—there is communication.

The implications of this principle are far reaching. To understand human interaction, we need to look beyond what people *say;* we need to explore all the other processes by which we come to influence one another. These processes have been variously ordered under a rubric called *nonverbal com-*

munication. Nonverbal communication includes how and when people look at each other and what happens when their eyes meet—that is, gaze direction and eye contact. Nonverbal communication also involves how and how far apart people stand and how directly they face each other—that is, posture, interpersonal distance, and body orientation. And, since bodies move, the nonverbal takes in changes in facial expression, gestures, and body movements. Also, bodies touch, in different ways, on different parts, with different force.

Even when people talk, there is more to it than speech. People can say the same thing in different tones of voice. The term *paralanguage* describes vocal tone in terms of loudness, pitch, pause, and tempo; included in paralanguage are also vocalizations like yawning, sighing, laughing, and crying.

To call all these behaviors nonverbal communication is something of a misnomer. To be sure, they are *non*verbal in the sense of not being put into words. But they are much more than the absence or negation of something. This book is concerned with what these processes *are* and with their role in human interaction. As Birdwhistell (1970) says, we are all multisensory beings. We communicate in many ways; occasionally, we verbalize.

Nonverbal Behavior Is Report and Command

Let's assume that a camera had been placed in the classroom we described at the beginning of the chapter and that we now have a film clip showing only your glancing down, folding up, and turning away. How might viewers interpret that film clip? More specifically, what would they think it says about you? Teachers would be likely to think that your behavior reports the kind of student you are—uncooperative, probably not very bright, and uninterested in learning. There may be something to this interpretation, but there is more to be seen in that film clip. Movements of the kind we have described are expressive of your personality, of your immediate feelings, and of your more characteristic ways of responding. But such movements are also statements about events going on around you. You are part of a situation and of a relationship. Not only are you reporting who you are by glance, posture, and movement; you are also making statements about what place this is, what activity is going on, and what relationship you're in. Among the nonverbal statements you may be making are "I am a student," "This is a classroom," and "A question-and-answer sequence is beginning." You may also be commanding "Don't focus attention on me."

In addition, a contract about the student/teacher relationship is being negotiated. You are saying to the teacher "I know that you know that, when I adopt this look and posture, I want you to pass me by. I want you to know also that, if you don't pass me by, you have chosen to expose my lack of preparation."

What is complicated and fascinating about even so brief a glimpse of an individual's nonverbal behavior is that it is a message both *about* and *toward.* It is simultaneously a report about who you are *and* a command toward others about how you wish to be taken and about how you are taking them. And, what's more, all parties in the interaction are making such multiple-purpose statements. The teacher cannot *not* respond to your message. He or she can deny, ignore, confirm, or confront the message, but there is always a reply. The teacher, too, is reporting things about self and prescribing the relationship between the two of you.

What the foregoing illustrates is that every communication has both a *report* and a *command* aspect (Watzlawick et al., 1967). The report is the *what*, and the command the *how* of communication. The report conveys the content, information, or description; the command is the instructions about how this content is to be taken (Ruesch & Bateson, 1968). Consider someone patting you on the shoulder. If you were to describe what the action was, you would report that someone patted you—say, as opposed to hugged or shoved you. But pats can be taken in very different ways, and this is where the command aspect enters in. In one situation, it is to be taken as light-hearted affection, but, in another, the message may well be patronizing condescension.

This distinction between report and command is vitally important in understanding nonverbal behavior in human encounters. The idea is hard to grasp at first because you expect the literal content to be all there is. But the command aspect is crucial in understanding how the report is to be taken. This book deals with what happens when people interact nonverbally with others—their nonverbal behaviors as well as how these behaviors are to be taken.

Nonverbal Communication Is between People

Although you may find the distinction between report and command new and intriguing, you may also be thinking "That's all very well, but what of the nonverbal things that seem to speak for themselves?" Aren't some reports so obvious that you don't need commands about how they are to be taken? Aren't there angry glares, seductive glances, sad looks, and twinkly eyes? Novelists (and the rest of us) certainly use such phrases in describing nonverbal behavior, and their descriptions are often intended to be reports about personality. New characters enter the narrative with posture, gesture, facial expression, tone of voice, or other nonverbal elements described so as to tell you who the characters are.

It is a temptation to take these postures and facial expressions as cues only about the person who adopts them. But consider what happens when you are not just a reader or the passive observer of nonverbal behavior. No doubt you know when a comment is made in a hostile tone. Often your reaction is to think or say "Don't use that tone of voice with me," thereby acknowledging inevitably something beyond the content of the tone of voice. The hostile tone is more than a simple report; it also says "I want *you* to take this remark as an angry one." Most of the time such commands are not conscious either for the person who conveys them or for the one who receives them. Communication is swift and automatic. The report and command aspects flow together rapidly. What we're attempting to do here is to make visible and accessible something that usually goes unnoticed in everyday interaction.

Encounters with others are complicated events. You react and are reac-

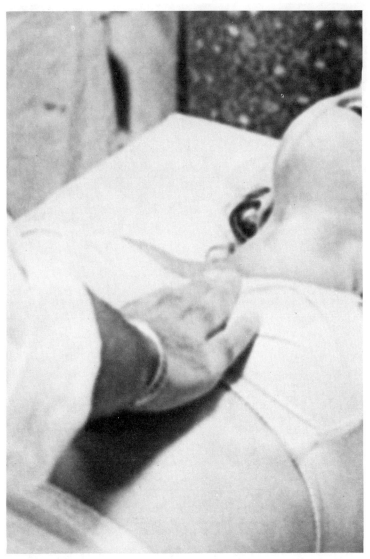

What is happening here? How are you to interpret the touch? Compare this photograph with those on the next two pages.

ted to and react back in turn. You send, receive, and interpret in lightning fashion. And only occasionally do you stand back and marvel at what has gone on. But in the heat of it all, you still try to make sense of the other's verbal and nonverbal acts. For example, what would you make of someone's turning away as you began to talk to him? Well, the track to the answer can go

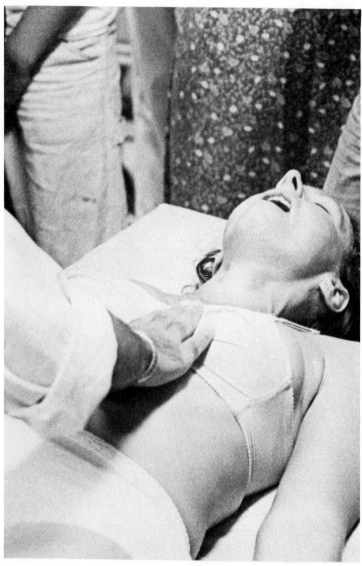

With more context, you see more of the two people involved. You also glimpse in the upper left that the two are not alone.

in a couple of different directions. One could be: he turned away as I began to speak. He did that because he is a shy, withdrawn person. He is like that because of events in his past. This kind of explanation, however, leaves out some important elements.

With yet a broader context, you see that several people are looking on. The touch acquires a different meaning: the toucher and the man on the right are teaching a class in massage.

Consider an alternative train of thought. The description of the act may remain the same: he turned away as I began to speak. The next step, however, is to wonder: Why here? Why now? Why with me? This route emphasizes mutual interaction at a specific time and place—that is, the relations between nonverbal acts and the contexts in which they occur. We believe that these relations are tremendously important, because—as we stress throughout this book—more attention to the context and field in which nonverbal acts occur increases the accuracy with which the command aspects of these acts can be understood. Although context is still a relatively neglected aspect in the study of nonverbal communication, its importance for understanding human behavior has long been recognized.

Context in Nonverbal Communication

Kurt Lewin (1951) showed that he was a remarkable pioneer in the young field of social psychology when he proposed that behavior is a function of the person *and* the environment. It is no exaggeration to say that social psychologists have been trying to grasp the vision and expanse of that proposition ever since. And the struggle is not made easier by the fact that Lewin's proposition runs counter to much of Western thought, which sees the individual as the dominant element in behavior, the causal force before which all else gives way. It is no accident that Lewin put the proposition in the abstract form of an equation: $B = f(P, E)$.

Let's look at each element of the equation more closely. B, which stands for behavior, is something that a person does. Eye blinks, hand movements, and posture shifts are part of behavior—to be exact, of nonverbal behavior. It is important to keep in mind, though, that it is *people* who behave. In other words, there is no behavior without a person doing the behavior. According to the equation, the behavior is related to both personal characteristics (P) and characteristics of the environment (E) in which the person operates. P includes enduring traits, needs, and values as well as more transient states like moods and feelings. P also covers the more visible attributes of age, sex, and culture. E refers to the environment, large and small. It includes the spatial location (for example, urban/rural, indoor/outdoor), the arrangement of the physical environment (for example, furniture placement), and the design features (like color and lighting). It also refers to social-psychological components such as the social setting (for example, a wedding or a concert), the interactional unit (twosome or group), and the social climate (rules and etiquette). Finally, the environment includes the timing or sequence of events. What comes before, during, and after a particular nonverbal act is often a neglected but important aspect of the environment.

A predominantly nonverbal conversation between strangers on an airplane is a good example of what we're talking about here. You approach your assigned seat and notice that someone—a woman—is already sitting in the window seat next to yours. In a quick glance you take in a great deal about her. She, on the other hand, notices your approach and can probably tell by the way you're moving and orienting that you're about to take the seat next to her. An ever-so-quick look of acknowledgement may pass between the two of you as you sit down. Perhaps you're feeling particularly communicative, so you lean over just a little and look out the window. Since she is looking out as well, you now say "It looks as though we've got a little wait ahead of us." She utters a subdued "Hmm" and picks up a magazine. It's not exactly a warm response. For the time being, you settle back.

Even so brief an interchange has a particular pattern, flow, and sequence. You cannot take the individual parts of the event and change their order without changing the whole event. What if the sequence had her first look out the window, then pick up the magazine as you approached and finally say "Hmmm" just as you sat down? This sequence is more an invitation to interact than the one above. An important element in understanding nonverbal behavior is understanding the *sequence* in which it occurs. Changing the sequence of events inevitably changes the meaning of those events. Hence to ask what behavior came just before and after a bit of nonverbal behavior is an essential step toward knowing how the event is to be taken.

The relation between P and E—that is, the interaction between the person and the environment—is represented in the equation by a comma. The comma conveys a multiplicative relation: P times E. We said multiplicative, not additive or subtractive. This is an important point. There can be no behavior in the absence of one of these two elements of the equation. If P or E were equal to zero—that is, if either were to be considered without the other—the equation itself would be zero. It's difficult to think of the absence of environment. You might think of a vacuum as zero environment, but even a vacuum is an environment, indeed a very special one in regard to its effects on behavior. Objects behave differently in a vacuum, just as subjects behave differently in a laboratory setting, because the research laboratory, like the vacuum—and, we wish to add, like any kind of environment—exerts a special pull on behavior.

Just as the environment influences people, people influence the environment. A game of chess is a good illustration of this point. The rules of a game are one part of the environment in which the game is played. In chess, if the players don't play by the rules, there is no game. But, although both players know and follow the rules in each game that takes place, no two games of chess are ever exactly the same. The difference lies in the players, their skill, their tactics, their motivation, and sometimes their dramatic ploys designed to confuse the opponent. In other words, the environment is not uninfluenced by the people participating in it.

The symbol f represents the complex notion of function. To put it in simple words, function refers to the variable and temporal nature of the elements in the equation. It establishes that P and E have no concrete, fixed nature of their own. People are forever changing. You cannot kiss the same person twice for the first time. Environments change as well. You can leave home for the last time only once. P and E are meaningless except in relation to each other. They are not isolated or absolute elements in any meaningful sense.

How does Lewin's formula help us to understand nonverbal behavior? It helps by making a general statement about nonverbal communication, which can be applied to a wide range of situations. If, for example, you see someone hunched over with knees on the ground, you reach a different conclusion about what he or she is doing if the behavior occurs in a church pew or on a sidewalk and if the kneeler is a child or an adult. Is the individual praying, playing marbles, having a heart attack, play-acting a marriage proposal, or looking for a lost contact lens? You take both the attributes of the person (P) and the characteristics of the setting (E) into account in deciding what behavior you are seeing and the reasons for it.

But what about those situations in which, instead of being an unobserved observer, you are actively interacting with another? Can the equation be of help then, too? Most of our discussion of the environment thus far has focused on the physical and social characteristics of the environment, which are by their very nature relatively static, relatively permanent, and relatively impersonal. We have described such features as buildings and social settings and have only hinted at another important aspect of the surrounding environment. And that is the presence of other people. You move around other people as they move around you. You are part of the environment for them as they are for you. To understand their behavior, you need to understand yourself; to understand yourself, you need to understand them.

Part of your interest in nonverbal communication comes from a desire to understand your own and other people's moves. In seeking such understanding, the natural inclination is to focus on the person—as did the teacher or the observer viewing the film clip of the student described at the beginning of this chapter. Their questions had to do with what made the student act that way. By introducing the Lewinian equation, we hope to show you that, if you want to understand the meaning of nonverbal behavior, it is necessary that you take into consideration the interactions between persons and environments. And the teacher, like any active interactant, must also see how much of the environment he or she represents for the student. In the pages to come, we discuss the essential role played by the presence of other people in creating the environment in which nonverbal communication occurs.

Meaning of Nonverbal Behavior

Not only is there no behavior without environment, but there is no meaning without environment. If you were to focus only on a nonverbal behavior, such as a smile, without taking into account the environment or context, you would have only the *report*. You could probably give a description of what happened, but you couldn't explain why it happened. To get to the *command*, you need to take the environment into account. To put it in even stronger terms, a person who fails to consider the situation, an observer who neglects the context, an interactant who does not see the effects of the environment, is going to make some serious interpersonal mistakes. To ignore the context is, for example, to risk seeing personal rejection where the other is simply in a hurry or personal invitation where the other is exhibiting the general friendliness required by a social ritual.

How do we reduce the incidence of such interpersonal blunders? By using our equation to understand the meaning of the nonverbal behavior in question. First, we identify the context. Where are we? What kind of situation is this? We have words for times and places that make up a context—nouns such as party, office, or bedroom and verbs such as play, work, and love. And each situation offers a variety of subtle and not so subtle clues that help us identify the *environment*.

Next we need to know something about the people present. Who are they? What are they like, in general and right at this moment? What are their roles? What is their relationship to you—teammate, supervisor, lover? Equally important is the recognition of your own characteristics and role. Who and what are you to these people? All these are the characteristics of the *person*.

And then there are those various components of the *behavior* that we are trying to understand—a pregnant pause, a fleeting smile, an unexpected move. Note that all of these components, as well as the resulting behavior, become interpretable only when you know what is going on around them and that, if you change the context, the meaning of the behavior changes, too. Let's use a verbal example to illustrate how changing the context changes the meaning. A word standing alone can have a number of different meanings. Take the word *cup*. "Will you have a cup of tea?" "Cup your hands to drink from the stream." "They won the Stanley Cup." It is the specific context that gives specific meaning to the word. Without context, it is often hard to know what a word means. Sometimes, when you encounter an unfamiliar word, you turn to a dictionary for help. And then you discover that the dictionary doesn't give you the meaning of the puzzling word in the situation in which you came across it. In a dictionary, words are usually followed by several definitions, and sample phrases are given to place the word in context. To know which of the various meanings fits your case, you try to find some similarity between the examples and the specific context in which your word appeared. The less you know of the context, the more uncertain you are about the meaning. And, conversely, the more you know about the context, the clearer the meaning becomes.

The meaning of a word derives from context not only in the sense that a word has different meanings in different contexts. Even a single context can give different meanings to a word by the different organization of the elements in it. Consequently, the contextual elements cannot be arranged and rearranged in random ways without altering the meaning of the word. Also, meaning does not arise simply by adding new information piece by piece. New information changes the meaning of the information that was available before. Gradually a pattern emerges. The word in question gets its meaning from the unfolding landscape around it. Consider the following:

tied

were tied by

couples were tied by bonds

the young couples were tied by bonds of obligation

By itself, the verb *tied* tells you very little. As the verb tense is added, you know whether the action is happening now, is already past, or yet to be. If the preposition following the verb were *to, after,* or *with,* instead of *by,* the meaning of *tied* would be different. Furthermore, if we were to alter the order of the words so they read "bonds were tied by couples," the meaning would again be different. What we are saying is that each new element of context changes the meaning of the preceding words.

You need more contextual cues to interpret this wink.

Context is essential in establishing the meaning of nonverbal behavior as well. A small bit of movement taken out of context is as meaningless as the single word alone. And there are no dictionaries of American (or any other) body language to help you identify the meaning you're looking for. Picture the face of someone in the process of closing one eye. What does that gesture mean? What elements of time and space do you need in order to know? You might note, for example, that the person is walking along a street and that a gust of wind has just blown dust into the air. As the person quickly raises a hand to rub his eye, you decide that the eye shutting "meant" that a bit of dust had settled in the person's eye. But what if the person is seated in a room where a meeting is going on? You see the eye closing and follow the direction of the gaze to notice that the person is looking at someone. Now you decide that the gesture you have observed is a wink. Different contexts of time and space suggest different meanings.

Having decided that the eye closing is a wink, you want to know what the wink means. To do that, you need to consider the other elements in the context—what Birdwhistell (1970) calls the *interactional flow*. There are now two people in the interaction, and the wink can convey a range of messages, from question to agreement or collusion. You can narrow down these possibilities by looking at the other elements in the situation. If the winker is speaking, the wink may be a command to the recipient that the verbal statement is to be questioned. If the speaker is the person winked at, the wink may signify

Body movements—as broad as running to greet someone and as small as a wink—are the topic of this book.

agreement with the verbal statement. If the speaker is instead a third person, the wink may be taken to mean collusion by the pair to disagree with the speaker.

Summary

This chapter has touched upon several themes that recur throughout the book. Whenever and wherever people interact, there is nonverbal communication. Such communication has report and command aspects; the former conveys information, and the latter tells how that information is to be taken. This book focuses on interaction between people; in that context, it is impossible not to communicate. Nonverbal communication is a function of both the environment and the persons and is subject to the changeable nature of each. The meaning of nonverbal behavior depends on context. No gesture, posture, or look means anything in isolation.

A recurrent problem in writing about nonverbal communication is inherent in the act of verbal description. To set something down in words is to fix it in time and space, to make a product of it so that this product can be looked at and analyzed. This static treatment distorts an essential aspect of nonverbal communication—namely, its dynamic, ongoing nature. As you read this book and think of moving bodies, try to see them as you would in film rather than in still photographs.

Chapter 2

Magnifying Movement

Multiple Channels

Three Analytic Perspectives

From Social Rules to Individual Behavior

Summary

When we first started studying nonverbal communication some years ago, we both found ourselves suddenly focusing on nonverbal behavior everywhere. We would go to a lecture and remember little of what was said, while many of the speaker's gestures and postures stood out clearly in our minds. What until then had been unseen became strikingly visible. Many of the students in our courses in nonverbal communication seem to undergo the same experiences and perhaps, as you read this book, you, too, will become very aware of nonverbal behavior. In classes, at parties, or at the beach, you will suddenly see how active the human body is. Once you shift your focus away from the verbal realm, you begin to sense a rushing stream of sounds and movements, large and small, all around you.

Perhaps your first reaction to all this will be self-consciousness. When you find yourself saying something that's coming out all wrong, you can stop talking. But what do you do about the direction in which your eyes are looking, the gestures your hands are making, and the way you're standing? You may become so self-conscious that you decide to stop moving altogether! As we said in Chapter 1, however, to stop moving is not to stop communicating. There is no silence in nonverbal communication.

Another reaction to the newly found world of nonverbal communication is an increasing awareness of what goes on *between* people. You begin to notice not only messages being sent but messages being received.

Multiple Channels

The term *channel* is used to refer to the various paths through which communication flows. For example, radio is primarily an aural channel, and television uses both aural and visual channels. As we have indicated, nonverbal communication is broadly inclusive and, as such, takes in a number of different channels. There is the visual channel through which you both send and receive a great deal of information about stance, movement, distance, and orientation. These are the kinds of things you can pick up by observing and by being observed. Vision is such a dominant channel because, unlike some other channels, it is not only a passage through which communications travel but also a form of communication in its own right. To look at another is to allow information to pass and is also information in itself. Someone who won't look at you is not just restricting his or her own access to visual information but is also sending a message closing you out. The aural channel contains more than speech; the sound of what is said is informative as well. Volume, pitch, and tempo of speech may not receive much conscious attention in everyday conversation, but they are essential aspects of the process. Finally, there are the channels through which touch and smell are transmitted.

In a conversation, people take turns in talking and listening; the impression is of orderly stops and starts. In the script of a play, each actor waits for another to finish before he or she begins to speak. Others wait in silence until their turn comes. But nonverbally there is no waiting; in the presence of others, you're on all the time.

Figure 2-1 shows a diagram of this process, adapted from Birdwhistell

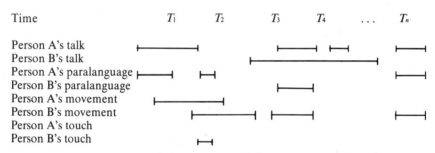

Figure 2-1. Communication as continuous process. (Adapted from *Kinesic and Context,* by R. L. Birdwhistell. Copyright 1970 by the University of Pennsylvania Press. Used by permission.)

(1970). In this diagram, the lines represent activity in each channel. For example, from Time 1 (T_1) to Time 2 (T_2), Person A is talking continuously while Person B is verbally silent. At Time 2, both are verbally silent. At Time 3 (T_3), Person B begins to speak while A is silent. But during the verbal quiet at Time 2, nonverbal activity is occurring, as it also is at other times. For example, Person A is making a brief paralinguistic comment at Time 2—perhaps a laugh or throat clearing—while finishing some movement begun during Time 1. Simultaneously, at Time 2, Person B begins some movement that includes a quick touch of Person A.

What this diagram indicates overall is that communication is a process in which there is always some channel (or channels) in operation. Communication is flowing in multiple paths. Thus we get patterns of cues rather than single behaviors. What's more, communication is occurring over time; communication cannot be described in a frozen instant, without taking into account what comes before and after. Lastly, you get a sense of people moving together in concert—a sense of moving bodies.

Three Analytic Perspectives

Although it is possible to say something about nonverbal communication by talking about single individuals, what we have tried to show thus far is that more is to be learned by looking at other aspects as well. The authors recall a striking example that the psychiatrist Albert Scheflen has used to illustrate this point. He speaks of a concert audience that includes both a noted musicologist and the father of one of the performers. These two people experience a very different concert. They look for and see different things. The father's eyes are upon his daughter, the cellist. He waits eagerly for her solo and shows pride when it goes well. His mind wanders to his daughter's childhood, her long hours of study and diligent practice, her persistence in pursuit of difficult goals. He sees the other musicians in relation to his daughter. He thinks he can pick out her bowing on the cello from the ensemble playing.

The musicologist has little interest in the individual players. He is interested in the composition being played, in the way the composer has combined musical parts to achieve a harmonious whole. He attends to the composition, picking out standard key changes, harmonic effects, and major and minor themes. The musicologist is an expert in musical form and structure; it is to these aspects of the performance that he attends.

What are some of the differences in the way these two people experience the concert? First, the father sees a collection of individuals on stage, while the musicologist sees the orchestra as a single unit. The father's perspective may be described as being at an individual level; he is interested in the characteristics of an individual and her needs, motives, and skills. The musicologist sees the orchestra as an entity governed by the rules and rituals of musical performance.

Second, the father sees the musicians as *creating* the performance. He thinks that today his daughter is playing better than usual and appreciates the keen sensitivity with which she expresses the mood of the composition. The musicologist pictures the musical score and sees the performers as executing their parts in a prearranged manner. Entrances and exits, brasses and strings, combine according to a plan. The difference can be described as one in which the father focuses on the person who causes the behavior to happen and the expert focuses on the musical parts as they are determined by a prescribed program. The father sees the parts as combining to form the composition; the musicologist sees the program as giving rise to the parts.

Third, when asked to recall the performance, these two observers organize their impressions differently. The father retains an impression of events in sequential order. His daughter's solo came after a long stretch of violin playing and before a trumpet fanfare. The musical expert remembers the piece in a hierarchical order. The measures become phrases, themes, movements, and finally a symphony. It is the structure of the piece that he recalls.

Researchers approach communication in similar ways. There are those who, like the father, concentrate on the individual level of analysis. They ask what the nonverbal behavior tells about the individual's experience with or participation in the communication. There are others who, like the musicologist, are concerned with the structure of communication. They treat nonverbal behavior as part of a larger system operating according to particular programs. Each of these viewpoints captures only part of the concert. In this book, we invite you to be both parent and musicologist, to value individual differences and shared realities.

We have organized our material to reflect these different perspectives. In the next three chapters, the focus is very similar to that taken by the father above. We concentrate on the individual's nonverbal behavior and on what that behavior says about feelings and personality. How do people's faces show what they're feeling? Do certain personalities have a special look or sound?

We also know that people have feelings about one another. You move close to some and away from others; you look up to some and down at others; you want from some and give to others. All these feelings are demonstrated nonverbally. Chapters 6 through 9 center on relationships between people and on how nonverbal behavior reflects the quality of these relationships. This perspective is similar to that of the parent in our example, in that it focuses on the psychological import of nonverbal behavior, but, at the same time, is quite different, in that it includes at least one other person. Do people in love look at each other more than people who are just friends? How do people show nonverbally that they're one up on you?

And, finally, we take a perspective like that of the musicologist. We shift our focus from the players to the rules that govern the concert—the concert of communication. For example, what are the nonverbal means by which people handle hellos and goodbyes? To some extent, who you are is determined by being part of a number of "communities"—communities of culture, gender, and age. Are women really more emotionally expressive than men? Are children really more sensitive to nonverbal insincerity than adults?

From Social Rules to Individual Behavior

Reading this book may be a little like looking through a microscope. On the slide is an entire communication. You adjust the microscope to get different levels of magnification. At different powers of magnification, you see different things. Figure 2-2, adapted from Ruesch and Bateson (1968, p. 275), illustrates this idea. Put yourself at the bottom of the diagram in the role of the observer who is looking at a particular person (represented by an x) in a social setting. When your focus is on a single person, you're at the *individual level*. However, if you broaden your scope, you see that this particular individual is in interaction with another person. You're now at the *relationship level*. And, if you then broaden your scope even further, you take in a number of other people; in our illustration, these other people are clustered in two groups, to the left and right of the two people you were observing before. This is the *social-rules level*. The twosome is set off from the other two groups, per-

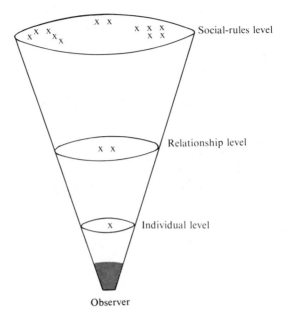

Observer

Figure 2-2. Levels of analysis in communication. (Adapted from *Communication, The Social Matrix of Psychiatry,* by Jurgen Ruesch, M.D., and Gregory Bateson, with the permission of W. W. Norton & Company, Inc. Copyright © 1968, 1951, by W. W. Norton & Company, Inc.)

haps by age (they're younger than the rest) or by culture (they're both American; the group to the left is British, and the group to the right is Italian). Only changes in magnification have occurred; the person who initially caught your eye remains the same throughout. But that person's nonverbal behavior "means" different things as you broaden the context.

What all this indicates is that you can analyze communication at three levels: the individual, the relational, and the social-rules level. Although all levels are present in any communication, you can look at only one at a time. Which you choose depends on what you are interested in. If you want to know how greetings are managed in this culture as opposed to another, you are concerned with the social-rules level of communication. If you want to figure out who is siding with whom in a group discussion, you are dealing with relationships. If you are wondering what mood someone is in, you turn to the individual level of analysis.

In communication these levels are closely intertwined. In contrast to popular descriptions of nonverbal behavior, which focus primarily on the individual level, we suggest that it is through the social-rules level that the individual level of analysis becomes meaningful. As Hoggart (1972) puts it, "The justification for learning more about social vocabularies is that, unless you understand what social signals you are responding to all the time, you will be less likely to see through the groups of a certain age and style and see the individuals within" (p. 22).

Social vocabularies or rules provide a sense of how things are usually done and thus reveal by contrast unusual or individualistic ways. Once you recognize a context, you have a pretty good idea of how most people appear and act in that situation. Some contexts are very rule-bound and allow little variation in behavior; others are less prescriptive. But, in most instances, you have some expectations or *baselines* to help you understand people's nonverbal behavior. You get these baselines by asking yourself two questions: "What would most people similar to this one person do?" and "What behavior belongs in this sort of context or environment?" To answer the first question, you draw on your knowledge of the rules of the "communities" to which the person belongs. You know what's typical of young and old, woman and man, native and foreigner. To answer the second question, you turn to your knowledge of contexts. What are the rules of greeting, mourning, or winning? It is this knowledge of the general that lets you make sense of the particular. When a person behaves as would no other, you see it clearly because you know what others would do under similar circumstances.

Let's look at a smile in terms of our microscope analogy. At the individual level, you might decide that the person is feeling happy. Upon widening the focus, you see that there's another person in the picture; maybe the smiler is indicating liking. At the broadest level, you see a social conversation in which a woman is listening to a man. Now it may be that the woman is following the gender rule that dictates that she should smile. In the absence of any other information, the safest guess about the meaning of the smile is at the rules level. More information from other channels or changes in context would help you decide whether she also likes the man and/or is feeling particularly happy.

Summary

Communication is not one thing. Several nonverbal channels combine with language to make communication. These channels operate interdependently and dynamically. Thus, while it is possible to think of one channel or one behavior at a time, more is to be learned by appreciating how they all operate together.

There is a great temptation to see nonverbal communication only for what it says about the psychology of the individual. We have suggested that it says a great deal more—for example, what is happening in a relationship and what rules guide interaction.

But, even more than that, we've argued for the importance of understanding the social rules, so that variation and uniqueness become visible and interpretable.

Chapter 3

Motion and Emotion

People find one another intriguing and often just plain confusing. There are feelings, wishes, and fears churning inside people that you would like to have access to. So you listen to their words but also watch their facial expressions and note how they move. It is not so much these cues in themselves that are of interest but the means they provide to get at the other's internal workings. Most of the research has been directed at finding out whether nonverbal cues could be used to know about another person. As we indicated earlier, this and the next two chapters focus on nonverbal events as they provide information about the individual. This chapter deals specifically with what is known about the nonverbal expression of emotion and feeling.

Emotion Shown and Observed

Nonverbal expressions of emotion are woven into the fabric of everyday life and seldom stand out as distinctive events. But despite their fleeting existence, emotional expressions have a life of their own. Consider the fate of an emotional message given off by one person in a group situation (Dittmann, 1972a). When people are working together, they are seldom conscious of sending and receiving emotionally charged communiqués. Suppose that a group of people are sitting around a table, each working independently at some part of a job, when one of them looks up and smiles. The obvious interpretation is that the person is pleased.

But often matters are not really that simple. People do indeed smile when they are pleased or happy, but they also smile when they want to convince themselves or others that they are pleased. The person smiling may be attempting to convey to others pleasure at the way the work is going, when in fact he or she is not happy at all. People can and do manage their facial expressions to mask their true feelings.

Some interpretations of emotional expression depend on how much one knows of the *baselines* for the expression. In this particular instance, does the person tend to smile a great deal, or is a smile rarely seen on his or her face? The rare, surprising smile is more likely to be taken as a sign of true inner feelings. *Sequence* is important, too. It helps to know how the now-smiling face looked just before and after the smile. Also, emotional expressions vary in *intensity,* from the slight smile of a Mona Lisa to the broad grin of a Jimmy Carter. Smiles of low intensity are more likely to be missed. Lastly, emotional expressions are brief, of no more than a few seconds' *duration.* The smiling face is constantly in transition from one expression to another, and it is change that you do in fact notice. Some expressions are so brief that observers cannot identify them; all they know is that something has changed.

Part of the problem in deciding whether the smiler is pleased is that people seldom express one, and only one, emotion. Life is complex, and virtually any emotional experience is at least double-edged. Emotional messages reflect this complexity. Facial and vocal expressions are mostly a matter of *blends*—combinations of feelings revealed in one configuration.

So far in our example we've been assuming that the smile was detected, and the question was whether the smiler was really pleased. But part of the course an emotional message travels depends on the perceiver as well. Some members of the work group may have been sitting where they couldn't see the face of the smiler at all. Others may have looked at the person but not noticed the smile, simply because people differ in the extent to which they notice feelings in others (Schiffenbauer, 1974). Some, wanting to get on with their work, were attending to the immediate activity, quite oblivious to other people's feelings. And even those who did attend to the smile may have been moved to interpret it according to their own emotional states, with little regard for what the other was indeed feeling. Some observers notice a smile but see it as something quite different from pleasure—for example, as smugness.

Let's now use some of the ideas suggested by this example to look at the research that has been conducted on emotional expression. Interest in this topic dates back to Charles Darwin (1872). Reading him today can be enlightening for the astute observations he made about us all—chimpanzees and humans alike. The research is presented here from the two perspectives we mentioned when we discussed the example above—that of the person expressing the emotion and that of perceivers trying to interpret that emotion. We begin with the research on expression and more specifically with the question of whether emotions such as fear or anger are always and everywhere expressed in the same way in face, voice, and body. Next, we consider how intricate emotional expression is; people manifest combinations of several feelings, and they also make incomplete or very brief displays of emotions. Also within the research on expression, there is consideration of the management of emotional display. People don't always show what they feel and don't always feel what they show. Then we look at research on the perceiver. Are some people more sensitive than others to what is going on emotionally around them?

Expressing Signs of Emotion

Sometimes you are with a friend and get a very strong impression that she is feeling something that she is not telling you about. Or you're sitting on a bus idly looking at your fellow passengers when you are struck by the notion that someone looks really sad. What are the nonverbal signs of particular emotions? The most important appear in the face, but voice and body provide information as well.

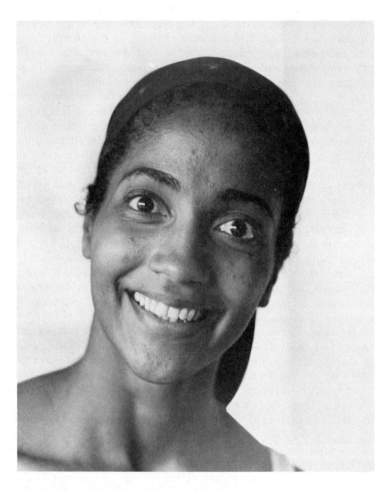

The simple smile is not so simple. It involves a number of changes in and around the eyes, the cheeks, and the mouth.

Facial Signs

In the example of the worker who looks up and smiles, you, as fellow worker, might conclude that the person is pleased. There are all kinds of happy states and all kinds of smiles, and the two go very much together. For example, children smile when they realize, even without being told, that they know the correct answers to difficult questions (Harter, Schultz, & Blum, 1971). The smile accompanying happy states would be recognized the world over.

The manifestation of happiness is marked by what we call a smile—corners of the lip drawn back and up; mouth parted or not, with teeth showing or not; a wrinkle running from nose to outer edge of lip; cheeks raised; lower-eyelid wrinkles; and wrinkles outward from the outer corner of the eyes (Ekman & Friesen, 1975, p. 112). You may have never stopped and analyzed a happy face in this amount of detail, especially since our perception of someone smiling or frowning or whatever is immediate and all of one piece. But, as Ekman (1972) pointed out, such details are essential to an understanding of facial expression of emotion.

In his view, once an emotion is elicited by some event, there is an immediate activation of what is called a *facial affect program.* This program connects each emotion with a particular and definitive set of neural impulses that transmit to the facial muscles. In other words, happiness—like the other primary emotions of anger, surprise, fear, disgust, sadness, and interest—has its own characteristic arrangement of facial muscles. These arrangements occur in three major parts of the face: (1) brows/forehead, (2) eyes/lids, and (3) lower face/mouth. Note that our description of the smiling face makes use of the lower two-thirds of the face.

Figure 3-1 represents the typical sequence that, according to Ekman, accompanies such expressions of emotion. On the left are the *elicitors*—events or stimuli that can lead to emotion. These include external things, such as witnessing or being involved in an accident, winning a prize, or being assaulted, and internal events, such as memories and fantasies. Immediately, an automatic appraisal mechanism, which is selectively tuned to different classes or groups of these stimuli, initiates a program for a particular emotion in a particular context. In other words, each emotion has its own program, or facial routine. This facial affect program is the central mechanism in the sequence connecting emotion to its nonverbal expression. Independent support for the existence of such programs comes from research findings showing that happy, sad, angry facial expressions are accompanied by electrical activity in four different facial-muscle regions (Schwartz, Fair, Salt, Mandel, & Klerman, 1976).

However, not every facial affect program is transmitted fully to the face. People qualify their emotional reactions according to a set of *display rules.* Hence, the resulting expression may be a much-reduced form of the internal experience, or it may be some other put-on expression that overrides the emotion altogether.

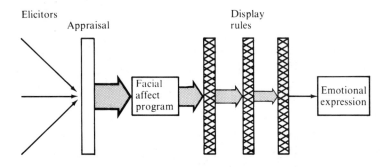

Figure 3-1. The course of emotional expression. (Adapted from "Universals and Cultural Differences in Facial Expressions of Emotions," by P. Ekman. In J. K. Cole [Ed.], *Nebraska Symposium on Motivation* [Vol. 19]. Lincoln: University of Nebraska Press, 1972. Copyright © 1972 by Paul Ekman.)

These display rules may be of three types: personal, situational, and cultural. The personal ones are unique ways each of us has developed to handle specific emotions. In other words, you may have learned very early not to be "afraid," so every time you are really afraid, your fear is overlaid by anger. Situational and cultural display rules are examples of the social rules we discussed in Chapter 2. Cultural display rules are the norms or conventions for emotional expression shared by all, or nearly all, members of a culture. That Latins are considered rich in emotional displays and Anglo-Saxons reserved is an example of cultural display rules. These are discussed in greater detail in Chapter 13. Context, therefore, enters in at both ends of Ekman's model; context determines what events serve as elicitors of particular emotions and what emotions can appropriately be shown to others in social interaction. A hundred years after Darwin, it can now be said with confidence that facial expressions are accurate reflections of internal states, at least for primary emotions simply expressed.

Vocal Signs

Although the face predominates in emotional expression, feelings are also expressed in the voice. No work as thorough and rigorous as Ekman's presently exists that links specific *tonal* elements to specific emotions. Fairbanks and Pronovost (1939) had actors read the same passage in tones intended to convey contempt, anger, fear, grief, and indifference. Listeners were able to distinguish these five emotions with degrees of accuracy ranging from 88% for indifference to 66% for fear. Another early study showed that contempt was the most easily identified emotion and fear the least (Dusenbury & Knower, 1939). Where emotions are similar (for example, joy and cheerfulness), their vocal expressions are hard to distinguish (Davitz & Davitz, 1959).

With regard to specific vocal cues, Davitz (1964) reported that emotions rated "active" (like anger) were expressed by a fast rate of speech, high volume of loudness, and high pitch, in contrast to "passive" emotions (like sadness), which were expressed in slower and lower speech. More recently, Scherer (1974) produced tonal variations mechanically, to which raters applied emotion labels. Using combinations of pitch, amplitude, and tempo, 64 tonal samples were recorded. Once again, anger, fear, and surprise were associated with fast tempo and high pitch, while boredom and sadness were linked to slow tempo and low pitch. In addition, changes in pitch characterized certain emotions; for example, pitch rose with fear and surprise. Recall the heroine's rising scream that greets the discovery of the corpse in murder mysteries.

Body Signs

The face and voice have been the most extensively investigated channels of emotional expression. This may be an accurate reflection of where in fact most emotional expression takes place, but it may also reflect a bias of Western philosophical tradition, which locates important matters in the head. The body then is implicitly regarded primarily as a platform on which the head sits. On the other hand, body movement is used to communicate feeling in Japanese theater and Indian dance, as well as French mime; it may be that movement plays a greater part in the expression of emotion than we yet know. In psychiatric interviews, for example, patients have been found to move more when discussing emotionally loaded topics (Sainsbury, 1955).

An attempt to untangle the relative contributions of different body parts to the expression of emotions was made by Ekman (1965). Following upon his interest in facial expression, he suggested that the head and face conveyed specific emotions, which were then qualified by body cues. Specifically, seeing someone in a tense, rigid posture might tell you that he or she was feeling something intensely, but you would need to see the head/face to know precisely what the feeling was. But this head/body division didn't seem to provide an adequate answer to the problem. A later formulation held instead that there are *body acts* and *body positions,* each of which can occur in any body part. The former are in constant change, while the latter are relatively still. Specific emotional information is conveyed by body acts, while emotional intensity is expressed in body positions (Ekman & Friesen, 1967). Bodies speak, as do faces and voices, with emotional overtones. In the very young field of nonverbal communication, researchers have just begun to listen to these messages.

In summary, signs of emotion are manifested in face, voice, and body. Most of the research has concentrated on one of these modalities at a time, although it is evident that emotional expression is intricate and patterned. As mentioned in Chapter 2, nonverbal communication uses multiple channels, usually in simultaneous, ongoing display. For example, when disgust is elicited, it is generally expressed by the familiar eyes-closed, tongue-out face, likely accompanied by vocal sounds like "ugh" and by movements and body orientation away from the elicitor of disgust. What the research has shown is that clear-cut linkages exist between certain specific emotions and their nonverbal expressions. Context is important both in what is reacted to and in what is expressed emotionally. One might even speculate that the emotion cues themselves are the report of the nonverbal communication but that the display rules are the command of how the expression is to be taken.

Emotional Blends

Although the research described above has isolated a few primary emotions and studied them one at a time, human experience seldom provides such simple, pure reactions. As you follow your daily round of activities, most situations don't evoke a strong emotional reaction at all. Those that do are likely to evoke complex emotions. You feel many things at once, and your face, voice, and body express some of the mixture of feelings you have. You're sitting at home when the doorbell rings, and you find an unexpected guest at the door. Surprise! Your surprise is likely to be mixed with other feelings, and your face will show this blend of emotions. Your surprise may be mixed with glee (a long-lost friend), or annoyance (a nosy relative), or interest (an attractive new neighbor). The displays of two or more emotions, either in rapid succession or simultaneously in different parts of the face, have been called *blends* by Ekman (1972).

True emotional expressions are quick to appear and equally quick to dissolve. In fact, most facial marks of emotion last barely a second or two. To get some sense of this, try to maintain a surprised expression for more than a few seconds. Is it convincing? And there are emotional reactions that last even less than a second. These, called *micromomentary* expressions, appear and disappear within 1/5 to 1/8 of a second (Haggard & Isaacs, 1966). Too fleeting to notice in everyday interaction, they can be clearly seen on slow-motion film. But even in ordinary conversations, these quick changes leave their mark. You perhaps can't say that the other's face looked happy or sad, but you get a clear sense that something has changed. Very similar to micromomentary facial expressions are what Ekman (1972) calls *partials*. During a partial, only part of the facial program registers on the face. The effect is something like seeing a half-finished portrait. Expressively, a person may smile only with his mouth and not with his eyes.

Emotional Put-Ons

Having reviewed the evidence for the case that the worker who looks up and smiles may be feeling happy or at least partly happy, let us now turn to another alternative. People can and do smile when they are in fact feeling something other than happiness. People have the capacity for both genuine

Cover the upper half of the woman's face; the smile alone can be taken as an expression of happiness. Now cover her mouth; the eyes and brows reflect sadness. The expression as a whole is a blend of the two emotions. Look at the man's face in the same way. His face shows an emotional blend of mild happiness (slight smile) and anger (eyes and brows). In both pictures, the brows are lowered; the difference is found in the inner corners of the brows, which are raised in sadness and lowered in anger.

expression and managed impression. In many occupations and even in family life there is a difference between onstage behavior toward the client or visitor and backstage behavior among the workers or family members (Goffman, 1959). The mechanic may be bored by your recital of automotive woes, but he keeps his face attentive, respectful, and friendly until you leave, after which he may show his true feelings to his co-workers backstage.

This distinction has also been characterized as one between *presentation* and *representation* (Spiegel & Machotka, 1974). The presentation is a performance, an arrangement and appearance designed to be seen. Its connection is less to inner feeling than to outer effect. In contrast, the representation refers to the expression of inner feelings. Because emotions are often not addressed to a specific other, they tend to be seen solely as representations of the feelings of the person who speaks or acts (Ruesch & Kees, 1956). However, in experiments that used painful electric shocks, the subjects showed much less nonverbal expression of pain when an observer was present (even when that observer was a scientist watching the experiment) than when they were left alone (Kleck, Vaughan, Cartwright-Smith, Vaughan, Colby, & Lanzetta, 1976).

What these findings indicate is that facial expressions can be put on or taken off much as one wears a suit of clothes. How can you tell a genuine expression from a mask? Clearly, it helps to know what makes up a facial expression of an inner feeling. For example, the face with the managed smile may contain traces of other feelings the person is trying to conceal. The genuinely happy smile does not involve the forehead or eyebrows (Ekman & Friesen, 1975). Hence that portion of the face may be a site for the expression of other emotions. If a smiling face involves eyebrows drawn down and together, it may be that the smile is a cover for anger. If the inner corners of the eyebrows are raised, the undercurrent of the happy face may be sadness.

But these signs are subtle and often hard to notice. There are easier ways to tell when a smiling person is not in fact happy. Look to the body. The body often offers information about the feelings a person is trying to conceal, because people don't try as hard to manage their bodies as they do their faces (Ekman & Friesen, 1969a). You learn to put your presentation efforts to work on your face because, not covered by clothing, the face is so visible and exposed. Also, from early childhood on, you find that others comment on your face as a clue to your feelings. They say things like "Let's see a smile from this happy girl" but rarely say "Why are you sitting so angrily with your arms crossed?"

From Representation to Emotion

The fact that people both express inner states *and* manage their behavior in order to appear to be feeling certain things is often greeted with dismay by others. The managed impression is dismissed as mere deceit, and the search is on to detect what the "real" feeling might be.

But there is another view. This one suggests that nonverbal expressions may precede emotion, rather than the other way around. In other words, facial expressions or body movements adopted for a variety of reasons may come to influence a person's inner state. Based on the James-Lange theory of emotion, the view is that bodies react to situations and people take note of their bodily reactions to decide what emotion they are experiencing.

In a number of interesting studies, people have been asked to move their facial muscles in particular ways according to a researcher's instructions. The effect was something like having a makeup specialist create a nose wrinkle here, raise an eyebrow there, and smooth a facial line somewhere else. The results of the research are interesting. Laird (1974) found that people whose facial features had been molded into a smile or frown reported feeling happy or angry, respectively. Izard (1975) used much the same approach and obtained much the same results. His reasoning is that neurological impulses can travel both ways on muscle-to-brain pathways. Where Ekman believed that the neural impulses travel from the brain to the facial muscles (see p. 27), Izard saw the nervous system as allowing two-way traffic; that is, impulses can also go from the facial muscles to the brain. In a more "emotional" test of these ideas, male college students who were to undergo electric shock were divided into three groups: the first group was instructed to express no pain, while the second and third groups were asked to show intermediate and high levels of pain, respectively. Results showed that the facial expressions thus adopted affected the subjects' physiological responses to pain. Those who put on the most pain showed the highest physiological reaction (Colby, Lanzetta, & Kleck, 1977).

Similar effects have been noted with respect to the relation between posture and thinking. Schulman and Shontz (1971) positioned students into four postures—standing erect, sitting erect, sitting bent, and lying down—and observed subsequent effects on thinking processes. On problem-solving tasks, students performed much better sitting erect than in any other position. However, creative efforts were uninfluenced by body position.

So it now appears that the connection between inner feelings and outward signs is not a one-way or a simple one. Putting on an expression will not create an emotion for which you have no internal basis, nor can you completely alter your experience of an inner state by putting on a different face. The communicational effect on others of your putting on a different face may nonetheless be powerful. If they take you as you wish (that is, follow the command aspect of the communication), the context may be sufficiently changed so that your actual experience changes.

Interpreting Signs of Emotion

Emotional Baselines

When you describe someone, you often resort to comparisons such as "He's young for his age" or "She's taller than most." Sometimes the comparison isn't obvious, but it's still there. If you were in the work group in our earlier example and you were trying to decide whether the person who smiled was really happy, you would automatically make some mental comparisons. You have a built-in sense of how much people smile. This gut sense provides you with a baseline with which to compare the smile you're looking at. One kind of baseline you're probably not aware of has to do with where you live or, what's more important, where you grew up. How much people smile varies, for example, from one part of the United States to another. Middle-class New Englanders walking along the street hardly smile at one another (Birdwhistell, 1970). Southerners smile the most. Knowing that this difference exists wouldn't lead you to think that Southerners are necessarily the happiest Americans, since you also know that this kind of smiling is more a matter of a social rule or custom. In the South the unsmiling person might be asked "Why so glum?" where the smiling face in New England is greeted with a suspicious "What's so funny?"

Your built-in sense of how much people smile isn't just a matter of place. Other social rules play a part. What you make of your co-worker's smiling also depends on whether that person is a man or a woman. Women in this society smile more than men (Bugental, Love, & Gianetto, 1971). Just as a lot of smiling by Southerners doesn't necessarily signal their happiness, so doesn't women's smiling reflect widespread joy and pleasure. We discuss gender differences in more detail in Chapter 12. Suffice to say here that, if your co-worker is a male, you might make more of his smile. The man's smile, being rarer, is noticed more and more likely credited to corresponding inner feelings. The woman's more common smile can reflect any number of emotions—or none at all.

Your emotional baselines are not derived from social rules of sex or culture alone. You develop a baseline for comparing people with themselves. The better you know someone, the more finely tuned these comparisons become. You come to notice not only the major shifts in mood but the slightest changes in feelings as well. Subtle alterations in expression, imperceptible to most others, signal to you that something has happened with an intimate. Deep understanding of another means knowing the usual so well that the unusual can be known.

In such intuitive comparisons, sequence is a most important thing. To know the meaning of a tone or look, you need to know what came just before that tone or look. The slight, tentative smile coming out of a sad expression may have more impact than a smile that grows broader. The contrast in expression makes the change stand out. The more a cue differs from the preceding one, the clearer its meaning (Grant, 1971).

But contrast is not all there is. People are sensitive to remarkably small changes in nonverbal behavior. Very quick, very tiny movements alter the impressions being formed. Tightening just a few muscles can change a posture from relaxed to tense, and a slight shift can turn an attentive look into a blank stare. Some interesting studies of such small changes in the appearance of the eye have been done by Hess (1975). He found that the pupil of the eye dilates when people look at pictures that interest them and constricts when people feel negative. These changes are very small. The pupil of the eye ranges in size from 30 to 80 millimeters, and the typical change from dilation to constriction is no more than 20% of that amount. Yet perceivers respond to such small changes. Men shown a woman's photograph retouched to enlarge the pupils reacted more positively than those who saw the same picture with constricted pupils. The men couldn't say what caused their reaction, but they described the woman with small pupils as cold, selfish, and hard, while those who saw the photograph of the same woman with enlarged pupils described her as soft, loving, and warm.

You might experiment with this yourself the next time you see a suitable portrait of a woman in a magazine. Use a felt pen to enlarge the pupil and look at the picture again. Or get two copies of the magazine and try the original and your retouched version on some unsuspecting male friends. You may find, though, that the photographer has beaten you to it; increasingly, advertisements have been making use of these findings to make their products more attractive (Hess, 1975).

Individual Differences in Sensitivity

By now, you have probably gathered that establishing the "real" meaning of an emotional expression is a pretty complicated affair. Yet we all rapidly and automatically make decisions about nonverbal cues all the time. If the cues are so very small, so very fast, and represent such blended portrayals of mixed emotions, how do people manage to get the "real" meaning behind another person's nonverbal behavior? Some people seem to be better at it than others. The search for the sensitive, accurate perceiver of nonverbal behavior has fascinated researchers for some time. In part, this search is a by-product of research dealing with the more general area of how people form impressions of others (Hastorf, Schneider, & Polefka, 1970). But the question of accurate perception is now getting the attention of psychologists interested in nonverbal behavior, who want to know more about what makes some people good at receiving and interpreting nonverbal messages.

Recall our example of the smiling co-worker and what happens on the receiving end. Some people simply don't see the smile. They may be engrossed in their task and not be looking at all or be looking but not at the face. Others see the face but don't notice the smile. One interesting possibility is that people pay attention to different nonverbal channels. Robert Rosenthal and his associates (Rosenthal, Hall, DiMatteo, Rogers, & Archer, 1977) have developed the Profile of Nonverbal Sensitivity (PONS test) to measure people's capacity to receive messages from the face, voice, or body. The PONS is a 45-minute film showing 2-second segments drawn from 20 different situations. There are 220 segments in all, showing a woman's face only, body only, or face and body combined, as well as two kinds of voice samples treated to obliterate the content while retaining the tone and rhythm of her speech. Viewers read two verbal descriptions of situations and must choose the one that describes the segment seen or heard. For example, they must decide if a given facial expression goes with "leaving on a trip" or "ordering food in a restaurant" or if a vocal segment is "criticizing someone for being late" or "expressing gratitude."

Preliminary results with this test indicate that women are generally more accurate than men in interpreting these cues across all channels. Beyond this, no overall skill in interpreting nonverbal behavior has been found. The PONS demonstrates that there are individual differences in what channels people attend to; people who are accurate interpreters of nonverbal behavior using the face are not necessarily accurate when presented with vocal or body cues (Zuckerman, Lipets, Koivumaki, & Rosenthal, 1975). Thus it may be that some people don't see our worker smiling because they just don't pay much attention to visual information. They might be more likely to pick up emotional information through the sound of the voice. Others may look at the body but not at the face. One study comparing psychotherapists and dancers found that the dancers paid more attention to the body in reaching decisions about what a person was feeling (Dittmann, Parloff, & Boomer, 1965). Try to remember a recent encounter in which you knew that your friend was very sad. What specific image comes to your mind most distinctly? Your friend's face? A particular inflection of her voice? Your mental image may give you a clue as to which channels you heed in decoding emotional messages.

Nonverbal messages can be missed not only because the receiver is sensitized to another nonverbal channel but because the viewer is not looking at the right time. As mentioned in Chapter 2, nonverbal behavior is as continuous as it is multichanneled. There is so much information available all the time that people necessarily sample from it. You tune in at certain times and not at others. So a smile which occurs when you're not attending is likely to be missed. But tuning out some nonverbal cues is not just a matter of amount. Sometimes people fail to notice because they don't want the responsibility of dealing interpersonally with the emotional information they would get by looking.

Noticing and dealing with the emotions of others is not a matter of personal choice alone. There are social rules about when to look and how much to see. Take embarrassment, for example. Not only are there display rules for senders, suggesting that they play down their embarrassment, but there are social rules for perceivers, suggesting that they look away for the moment. Once again, interaction between people emerges as an important element in communication.

Summary

Emotional expressions are conveyed nonverbally. They are brief and usually multichanneled, involving several modalities simultaneously. Furthermore, there are distinct and different patterns of facial movements associated with distinct and different emotional experiences. In their pure report form, they cannot be confused with one another.

In their more everyday occurrence, however, emotional expressions can be highly transient, sometimes incomplete, and often occurring in mixed combinations. In addition to these variations, emotional expressions are intimately involved with contextual features. They can be dampened by the sheer presence of others or altered to fit the definition of the social situation.

As perceiver, you are helped enormously by knowing not only what to look for but when and how to interpret it. These built-in baselines increase your chances of interpreting correctly. It is true that people differ with regard to what channels they respond to, but it is probably also true that the accurate perceiver is one who knows not only what is going on but how to take it as well.

Chapter 4

Personal Signatures

In Chapter 3, we talked about changes in facial expression, body postures, and voice tone that reflect the quick but significant changes in a person's internal state from one moment to the next. But there are some people, perhaps many, who appear to be permanently frowning or constantly tense. It's almost as though the fleeting had become forever etched in their faces and often throughout their whole bodies.

Nonverbal behavior is of interest for what it says not only about a person's feelings right at the moment but also about that person in general. You meet people for the first time, and you try to figure out what they're like. You ask yourself not just whether they're angry, sad, or happy right then but whether they're that way most of the time. People wonder, in the words of the comedian Flip Wilson, if "what you see is what you get." Where Chapter 3 dealt with the nonverbal behavior associated with transient emotional states, this chapter presents information on behaviors that reflect more enduring personality characteristics and differences. For example, a person might be feeling temporarily shy or anxious before giving a report in class, in contrast to someone who is nearly always shy and withdrawn with people. Temporary feelings are called *states,* and the more permanent qualities are called *traits*— a distinction that is important to keep in mind throughout this and the next chapter.

PERSONALITY TRAITS

That there might be connections between features of the face and body and patterns of personality is not a new idea. Speculations about physique and character are found in the Bible and in other writings of antiquity. It was in the 19th century that physicians and anatomists began to describe specific body types that went with different psychological orientations. Artists and writers have often relied on descriptions of physical appearance to convey nuances of character. One of the authors, indulging an addiction to detective fiction, has become fascinated with the physical description of the criminal when that character is introduced for the first time. Would you be suspicious of a "born gossip" whose "heavy red face became animated" and who "cocked his curious pear-shaped head" (Allingham, 1950)? How about an actor who "was not a preposterously good-looking man," whose "eyes, scarcely the width of an eye apart, were surprisingly blue," and whose "mouth, generously large and curiously folded in at the corners, was a joy to newspaper cartoonists" (Marsh, 1963)? Writers evidently use nonverbal cues to draw a framework from which the reader is to gain a sense of character.

Notice how often these descriptions imply that physical features somehow connect automatically to psychological traits. If some facial or bodily part is "surprisingly" or "curiously" formed, you are led to expect that there are likely surprising or curious psychological traits as well. Such connections, although they may seem self-evident, seldom turn out to be very accurate. For example, when people try to guess someone's personality after hearing a short speech sample, there is considerable agreement among listeners about what vocal sounds go with what traits. But, when you compare these impressions with what personality tests show about the speakers, there is little overlap (Kramer, 1963, 1964). It seems that there are stereotypes of voice tones and speech mannerisms that, although widely shared, don't correspond much to reality. Persons with low vocal volume and slow speech tempo aren't necessarily shy and withdrawn. They may be in a noisy place saying something they want to have clearly understood but not overheard. Their vocal tone is determined as much by the situation they're in as by any of their personal characteristics. In terms of the description of behavior presented in Chapter 1 and of Lewin's equation, this nonverbal behavior is a function of both the environment and the person. The contribution of "person," in this instance, most likely stems from a temporary state of being; that is, the person might be feeling shy right then in that encounter. Accuracy drops off when one ignores situational aspects and ventures predictions of permanent traits.

In the next few sections, we review the research evidence on whether particular nonverbal behaviors reflect underlying personality traits. The personality traits, or characteristics, we examine are the tendency to move toward or away from relationships with people (extraversion/introversion), the tendency to try to influence others or to be influenced by others (control), and the tendency to rely on self or on others for information about the world (field independence/field dependence). We selected these dimensions first of all because they strike us as the most interpersonal and hence the most applicable to nonverbal communication, which is between people. Secondly, research using these dimensions has yielded a modest consistency with regard to nonverbal behavior. Regrettably, many studies apply a personality test measuring a single trait or dimension to a group of people and then measure some single aspect of the nonverbal behavior of those with highest and lowest scores. The results of such studies are typically inconclusive. In reconciling these mixed results, we will be stressing the importance of context and environment and how these mesh with particular personality types.

Orienting toward Others

Extraversion/Introversion

A dimension based on Jungian psychology that has received considerable attention with regard to nonverbal behavior is that of extraversion—the tendency to turn outward to other people for personal rewards and satisfactions. It seemed likely to most researchers that extraverts might be more nonverbally tuned to other people and therefore might look more at and move closer to others. Most researchers have been interested in gaze. Comparing people who scored high, moderate, and low on an extraversion scale, extraverts (that is, those who scored high on the scale) were found to make more eye contact when engaged in conversation (Kendon & Cook, 1969; Mobbs, 1968). But a later study showed that extraverts look more at a conversational partner only if that partner is of the same sex (Argyle & Ingham, 1972).

Several investigators were curious about whether extraverts would allow others to come closer to them than would introverts. Although one study found that extraverts sat closer to their conversational partners and allowed the experimenter to get closer to them (Williams, 1971), there is more evidence that there are no differences between extraverts and introverts in interpersonal distancing (Fromme & Schmidt, 1972; Meisels & Canter, 1970).

Your intuition probably tells you that extraverts really do differ from introverts in their nonverbal behavior. Why, then, do the results of these studies seem qualified at best or even washed out altogether? Part of the reason may stem from the environments in which the research took place. These studies have all been conducted in psychological laboratories, which, as we mentioned in Chapter 1, affect behavior in different ways than other environments. (Although the assumption may be that, if everything is held constant, the real behavior of interest can be studied with great precision, the controlled procedures of the laboratory do not constitute absence of environment and do indeed affect behavior.) It is, therefore, plausible that both extraverts and introverts, in the "serious" climate of a psychological investigation, modified their behavior. Specifically, it may have been that extraverts' "usual" outgoingness was dampened by the need to adapt to the contextual demands of a laboratory.

Need for Affiliation

A personality dimension somewhat similar to extraversion is the need for affiliation, which, like extraversion, taps the degree to which a person needs and wants relationships with others. The priority of this need is examined in relation to a person's other needs—for example, the individual's need to seek affiliation rather than achievement or control.

Among researchers who have used the FIRO test (Schutz, 1966) to measure affiliation (FIRO stands for Fundamental Interpersonal Relations Orientation), one study found that the affiliative maintained more eye contact in conversation (Exline, Gray, & Schuette, 1965), but another study did not (Kendon & Cook, 1969). Other studies, though, showed more consistent results. Using a personality scale other than the FIRO test to measure the orientation toward others described as nurturance—which combines both affection toward and control over others—Libby and Yaklevich (1973) found that the highly nurturant maintained more eye contact with the interviewer. Measuring affiliative tendency with an instrument of his own devising, Mehrabian (1971b) videotaped students in a waiting situation. The more affiliative students were more positive in their nonverbal behavior and particularly so with friendly experimental confederates. Specifically, they looked more, talked more, said more pleasant things, and nodded and gestured more. The overall pattern here suggests that a personality tendency to orient toward others goes with some nonverbal signs indicative of such tendency.

When context and social rules are taken into account, however, a greater complexity emerges. One study, for example, revealed that women who were high in need for affiliation looked more while speaking and maintained more eye contact than women low in this need; the findings for males, on the other hand, were the opposite (Exline, 1963). Furthermore, when one more contextual factor was introduced—namely, competition—pairs of women with high need for affiliation shared more mutual glances in a noncompetitive situation than did women with low need for affiliation. The latter, however, established more eye contact in competitive situations than did the former. Male pairs showed only a slight tendency along these lines. When personal characteristics (like affiliation) and environmental characteristics (like cooperation) match, the link between trait and behavior is enhanced. When the personal and environmental characteristics are at odds, either no clear relation emerges or the environmental traits predominate.

Controlling Others

We've all been in the position of taking orders or, at the very least, following someone's instructions. Whether that person be teacher, employer, parent, or friend, he or she usually gives off signs of being in control and of exuding confidence—more generally, of being a dominant force. If he or she does not, it may be very difficult to take the person seriously.

What are the "signs"—specifically, nonverbal signs—that these dominant personalities give off? For one thing, the high controller's pattern of looking is different from that of the nondominant person. Those who describe themselves as wanting very much to control others tend to look more at the other person when speaking than when listening. In contrast, those whose inclination to control others is quite weak look a great deal when listening but much less when talking (Exline, Ellyson, & Long, 1975). In other words, high controllers attend to the other when they're talking and not when they're listening. This style is called a *visual-dominance pattern*.

And when they talk, those exuding confidence sound very different from those experiencing doubt or hesitation. Analyses of the same speech delivered by an actor portraying a confident person and a doubtful person revealed that the confident voice was marked by greater energy, higher pitch, and faster rate of delivery. In addition, there were fewer pauses, and, when they occurred, they were of shorter duration (Scherer, London, & Wolf, 1973). It is interesting to note, however, that raters, while distinguishing confident voices from doubtful ones, didn't see the person with a confident voice as being any more competent than the person with a doubtful voice.

Even during silence, high-dominant personalities are different from low-dominant ones. When looked at steadily by another and asked to approach, dominant people approach the other person more closely and more quickly than do nondominant people (Fromme & Beam, 1974).

But here, too, other results suggest that things may not be quite so simple. Exline and Messick (1967) found a difference between dependent and dominant subjects only under a condition of little responsiveness from an interviewer. Under such condition, dependent subjects engaged in significantly more eye contact, presumably because they were seeking approval that was not forthcoming. And a recent study found that people who described themselves as capable of controlling their own outcomes were more vocally assertive than people who viewed events as being beyond their personal control. This effect, however, occurred only in a "free" interaction; there were no vocal differences when the subject was in a supervisory role (Bugental, Henker, & Whalen, 1976). It may be that personality dimensions are most likely to be manifested in nonverbal behavior in those situations that have little structure. In other words, where social rules and contextual constraints are low, people are freer to express their personal dispositions.

Thinking about Others

Field Dependence / Independence.

The way an individual looks at and thinks about the world has been seen as reflecting a stable personality disposition. Specifically, the relation of self to the external world has been described as leading to two different orientations: field dependence and field independence (Witkin, Dyk, Faterson, Goodenough, & Karp, 1962). The field-dependent person tends to rely more on cues from the environment, including those from other people. Field-independent persons, instead, govern themselves more from internal cues and tend to be less influenced by others. Thus, field-dependent children look more at the teacher while taking a test than do field-independent children (Konstadt & Forman, 1965). This effect, too, is shaped by context, being more pronounced in women (Nevill, 1974) and less pronounced when the field-dependent person is in the speaking role (Kendon & Cook, 1969).

Cognitive style seems to affect body movement as well. Field-dependent people make more body-focused gestures (Freedman, O'Hanlon, Oltman, &

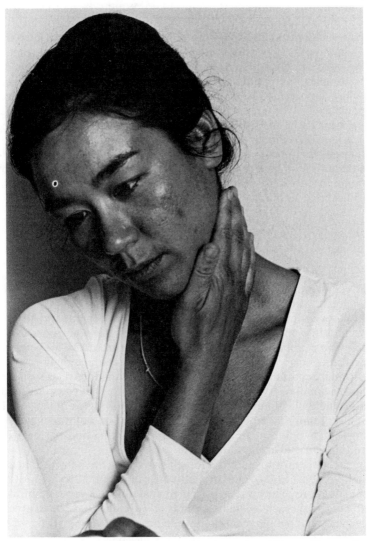

Body-focused movements, such as this woman's rubbing of her neck, are more often found in field-dependent people.

Witkin, 1972); in interviews, they squeeze, rub, or scratch parts of their bodies more than do field-independent persons. Specifically, field-dependent people are more prone to use hand-to-hand movements (rubbing and squeezing their hands together) while they speak. They also make more pointing or groping movements when at a loss for words. These same behaviors, however, did not distinguish field-independent and field-dependent women in a more recent study (Greene, 1976). What Greene found, instead, was that field-independent women showed more "distancing" (that is, arm and leg crossing, shoulder shrugging, absence of forward lean, and smiling) toward a male interviewer than did the field-dependent women, especially when the male was giving praise and showing acceptance.

In summary, the research on personality in nonverbal communication makes clear the need to take both person and environment into account. More specifically, you can expect to find "outgoing" nonverbal behavior among extraverts in friendly social situations. Similarly, you can expect to find assertive and dominant nonverbal behaviors among high controllers in free situations that presumably allow them to take charge. Just as people influence the environments in which they find themselves, they also select situations that fit themselves. But environments, too, make selections; some are so structured that virtually everyone knows what to do—and does it.

EXPRESSIVE STYLES

Movement Dynamics

Instead of grouping individuals according to a common personality trait and then looking at nonverbal behavior, some researchers have done just the opposite; they have sought to identify patterns of movement and glean from them insights into personality. When you are working in your room, can't you often tell who is approaching from his or her footsteps? Or, looking out the window, can't you spot a friend from the back by a characteristic posture and walk? Human beings have nonverbal signatures as distinctive as their written ones. Sports announcers can identify different football players on a team by their movements, without ever seeing their identifying numbers. Children declare their family memberships with distinctive ways of moving, as in the arresting sight of a 6-foot father and 3-foot son walking side by side, with the same rolling gait and arm swing.

An early attempt to study such expressive movements was that of Allport and Vernon (1933), who studied consistency of movement styles in different situations. They watched 25 men enacting a variety of familiar acts involving mobility, such as shaking hands or walking. They found great consistency over time; people seem to shake hands in the same stylistic way from day to day. Allport and Vernon also found consistency across different parts of the body—a consistency relating to the three dimensions of *area, centrifugality,* and *emphasis.* The first dimension refers to the area covered by the movement and describes the fact that people who walk with long strides also make large arm movements. The second dimension, which is related to the first one, refers to the tendency to direct movements outward away from the body rather than toward it. The last dimension refers to the sharpness with which the movements are made.

Not surprisingly, it is dancers who have paid the most attention to the

This boy is beginning to adopt movement patterns similar to his father's.

"how" rather than the "what" of body movement. Quality of movement has long been used in dance to convey character and personality. Expressive movement has lately been employed in the form of dance therapy to effect personality changes. Also in connection with dance, a system of description and analysis of movement, called *effort-shape* (Lamb, 1965) and based on dance notation (Laban, 1956), has evolved. This system taps some of the same dimensions identified by Allport and Vernon. For instance, *effort flow* refers to the relative freedom of movement and seems to combine elements of emphasis and control. Persons whose movements are less constricted are seen as more spontaneous and creative than those whose movements are more constrained. *Shape flow,* instead, refers to the body's use of space—what others have called expansiveness. Body movements are seen as they would be seen in dance—narrowing or widening, rising or sinking, advancing or retreating.

Idiosyncratic Variations

Self-Confrontation

Most of us react with curiosity to seeing ourselves on film for the first time; we suddenly become aware of mannerisms and of peculiar ways of moving our bodies we never knew we had. Such reactions were particularly evident among the subjects of a study who were shown films of themselves engaged in a heated philosophical debate with a challenging experimental confederate. These subjects (22 young men) were later asked to comment on the confrontation that they had just seen on film (Nielsen, 1964). The "particularities" that the young men's movements showed, especially at stressful times in the discussions, were classified, on the basis of the subjects' own explanations, as physical or psychological in origin. For instance, a young man's characteristic ways of moving his hands to conceal the fact that two of his fingertips were missing (as a consequence of an accident) were classified as physical in origin. Those of another young man, instead, who repeatedly touched or covered his mouth—a characteristic movement associated with his need to repress or deny his feelings—were identified as more psychological in origin. These idiosyncratic movements appeared as they did perhaps because, under stress, people become less aware of the environment and more self-absorbed. Under even greater and constant stress, as in the case of psychologically disturbed persons (see Chapter 5), the unique aspects of an individual's nonverbal behavior become even more evident.

Self-Manipulation

Similar reasoning, based on a similar method, was used to explain autistic (body-related) gestures associated with tension and conflict (Krout, 1935). Students asked to comment on the movements they made while free-associating in response to conflict-inducing words were often able to name the conflicts they felt. It is important to note that the same word led to different conflicts and different gestures in different students. Despite this variability, Krout (1954) made extensive assumptions about the meaning of particular gestures such as hand to nose (fear), finger to lips (shame), and clenched fist (anger). Although it is unlikely that such specific interpretations can be generalized beyond a point, probably there is some systematic difference between movements directed toward and away from the body. De Lannoy and Leyn (1973), for example, found that withdrawn adolescents engaged in almost three times more body-focused movements than the more popular boys.

During a recent television interview with a well-known political figure, the camera was placed so as to reveal from time to time a nonverbal activity not usually seen in such context. From the front view, the senator appeared relaxed and still, but, from a back view, his hands were clearly active, with the fingers of the left hand digging and picking at the back of the right hand. Self-manipulations of this type have been called *body-focused movements* by Freedman, Blass, Rifkin, and Quitkin (1973) and *self-adaptors* by Ekman and Friesen (1969b).

For both groups of researchers, the kinds of movements we just described (that is, hand movements directed *toward* the body) must be distinguished from hand movements orienting *away* from the body during speech. For Freedman and his associates, self-manipulation such as hand-to-hand movements represents covertly expressed hostility. For Ekman and Friesen, self-adaptors are movements first learned as part of an effort to satisfy particular self-needs (such as the need for protection) or body needs (such as hunger and pain) and later used in response to a variety of problems or needs. For example, Ekman and Friesen found that observers rated people who scratched or picked at their bodies as hostile or suspicious. If one applies this view to the senator's televised behavior, one might speculate that the senator was angry at himself or at the interviewer and was disinclined to express his hostility directly.

Movement and Meaning

Descriptions of expressive styles can be fascinating, especially when you look to see whether these descriptions fit you or your friends. You are also likely to wonder how and when these mannerisms began. So the question "Why am I like this?" gets easily translated into "Where did that behavior come from?" The search for causes in the person's past life leads, however, to quite unreliable answers.

This unreliability is due in part to the fact that people don't always remember past events accurately. Furthermore, whatever one person reports about his or her past to another is also influenced by the ongoing relationship between these two persons. So, while there is little argument that the present action is at least partly determined by past events (that is, personal characteristics), there is also little argument that the present condition (that is, the environment) plays a crucial role in the present behavior. In other words, behavior cannot be explained solely by reference to its origin; behavior must be explained also in terms of the context that exists at the time when the events occur. No matter how unique the behavior and the circumstances that originated it, the role of context can never be ignored. Just as Lewin (1951) found statements such as "He is psychotic because of his heredity" unacceptable, we, too, find statements such as "She gestured that way because of a traumatic childhood event" equally unacceptable.

Summary

There are individual differences in nonverbal behavior that seem to be relatively stable and enduring. It is true that the extraverted and the affiliative are nonverbally engaging, that high controllers are dominating, and that independents are nonverbally distancing, but only when the environment is conducive to these behaviors. Social rules and the purpose of the interaction are but two of many contextual features that can alter the emergence of individual nonverbal behavior.

Although relatively little is known about how nonverbal styles, as opposed to specific behaviors, relate to personality differences, there is nevertheless some indication that they may be more informative than isolated behaviors. Style is, by definition, patterned. Nonverbal behavior cannot be explained solely in terms of personal history; there is always a contemporary context that contributes to the observed behavior.

Chapter 5

Psychopathological Presentations

Cues to Psychological Disturbance

> *Depression*
> *Schizophrenia*
> *Anxiety*

Nonverbal Sensitivity of the Psychologically Disturbed

Changes with Treatment

Interactions in Therapy

Summary

When it comes to the nonverbal behavior of psychologically disturbed people, it seems that few of us have any doubts about it. We may have some vague sense that extraverted people behave differently from introverted people, but we are a lot surer that a mentally disturbed person behaves quite differently from the rest of us. Try, for example, to picture some of the photographs that often illustrate the need for mental-health associations. What comes to your mind is probably the image of a person sitting alone, gaze averted, head bowed, arms and legs drawn close to the body, in a fetal position.

If you analyze the description above, you will notice that the picture we have drawn is a composite of several postures characteristic, at one time or another, of all of us. There are times when you let your head droop or hug your body closely, and there are times when you avoid another's eyes. What we are trying to say here is that what differentiates the nonverbal language of the mentally disturbed is not the use of "crazy" gestures or other strange nonverbal behaviors but, rather, the different ways in which these nonverbal signals are used. Psychiatric patients basically do the same things the rest of us do, but they do them much more or much less than the rest of us. For instance, they either look at another person too much or hardly at all. They remain very still or move about in agitated fashion. In addition, the timing of their nonverbal behavior is frequently off. They may do the right thing—smile or gesture—but at the altogether wrong time. They look or move when least expected or fail to respond when others would. Imagine someone who applauds a speech in midsentence instead of waiting for a pause or responds to a question with a blank smile. Also, the psychologically disturbed sometimes don't look all of a piece, so to speak; the rhythm of their movements is choppy and disorganized.

These examples suggest three ways in which the nonverbal behavior of the psychologically disturbed is different from normal behavior. First, it often violates the *baselines* on which expectations for behavior are built. The average person has learned from past experience what range of behavior to expect from others in a given situation. The sense that the psychologically disturbed do too much or too little is based on such baselines; that is, their behavior goes beyond the permissible range. Second, the psychologically disturbed don't seem very responsive to the salient characteristics of the *environment* they're in. Their self-absorption is such that they fail to notice or to respond to some important things going on around them. Finally, their nonverbal behaviors don't appear to hang together in a *pattern*.

This chapter deals with what the nonverbal cues to psychopathology are—that is, how different kinds of patients move, look, and sound. We also discuss how the psychologically disturbed respond to the nonverbal behavior of others—a point that is the object of conflicting opinions among the public. Some believe the psychologically disturbed to be extrasensitive to nonverbal cues, so that they see and feel what more normal people tune out; others see the psychologically disturbed as handicapped and limited in interpersonal perceptiveness. Finally, we discuss some research on the effects of psychological treatment on nonverbal behavior. Do the changes brought about by treatment in the patient's overall behavior extend to his or her nonverbal behavior as well? In this chapter, as in the preceding ones, you will find inconsistencies among the research findings. Here, too, as with research on personality, one mode of understanding these differences is to attend more closely to the importance of the contexts in which the research was done.

Cues to Psychological Disturbance

Depression

How do you know when someone is severely depressed? Sometimes you are told, but more often a close look will give you some rather clear clues that leave little doubt. It's partly in the eyes. Acutely depressed people have literally downcast eyes—what psychologists call the *averted gaze* (Riemer, 1955). They engage in little eye contact (Hinchcliffe, Lancashire, & Roberts, 1971; Waxer, 1974) and often reduce this contact even further by passing a hand over their eyes (Ekman & Friesen, 1969b). When we ask whether someone is "down," we are apparently posing a literal as well as a psychological question. It has been found, for example, that depressed people droop their heads and their mouths in addition to their eyes (Waxer, 1974).

Voices can give away depression even when the verbal content indicates that everything is just fine. Whereas everyday speech shows a fair amount of paralinguistic (tonal) variation, electronic analysis of depressed voices shows a notable reduction of the normal range of variation in pitch, loudness, and length of utterance (Hargreaves, Starkweather, & Blacker, 1965). In addition, resonance is lacking, faint quavering is present, and tempo is reduced (Condon & Ogston, 1966; Newman & Mather, 1938).

This man's downcast posture, head, eyes, and mouth reveal his depressed state.

Schizophrenia

Most nonverbal research into psychopathology has focused on schizophrenic patients. Schizophrenia is a mental disorder characterized by apathy, withdrawal, minimal social contact, and sometimes delusional thoughts and hallucinations. Nonverbal research has concentrated on schizophrenics for a number of reasons. For one thing, schizophrenics constitute the largest diagnostic group in most mental hospitals; for another, the verbal communication of many schizophrenics is nonexistent or, at least, hard to decipher. It is this latter reason that has moved psychotherapists to look more closely at the nonverbal behavior of schizophrenics (Fromm-Reichmann, 1950).

As with personality research, the assumption underlying the studies on schizophrenia is that the psychological withdrawal and social isolation that characterize the disorder are also manifested in nonverbal behavior. Schizophrenics are presumed to look less at others, move less, and be paralinguistically unresponsive.

With respect to gaze behavior, research initially revealed that schizophrenics, like depressives, do not attend visually as much as normal people do (Lefcourt, Rotenberg, Buckspan, & Steffy, 1967; Rutter & Stephenson, 1972). More recent research, however, has shown that schizophrenics do not differ from normals in their gaze behavior (Rutter, 1976). This may be due to the fact that the element of context in this latter research was different from that in most of the earlier work. Specifically, it appears that schizophrenics look less when they're talking to psychiatrists about personal topics but look as much as anyone else when they're talking to other schizophrenics or normal people in free conversation about relatively impersonal topics. This may indicate that the report aspect varies with changes in context and that the command aspect in interviews concerning personal topics is that the schizophrenic is unwilling to be engaged. But even in casual encounters, schizophrenics tend to avoid interacting. A study by Williams (1974) has shown that, if schizophrenics are given a choice about interacting with someone or watching television, they'll choose the latter.

It is not clear from these results whether the lack of visual attention to other people is an attempt to avoid the information and stimulation that come from attending to others or whether it is an attempt to avoid human contact in particular. Some clarification on this point was provided by a study in which schizophrenic boys were left alone in a room that had five masks mounted on the walls. Two of the masks represented human faces—one sad and one happy—one mask was just a blank in the shape of a face, and two of the masks represented animals. Observers noted that the schizophrenic boys, in comparison to boys in a control group, looked less at the masks of happy and sad human faces. They spent about the same time as normal boys gazing at the blank human mask and at the animal masks, but they spent more time looking at and touching physical features of the room, such as light switches and water faucets (Hutt & Ounsted, 1966). Here, too, it seems that, if given a choice about "interacting" with people, schizophrenics will choose not to do so. This is particularly true when the command carried by others' nonverbal expressions is to do something. Happy or sad faces command more response than blank or animal faces.

Voice characteristics of schizophrenics are different as well. College students rating voice qualities were able to determine whether the same verbal passage was read by a schizophrenic or by a nonschizophrenic patient (Markel, Meisels, & Houck, 1964). If such global differences exist, it is important to know what aspects of the voice reveal to psychologically untrained listeners that the speaker is a schizophrenic. A structural analysis of the pitch, loudness, and tempo of the voices of psychiatric patients was compared with clinical scale scores on the MMPI test (Markel, 1969). Speakers whose voices were rated as having loudness and tempo lower and slower than average and pitch above average had personality profiles characteristic of schizophrenia. Markel called this a "peak-pitch profile." Those whose voice profiles had higher-than-average loudness and lower-than-average pitch and tempo corresponded to the psychoneurotic diagnosis of depression. Peak tempo was not associated with any particular psychological disturbance.

In another area of speech, Mishler and Waxler (1970) noted that a *smaller* number of speech disruptions (such as pauses, repetitions, and incomplete words) occurred in discussions among family members one of whom was a schizophrenic than in discussions not involving a schizophrenic. Since speech disruptions of this kind are sometimes regarded as helpful in problem solving (in that people pause and repeat themselves as they search for the right words), their absence when the discussion included a schizophrenic was interpreted as a deficit in problem-solving skills.

The research on paralinguistic variations in schizophrenic speech reflects the importance of *baselines* for understanding psychological disturbance. The tonal variations go higher and lower than usual, the pauses are fewer; expectations about how voices are supposed to sound are disconfirmed.

Within the general category of schizophrenia, a particularly severe form is catatonia, which is characterized by long spells of body immobility. The stillness and rigidity have often been taken to represent complete social withdrawal. They can also be seen as a clear attempt to stop communicating. But, as we indicated in Chapter 1, one cannot *not* communicate. The very attempt to convey uncommunicativeness is a powerful communication in and of itself.

A fascinating finding concerning the body movement of normal people has been instructive about the movement patterns of schizophrenics. You might have had the experience of being with someone who seemed to be out of step with everything around him, including himself. Condon and Ogston (1966) have described this phenomenon as "self-dyssynchrony"—a condition in which the movements of certain body parts are out of phase in relation to one another. (In normal people, movements of body parts are rhythmic and coordinated; that is, parts move together.)

As a normal person speaks, the body moves in patterns of change that are synchronized with the speech stream. The body parts change direction of movement at the same time, and the boundaries of movement thus established correspond to the change points in speech. Even in the absence of speech, the body parts move in a coordinated and coherent fashion. The movements of some schizophrenics, however, are uncoordinated and lack a coherent pattern. The impression one receives is that the various parts of the body are separately controlled by several different people housed in the same body (Condon & Brosin, 1969).

Condon and Brosin also applied a frame-by-frame analysis to a film of the patient described in *The Three Faces of Eve* (Thigpen & Cleckley, 1957). This patient had three distinct personalities, which emerged at different times, and the distinctive presence of one or the other could be noted from the patient's facial expressions. For example, the analysis revealed a "transient eye strabismus"—a rapid eye movement in which one eye deviates from the direction in which the other eye is focused. These independent movements of each eye coincided with the presence of one of the two dominant personalities; when the left eye tracked away, Eve White was present, and when the right eye deviated, it was Eve Black who predominated. Therapists had noticed before something peculiar about the gaze of patients with multiple personalities, but, until Condon and Brosin's (1969) analysis, the precise nature of the disturbance was not known.

Anxiety

Another psychological disturbance that has received attention from researchers of nonverbal behavior is anxiety. In Chapter 4, we made a distinction between states and traits from the point of view of personality characteristics. Here we apply that same distinction to anxiety by differentiating between state anxiety, which is a temporary state brought on by a stressful situation, and trait anxiety, which is an enduring condition.

Most of the research on anxiety, both state and trait, has dealt with vocal characteristics, particularly speech disturbances. A large number of studies (for example, Dibner, 1958; Kasl & Mahl, 1965; Pope & Siegman, 1962) has found a relation between state anxiety and speech disturbance, specifically the presence of repetitions, stutters, word omissions, and slips of the tongue. With respect to trait anxiety, however, the speech disturbance called the *filled pause* (that is, "ah," "er," "um") does not occur more frequently in anxious persons than in normal persons (Kasl & Mahl, 1965; Krause & Pilisuk, 1961). A rare study comparing the effects of state and trait anxiety on speech disturbance found no effect of trait anxiety on filled pauses, speech rate, or other speech disturbances (Cook, 1969). State anxiety, on the other hand, was associated with more stutters, omissions, and other disturbances, thus confirming previous findings. Comparisons of speech samples obtained from patients on days when they were very anxious and on days when they were less so showed that more speech disturbances, a slower speech rate, and more silences characterized the days of greater anxiety (Pope, Blass, Siegman, & Raher, 1970). It would appear from these findings that a state of anxiety, like a state of happiness, has characteristic vocal features.

Nonverbal Sensitivity of the Psychologically Disturbed

As mentioned earlier, there is some disagreement in popular views about how sensitive the psychologically disturbed really are. On the one hand, the psychologically deviant are thought to possess special perceptive capacities not available to or used by the average person. On the other hand, there are those who stress the self-absorption of the psychologically disturbed and, consequently, see them as less sensitive than average.

A study comparing schizophrenics with medical and surgical patients found that the former were generally poorer at identifying emotions in speech sounds. There was, however, much more variability in the schizophrenic sample than in the normal group, leaving open the question that some schizophrenics may indeed be more sensitive to emotional expression than the average person (Turner, 1964). A similar comparison found both psychiatric and medical/surgical patients poorer at identifying ten emotions conveyed with a standard sentence than either hospital-staff members or healthy adults not associated with hospitals (Nash, 1974). The fact that both sets of patients were equally poor at this task suggests that there may be something self-absorbing or disorienting about hospitalization that affects the judgment of emotion in others. In judgments of facial expression, schizophrenics were poor at identifying faces depicting disgust, contempt, shame, and humiliation and tended to label a large number of pictures as representing joy (Dougherty, Bartlett, & Izard, 1974).

Given the scarcity of research on this topic, it remains unclear whether the psychologically disturbed are generally impaired in their sensitivity to others' nonverbal behavior. It may be that they attend more to some nonverbal channels than to others or to some emotions than to others. In Chapter 3, evidence was presented that the normal population differ in this regard, and it is likely that the psychologically disturbed do so as well.

Changes with Treatment

Just as there are nonverbal signs of the onset of psychological disturbance, so there are signs of its abatement. As people feel less troubled, their nonverbal behavior, too, shows signs of improvement. Thus, an increase in the amount of eye contact that schizophrenic and depressed patients make with an interviewer can be used as an indicator of improvement in the patient's condition (Hinchcliffe, Lancashire, & Roberts, 1971). Similarly, the amount of space patients require around them can be taken as an indication of change. In one study, schizophrenics who were about to be discharged from the hospital allowed an experimenter to approach them closer, from all sides, than they had on admission (Horowitz, 1968). Presumably this tolerance for closer distances reflects a more general willingness to engage others. At admission, the reluctance to interact with others is reflected in maintaining greater distance, avoiding eye contact, and using other nonverbal ways of saying "Leave me alone."

In psychotherapy, the nonverbal channels of gaze, facial expression, voice characteristics, hand gestures, and seated posture provide the therapist with information about the state of the patient and the progress of the interaction. Dating back to Freud, psychotherapists have used nonverbal behavior to make inferences about the patient's thoughts and feelings—usually about material the patient could not consciously recall or describe. Playing with a wedding ring, foot wiggling, and other nonverbal activities have been linked to fantasies and feelings that the patient found it hard to talk about (Mahl, 1967). It must be stressed again that these particular gestures have meaning for a particular patient at a particular time and cannot be taken as generally meaningful cues. Not all people who play with rings on their fingers are concealing marital tension.

Change in psychological state is inferred when a particularly notable nonverbal cue by a patient changes in form or frequency. For example, a group of college students was shown films of depressed women patients made when the women were admitted to the hospital and, again, when they were discharged. On the basis of the women's nonverbal behavior alone, the students described the same patients quite differently at the time of admission and at the time of discharge (Ekman & Friesen, 1968). Where the students saw one woman as suspicious, bitter, and tense on admission, they described her as friendly, calm, and gentle on discharge. Another, who was seen as despondent, fearful, and unstable when admitted to the hospital, was later called active, impulsive, and cheerful. Careful analysis of these films revealed which specific body movements were different on the two different occasions. For example, the film of the woman who on admission was judged despondent and fearful showed one very repetitious foot action; the woman constantly slid one foot back and forth on the floor. At discharge, foot movements were about the same in number but they were much more varied, with legs crossed and uncrossed, ankles bent or not, and feet tapping and swinging. Hand actions also changed in the course of treatment. Overall, it was the restoration of a greater range of gestures and movements that signaled these patients' return to normalcy.

Psychological disturbance affects the entire person, mind and body. When treatment is primarily verbal, changes in nonverbal behavior are regarded as following upon changes in feeling and outlook expressed verbally. Recognizing the inextricable connection between mind and body, other therapists, however, have suggested that changes in thinking might accompany induced changes in nonverbal behavior. For example, "character armor"—involving rigidity in posture, gait, and gesture—can be reduced by direct intervention with that "armor" (Reich, 1949). Body-movement therapies are guided by the belief that loosening up the body through exercise, massage, and prescribed movements can yield concomitant changes in mood and self-perception. The relaxation procedures of behavior-modification therapies are also based on the notion that the anxiety and fears associated with certain experiences can be reduced if the body can be trained and maintained in a state of relaxation during the experience.

Interactions in Therapy

We've been talking for most of this chapter about what nonverbal cues can tell us about an individual in psychological distress. The focus has been on the individual and on the cues that the individual provides for the psychotherapist about his or her internal dynamics. But nonverbal cues emanate from the therapist as well, and the disturbed individual responds to them. Some argue that patients generally prefer to be quite close to the therapist (Kelly, 1972), but others recognize that some distances can be altogether too close for comfort (Boucher, 1972). The general consensus seems to be that a distance of about three to four feet is just right (Engebretson, 1973). Reducing it to what Hall (1959) calls an "intimate distance" (18 inches or less) would produce more anxiety than rapport. A similar effect is produced when the distance is increased, as demonstrated by a study in which increased distance (6 to 9 feet) was accompanied by increased speech disturbance on the part of the patients, which reflected increased anxiety on their part (Lassen, 1973). Another problem presented by the greater distance was that the patients didn't feel that they were getting their points across.

With regard to vocal behavior, Mehrabian (1972) has suggested that the therapist should use a high degree of nonverbal responsiveness. Expressed through greater facial expressiveness, higher speech rate, and louder speech volume, such high responsiveness presumably signals to the patient that he or she is the center of the therapist's attention. But here, also, too much responsiveness by the therapist can be disturbing.

Another study, employing a highly detailed analysis of therapist vocal cues, uncovered some characteristic cues that go with peak and poor therapy sessions. One finding concerned the intonational patterns. Whereas the therapist's voice in the peak sessions conveyed the normal intonation that gives speech its rhythmic quality, the intonation in the poor interview either was flat or was overloud or overhigh (Duncan, Rice, & Butler, 1968). Other findings showed that certain vocal cues in and of themselves did not distinguish peak from poor sessions but in combination with one another produced significantly different effects.

One aim of therapeutic responsiveness is to bring the patient out of his or her social withdrawal and into an active involvement with other people. It now appears that the actual physical environment in which people interact can either aid this movement toward involvement or seriously hamper it.

Fixed seating arrangements, once thought to be irrelevant to social involvement, are now recognized to be an important factor in the communication between people. For example, Osmond (1957) distinguished between what he called *sociofugal* and *sociopetal* spaces. The former prevent the development of communication, and the latter encourage growth of relationships. Sociofugal spaces are characteristic, for example, of hospitals and hotels; sociopetal distances, instead, are exemplified by the setting of a teepee or an igloo. A hospital dayroom provided a setting in which to test the effects of sociofugal and sociopetal furniture arrangements (Holahan, 1972).

To test sociofugal spacing, two small square tables were placed in the middle of the room, with two chairs (far apart from each other) against each of the four walls. In the sociopetal spacing, the tables were again in the middle of the room, but the chairs were placed around the tables. The sociopetal arrangement produced a significantly greater amount of social interaction than did the sociofugal one.

Sociofugal spacing, like the seating arrangement in this airport waiting room, makes interaction more difficult.

Summary

Psychopathological nonverbal behavior doesn't essentially differ in kind from normal behavior. It does differ, however, in its deviation from expected baselines, unpredictable response to the environment, and disjointed presentation. Mostly it is a matter of inappropriate responses to current situations.

The initial research on psychological disturbance assumed, as did the initial research on personality, that abnormality, like personality, is relatively constant. In other words, it assumed that the relation between nonverbal behavior and psychological disturbance is always there (Dittmann, 1963). But we know know that, just as so-called "normal people" express different nonverbal behaviors depending on the situation, "abnormal people" may do so as well. The research on gaze in schizophrenics showed that avoidance was present under a particular set of circumstances. Much more needs to be known about the circumstances, people, and situations that may elicit, inhibit, and control the manifestations of disturbed behavior.

It is also commonly assumed that the relation between nonverbal behavior and some disturbed state is a one-way relation. But it is more likely that the connections are two-way. For example, it may be that disruptive behavior doesn't originate only from the inside but from the outside as well. Disturbed behavior can be learned and, once learned, creates havoc with interpersonal relationships, which in turn affect internal dynamics. Nonengagement with others may occur because someone has learned to stand at a distance, to avert gaze, and to act generally subdued. People who behave this way are then avoided, and this creates in them real feelings of isolation and depression.

Finally, we have seen that the environment can have real effects on behavior, either by exacerbating already present withdrawal tendencies or by creating an atmosphere that encourages approach and openness. Physical arrangements, as well as nonverbal interventions by therapists, greatly modify individual pathological behavior.

Chapter 6

Moving Toward and With: Positive Relationships

It's a noisy, crowded party, and you're a little tired and bored. You're being "talked at" by someone who doesn't have much to say, and you're considering leaving. Then, suddenly, you catch a pair of eyes looking at you from across the room. For a moment your eyes are held, then you move on. But something made that contact different from the usual party scanning, so, after a moment, your eyes return to that face in the crowd. And there, again, is the other looking at you. Your eyes are held longer. A message sent is received and answered. Sometimes that's all there is to such encounters. Sometimes there is more. You realize you've lost track of the conversation you're in and return your attention to it. But the nonverbal dialogue with the stranger goes on. As you try to keep your attention on the conversation, you shift your position so that your body is now turned toward the stranger across the room. The next time your eyes meet, the mutual look is longer, and the other smiles. Slowly and slightly, you return that smile and look away again. You say to your partner that you wish to refresh your drink, so the two of you move across the room, thereby narrowing the distance that separates you from the stranger. Again, sometimes the sequence ends there; the next time you look, you find yourself facing the back of the stranger, who is in animated discussion with someone else. But, again, sometimes the sequence does not end there, and your eyes meet again. Now, the stranger comes near and, touching your arm, says "Let's go somewhere and talk." You both know that the mutual attraction was affirmed and confirmed long before those words were spoken.

The script for this scene introduces some new elements into our discussion of nonverbal communication. In the last three chapters, we've been dealing primarily with the individual—that is, with behavior that can occur even when the individual is alone. Now we turn our attention to what goes on between and around individuals. Instead of private preserves, it is shared grounds that we now seek to understand. In addition to cues rendered in solitude, there are cues directed to others, received from others, and exchanged with others. In the next four chapters, we examine the role of nonverbal behavior in a number of different relationships, including those characterized by attraction, aggression and competition, and power and influence. In this chapter, we consider "positive" relationships—those that involve movement toward and with other people.

Nonverbal Indicators of Attraction

You can look at the nonverbal indicators of attraction from two perspectives—as a participant and as an observer. That is, you can look at behavior that indicates attraction from the viewpoint of those feeling mutually attracted or from the perspective of an observer trying to decide by the nonverbal behavior of interacting people whether they are attracted to each other. Therefore, you can ask questions about how people who are attracted to each other look and move or about what inferences you can draw from the fact that two people stand close to or look at each other a great deal. Take our description of the nonverbal encounter at the party, for example. If you were one of the pair in the situation we described, you would be looking at that nonverbal encounter from the viewpoint of the participant. The looks you exchanged and the moves you made, however, would be automatic, done without awareness, because that's how we've all learned to respond when we feel attraction toward someone. Keep in mind, though, that the script involves two actors; without the countermoves, there can be no relationship. If, instead, you read about the encounter at the party, you would see that encounter from the observer's perspective; watching people at parties offers many opportunities of this kind, which tell you that you're observing attraction at work.

These two perspectives have been termed *encoding* and *decoding* (Mehrabian, 1969). People encode when they *act* on their attitudes in a relationship by their nonverbal behavior; they decode when they *interpret* these attitudes from the behavior they observe. Obviously, both perspectives are used in communication, since people take both the role of participant and that of observer. When you're attracted to somebody, the attraction you feel comes out in your nonverbal behavior. You look longer and move closer. When someone moves closer to you in a conversation, you may not notice that move specifically, but from the constellation of the other's behaviors you may form the impression that he or she likes you.

In the pages to follow, we review the research on nonverbal cues to attraction from both perspectives. Material on gaze, on distance, and on touch is presented in three separate sections, because the research typically considers one variable at a time. Keep in mind, though, that these three channels do not ever function in isolation and that nonverbal behavior in positive relationships flows together from several channels.

Gaze

As our example suggests, gaze and eye contact provide very powerful cues to attraction. Poets and writers have long celebrated the power of the look between lovers—a phenonemon called *overgaze* by researchers, who note that eye contact is greater between those highly attracted to each other.

In social interaction, people look at each other for periods of time that vary in length from 1 to 7 seconds (Argyle & Kendon, 1967). This indicates that the amount of time a person spends looking at the other may be small or large; but what is interesting to note here is that the amount of time spent in eye contact is virtually always less than the time each person individually spends looking at the other. Of course, unless both pairs of eyes meet and hold, no eye contact occurs. It is the mutuality that characterizes the heightened gaze in attraction. A given person's tendency to look or not to look at others is fairly stable over time, but the amount of mutual gazing in different encounters varies a great deal, since it depends on the coordination of two individuals (Kendon & Cook, 1969).

Mutual gaze at this close distance is characteristic of people in love.

Do people look more at those they like than at those they dislike? Research findings provide evidence that it is so. In one of the first laboratory experiments on attraction and gaze, Exline and Winters (1965) observed the visual interaction of students before and after being praised, criticized, or not evaluated by an interviewer. The students who had been criticized looked less at the interviewer than those who had been praised or those who had not been evaluated; later they also said that they disliked the interviewer. In a second study, the students interacted with two interviewers, and midway through the conversation they were asked which of the two they liked better.

It was observed that, when the conversation resumed, the subjects looked more at the preferred interviewer. This might have been the result of the subjects having expressed their preferences, since, as Exline and Winters point out, no differences in visual interaction had been detected before the preferences were stated. The importance of sequence is quite clear in this experiment; the fact that you decide (and state) that you prefer one person over another does affect your subsequent behavior toward those two people. Other factors that contributed to the results of this study were the interviewer's sex and the conversational role (that is, speaker or listener). When speaking, women looked more at the person they preferred than at the other one; men, instead, looked more at the preferred person when they were listening.

Another factor that significantly affects the relation between amount of gaze and attraction is the content of the verbal interaction between the people involved. How would you feel about an interviewer who, upon learning that you're the oldest child in your family, looks you right in the eye and tells you that firstborns have a lot of negative traits? Such a procedure was used in a study (Ellsworth & Carlsmith, 1968) showing that, if an experimenter made a lot of eye contact while discussing a topic that was rewarding to the subject, she was evaluated very positively by the subject. But, if the experimenter made frequent eye contact while discussing something that had negative implications for the subject, her evaluation by the subject was quite negative.

Gaze is a way of signaling involvement with or focus on another person. This means that a person who feels attracted toward another gazes more because he or she is giving that person undivided attention. As the findings above indicate, when the visual attention (*report* aspect) combines with positive verbal content, the *command* is to take this attention positively. When the visual attention combines with negative content, the message is to take this focus negatively.

It is interesting that a replication of this study, using same-sex experimenter and subjects, found that, when the positive verbal content was of a more personal nature, the experimenter's intense gazing led to less positive evaluation on the part of the subjects than when the high level of looking was accompanied by equally positive but more impersonal verbal content (Scherwitz & Helmreich, 1973). The researchers' explanation for these findings was that in same-sex pairs the combination of high eye contact with highly personal positive comments constitutes a violation of expectations. In other words, too much involvement (that is, a lot of gaze and personal comments) in same-sex encounters is reacted to with a certain amount of suspicion and dislike.

In cross-sex encounters, however, a different set of expectations operates. Men and women seem to share the expectation that, when two people of opposite sexes meet for the first time, the woman should be expressive and responsive to the man. In a study (Kleinke, Bustos, Meeker, & Staneski,

1973) in which male-female pairs met for the first time, women rated male partners highest when they believed themselves to have looked at the man "more than most people." On the other hand, men gave the highest rating to the woman whom they believed to have looked at the least. These results confirm that people act upon observations of their own behavior and that they interpret this behavior according to the social rules they know. In Chapter 12, we present some of these rules and discuss how they regulate male/female encounters in our society. What the study we have just discussed suggests about such rules is that women are supposed to look at men and men are not supposed to look back too much. Indeed, the male subjects in this study rated low-gazing females as least attractive, and the female subjects rated high-gazing males as least attractive.

Most of the research presented thus far has dealt with encounters between strangers meeting in the research laboratory for the first time. The results have all been based on how much *one* member of such pairs looked at the other. Now we turn to a study that observed well-acquainted couples—rather than couples who had just met in the experimenter's laboratory—and found support for the expected tendency of lovers to gaze at each other (Rubin, 1970). Dating couples were compared, and those who scored higher on a scale measuring romantic love were observed to spend more of their looking time in eye contact than those who scored lower on this scale. An interesting sidelight of this finding was that the women spent much more time gazing into the face of the loved one than did the men. The social rules alluded to with regard to the Kleinke et al. findings continue to operate here. The difference in the gazing behavior of strangers and couples who are in love seems to be that a man in love returns the gaze of the loved one, thereby producing a higher amount of mutual eye contact. It appears, therefore, that among lovers it is the degree to which the man returns the woman's gaze that produces what we call the *overgaze*.

Distance

In our example of nonverbal exchange between strangers at a party, we saw that, once eye contact had been established across the room, the two parties involved began to close the distance between them. Interpersonal distance is most decidedly the result of an interactional process; what is too close for one person may be too far apart for the other, and the discrepancy must be negotiated between the two. In Chapter 7, we discuss what happens when someone comes too close for another's comfort; here we deal instead with interpersonal distances as they are mutually agreed upon. The anthropologist Edward Hall (1966) was the first to describe the spatial zones that reflect social rules for interaction. In our example of the party encounter, the eyes of the two people met at what Hall calls *public distance*—a distance from 12 to 25 feet—which characterizes formal encounters, lectures, judicial proceedings, and other public events. When the two started to move closer, they came to what Hall calls *social distance* (from 4 to 12 feet), which is typical of most casual social and business transactions. At this distance, you can easily see the other's upper body and hear most paralinguistic aspects of the other's speech. In our example, when something was actually said, the two people were at a *personal distance* (from 1½ to 4 feet), which allows for touch as well as a richer exchange of sight, sound, and smell. Closer still lies *intimate distance* (from 0 to 18 inches), which signals unmistakable involvement. This distance allows for maximum sensory information, with sight, sound, smell, touch, body heat, and feel of breath all engaged. It is the distance for lovemaking and comforting but also for some contact sports or for riding in crowded buses and elevators, where steps must be taken—whenever possible—to reduce the intimacy.

What Hall's classification indicates is that there are appropriate spacings or suggested baselines for different kinds of encounters. It has been found, for example, that the optimal distance for interacting friends is smaller than that for interacting strangers (Sundstrom & Altman, 1976). When Little (1968) asked people to imagine encounters between strangers or between good friends and to place dolls on a piece of newsprint to represent these encounters, the dolls were placed significantly closer in the situation involving friends. Similarly, when people were asked to place themselves with respect to imagined liked and disliked others, they placed themselves closer to those they imagined liking better (Mehrabian, 1968b). Also, if asked to imagine someone standing 3 feet rather than 7 feet away, subjects inferred that the person imagined to stand closer liked them better than the person at a farther distance (Mehrabian, 1968a).

In a relatively more realistic setting, distance was found to depend on the attraction people felt toward each other. Pairs of college students were selected, after being tested with an "attitude scale," to represent high or low degree of agreement. When the couples returned to the experimenter's office after spending a little time together on a "Coke date," the distance the subjects maintained between them was measured. Couples who had initial high attitude agreement reported liking each other more and stood closer than those with low agreement (Byrne, Ervin, & Lamberth, 1970).

It would seem, therefore, that the relation between distance and attraction is pretty straightforward. But here, too, things are not as simple as they may appear. It has been found, for instance, that closer distances do not always signal greater liking. They do signal greater intensity and involvement, which can then be differentially interpreted depending on other contextual cues. For example, Schiffenbauer and Schiavo (1976) found that, if an interaction has a negative tinge, a closer distance makes it even more negative. If the interaction has a positive cast to it, then close proximity accentuates this positive quality. The practical implication of these findings is that your getting physically closer to someone who doesn't particularly like you will not automatically turn the situation around and make the person like you more; as a matter of fact, it may do quite the opposite.

Touch

Touch is a nonverbal dimension that seems to signal intensity in a special way. Someone can look at you without your looking back, but touch is necessarily connection. It can be seen as the zero point of Hall's "intimate distance." Given the inescapable intensity of this dimension, context is very important in the positive or negative interpretation of touch. Whether touch communicates liking depends very much on a combination of things: type of touch, body parts involved, kind of relationship, and the situation in which the touching occurs. You may tend to think of touch in so many positive contexts (such as touch between mother and child, lover and beloved, healer and patient) in which the intensity is welcomed that you may not be as tuned to contexts in which that very intensity is less positively greeted. Subjects who explored the face of another by touch under the guise of testing extrasensory perception liked the other better than did subjects who did not touch the other person (Boderman, Freed, & Kinnucan, 1972); but this effect was not found when touch was coupled with a distant manner (Breed & Ricci, 1973). On the other hand, when the context is clearly a positive one, touching is seen as indicating more positivity. For example, engaged couples who were observed to touch more were rated as more loving than couples who touched less (Kleinke, Meeker, & La Fong, 1974).

Touch was also found to have a powerful effect on liking, as a study by Fisher, Rytting, and Heslin (1976) demonstrated. The setting of this study was a university library; in the process of returning the library cards to the patrons, the library clerks briefly touched the hands of some of the patrons but not of others. All the patrons were interviewed as they left the library. Among the female patrons, those who had been touched expressed more positive feelings toward the clerk and the library than those who had not been touched. Male patrons did not express similar feelings. These findings would seem to provide evidence that even a slight impersonal touch (unnoticed by most subjects) had a positive effect on women but not on men.

We have reviewed the research on the connection between attraction and gaze, distance, and touch. As you have probably noticed, most studies deal with only one of these variables. But in our example of the party, it was clear that the nonverbal dialogue involved more than just one cue. There were looks across the room, body orientations toward each other, smiles, and, finally, touch. It is quite likely that there were other cues as well, which, together with those we have analyzed, blend in a communicational event of considerable complexity. Relatively few studies have tried to deal with the complexity that often characterizes nonverbal encounters. However, in the section below, we present two conceptual approaches—the intimacy-equilibrium model and the arousal model—that have been offered to account for the way in which different nonverbal behaviors combine and interact with one another.

We may conclude at this point that the nonverbal cues of increased gaze, decreased distance, and touch are indicative of greater liking and closer acquaintance. This conclusion, however, is valid only when the environment has already set a positive stage for the proceedings. Gaze, distance, and touch are all powerful reports of involvement and focus, but it nevertheless falls to the context to issue the commands as to how the involvement is to be taken.

Intimacy-Equilibrium Model

Given that every real social encounter involves a multiplicity of nonverbal cues, unraveling the interrelation of those cues poses quite a problem. One of the two approaches we are about to discuss suggests that nonverbal behaviors combine to produce a desired level of intimacy for any particular social encounter (Argyle & Dean, 1965). Every social encounter is seen as posing a conflict between *approach* forces (for example, love, security, and warmth) that draw the participants toward greater intimacy and *avoidance* forces (for example, fear of rejection and fear of loss of independence) that pull the participants apart. Intimacy is seen as cued by a combination of eye contact, interpersonal distance, body orientation, facial expression, and other related dimensions. The forces that pull people toward and away from intimacy tend to maintain a state of equilibrium. If the equilibrium is disturbed by too much intimacy in one dimension (for example, by too much gaze), it will tend to reestablish itself through a decrease in intimacy in another dimension (for example, by increasing interpersonal distance).

Looking away when another looks too long is an attempt to restore equilibrium within the same nonverbal channel in which the desired level of intimacy was upset. But restoration of equilibrium can occur in different channels as well. Equilibrium can be restored by maintaining the same degree of eye contact but shifting one's posture away from the other person, leaning back, and changing the topic of conversation to a more impersonal one.

This intriguing model has been subjected to considerable empirical testing. The support for the theory is strongest for the relations between eye contact and distance and between distance and body orientation (Patterson, 1973). Specifically, it appears that, as experimental subjects interact at closer distances, the amount of their eye contact decreases (Argyle & Dean, 1965; Goldberg, Kiesler, & Collins, 1969). As interpersonal distance decreases, the body orientation of participants becomes less direct (Mehrabian & Diamond, 1971; Patterson & Sechrest, 1970; Pellegrini & Empey, 1970).

As we said earlier, the intimacy-equilibrium model holds that, when the equilibrium is disturbed, compensatory changes occur to reestablish it. Compensatory changes seem most likely to take place when the interactants are strangers of the opposite sex meeting in the context of a laboratory experiment (Jourard & Friedman, 1970). But it is also possible that, when the equilibrium is disturbed, the change is reciprocated rather than compensated for (Breed, 1972). At the party, for instance, when you first encounter the prolonged gaze of a stranger across the room, you break that eye contact fairly quickly when it exceeds the level of intimacy appropriate for visual exchange

The intimacy cued by being seated close together is offset here by reduced eye contact.

among strangers at a social gathering. If there is interest on your part in increasing the intimacy of the encounter, your eyes return. If this interest is reciprocated, still longer eye contact occurs.

What is comfortable equilibrium for a particular person in a specific encounter is influenced by the person's expectations about the encounter, his or her past experience with similar interactions, and the social customs governing such events. The importance of situational, as well as personal, factors in determining intimacy levels and the possibility that the intimacy level for a given encounter may change during the course of the encounter are recent additional components of this model (Argyle & Cook, 1976).

Arousal Model

Implied in the intimacy-equilibrium model is the idea that too much involvement too soon is uncomfortable. Verbal assertions of involvement pale beside the impact of nonverbal messages.

How do you respond to increased attention aimed in your direction? According to Patterson (1976), you go through a number of stages before responding. First, you may or may not notice the increased attention. If someone were feeling particularly attracted toward you but so downplayed the nonverbal display of attraction that you hardly noticed, it you wouldn't experience any change of arousal. But what if, instead, the focus came through unambiguously? Look at Figure 6–1. As you can see there, the next step involves your interpreting the arousal—that is, assigning an emotional label to it. Does the focus cause you to feel uncomfortable (negative emotion) or pleased (positive emotion)? The surrounding context helps you decide. If your reaction is negative, you probably then compensate by trying to increase the nonverbal distance—for example, by looking less or moving away. If, on the other hand, you regard the arousal positively, you are likely to reciprocate the involvement directed toward you by looking more or moving closer.

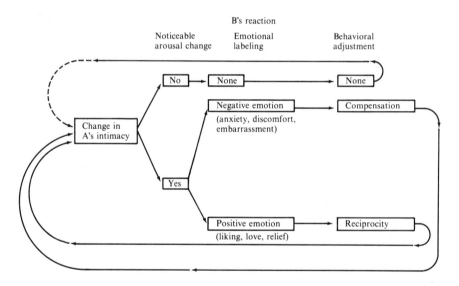

Figure 6-1. Diagram of the arousal model of interpersonal intimacy. (From "An Arousal Model of Interpersonal Intimacy," by M. L. Patterson, *Psychological Review,* 1976, *83,* pp. 235–245. Copyright 1976 by The American Psychological Association. Used by permission.)

Some indirect support for the arousal model comes from a field study investigating reactions to a very noticeable stranger. The findings of this study indicated that subjects maintained more distance from both male and female confederates standing in line to buy tickets when these persons wore bright clothing and strong cologne than when their presence was less arousing (Nesbitt & Steven, 1974).

Although, as a rule, people seem to try to reduce unwanted stimulation, there are instances in which people try to increase intimacy in response to an absence of the desired arousal. When conversational distance was increased between classmates who were good friends, they increased the number of mutual gazes (Russo, 1975). This may be an example of seeking to restore the intimacy level friends prefer.

A decided limitation of both the intimacy-equilibrium and the arousal models is that they don't take the nature of social interaction into full account. Each model is based on the existence of preferred levels of equilibrium or arousal inside the individual. This locates the changes within the individual rather than between participants. Yet social encounters are clearly joint ventures, processes of mutual negotiation, as our example of the party encounter suggests. A model that explains such interpersonal negotiations has yet to be proposed. One recent suggestion (Bakken, 1977) is that more attention be paid to the social rules governing intimacy for particular interaction contexts. Individuals' equilibrium-seeking or arousal-labeling tendencies may find expression only to the degree to which the rules allowed by the situation in which they find themselves permit. Some contexts call for intimacy, and in them you might find reciprocity; others call for more distance, and in them you might find compensation. In either case, *both* participants are responding to the same things.

Movement Synchrony

An attempt at taking more than a single individual into account has been made in research on people moving together in synchrony. Think of a scene from a movie or television show that was filmed in slow motion. Perhaps it was the idyllic coming together of two lovers across a springtime meadow or the members of a track relay team passing the baton from one to the other. What feeling do you get from such scenes? One vivid impression is that of the grace and flow of human movement. Another reaction stems from seeing people moving in unison, as though they were moving in time to the same music. What research on nonverbal communication is beginning to show is that we all, young lovers or not, often move in synchrony with others.

Do you remember when, engrossed in conversation with an intimate friend, all of a sudden you realized that both of you were leaning forward simultaneously to refill your coffee cups, so that your hands met on the coffee pot? That was the culmination of a synchrony that had guided your movements for some time, without your being aware of it. Have you ever noticed, for example, that long-married couples often show great similarity in their moves and mannerisms?

Perhaps imitation is not only the sincerest form of flattery but the harbinger of attraction as well. For example, Dabbs (1969) found that, when an experimental confederate mimicked one of a pair of subjects, the person who was being mimicked liked the confederate more than the person who was not being imitated. Similarly, Kendon (1970a) found that in a group discussion the movements of a speaker and those of the listener he addressed were sometimes mirror images of each other. This phenomenon was not as pronounced with other listeners who were not as involved in the conversation.

Posture Synchrony

Besides moving in unison and mirroring each other's movements, often people also imitate each other's postures (Scheflen, 1964). When you observe a group of persons interacting, you frequently see two people who are standing or sitting in identical positions. Both may have arms crossed or hands stuffed in their pockets. At times the mirroring is so literal that, if one person

People who have a common stance toward life often show postural mirroring.

is resting his right arm on the back of the couch, the other person will be resting his left arm on the back of the couch, and the two people will have their left and right arm, respectively, resting at the side. It is Scheflen's view that such shared postures may be indicative of a shared viewpoint.

There is research support for such speculation. Charney (1966) analyzed a film of a psychotherapy session and found that, at those times when in the therapist's opinion there was rapport between himself and the client, there was also a significant amount of posture sharing between therapist and client. Some other research has shown that the connection between posture sharing and rapport is significant even for groups made up of more than two people (LaFrance & Broadbent, 1976). In this study, the amount of posture sharing between students and professors was observed in seminar-size college classrooms, and class members were asked to indicate their level of involvement in the class. Results gave considerable support to Scheflen's notions. Classes in which the students described themselves as being involved showed more posture sharing between students and instructors than did classes that were described as producing low involvement. When this relation was examined over time—specifically, by looking at posture sharing and rapport over the course of a summer semester—posture sharing was found to precede rapport (LaFrance & Broadbent, 1977). It may be that those who begin by moving together come to find themselves involved in other ways as well.

Vocal Synchrony

Have you ever noticed that, when you're with some people, you seem to be very geared up (for example, you talk louder and faster), while the opposite is true when you are with some other people? Such behavior may be the result of another kind of synchrony, called *vocal convergence*. A variety of studies have shown that people being interviewed converge their vocal behavior to match the vocal behavior of the interviewer—specifically, the interviewer's length of speech (Matarazzo, Weitman, Saslow, & Wiens, 1963), frequency of interruptions (Wiens, Saslow, & Matarazzo, 1966), pause length (Jaffe, 1967), speech rate (Webb, 1970), and vocal loudness (Natale, 1975). You adapt to the other because you wish to communicate. You converge when you wish to be involved.

Summary

To talk about the role of nonverbal behavior in attraction is to talk about communication between people. In this and the next three chapters, we look at processes that make sense *only* when we consider the relationships in which people find themselves; that is, we deal with the interactional level of analysis of nonverbal communication.

Attraction is cued by the nonverbal behaviors of increased gaze, decreased distance, and touch. These cues actually signal involvement with another, and the context—such as the nature of the topic of conversation—

provides the guidelines concerning how the involvement is to be taken. The nonverbal cues themselves (eye contact, interpersonal distance, and touch) are not only indications of the nature of the relationship but also means through which a relationship characterized by attraction is negotiated. For example, if nonverbal involvement seems too much for one, he or she can compensate by reducing the involvement by looking away. If the signaled focus is welcomed, it can be reciprocated—for example, by moving closer—and this leads to a new level of interaction. Obviously, the cues of eye contact, interpersonal distance, and touch require at least two people. One alone can gaze; only two can have eye contact. One alone can move toward; only two can settle on an intimate distance.

Lastly, the phenomena of movement synchrony, posture sharing, and vocal convergence demonstrate dramatically that the boundaries of a relationship extend beyond any individual's skin. You do not only react to but respond with.

Chapter 7

Moving Away From and Against: Negative Relationships

The previous chapter began on a happy note. Attraction was the theme: a party scene, eyes meeting, and an acquaintance beginning. But not all nonverbal communication has a positive connotation. We all take part in encounters marked by slights, hostility, and rejection. This chapter presents the nonverbal behavior associated with competition, rejection, and aggression—that is, nonverbal behavior characteristic of negative relationships. Consider, for example, the nonverbal repertoire you call on when you're studying and a boring acquaintance drops by to chat. You're reluctant to tell the person straight out that you're busy and don't want to talk. Instead, you turn back to your desk, let your eyes drift to your work, and utter automatic "uh huhs" as the other talks. Most recipients of such communication do get the nonverbal message of rejection and depart.

Sometimes you make the picture more complex. As your acquaintance gets ready to leave, you might say "Hey, it was nice of you to drop by." Maybe that's conventional politeness, or maybe you're feeling a little guilty because you were cool to someone whom you don't like but who likes you; whatever the reason, you've sent contradictory messages; the verbal message was positive, and the nonverbal message was negative. The last part of this chapter takes a look at various kinds of inconsistent messages. Most people find inconsistency puzzling, and many resolve such contradictions by placing greater faith in the nonverbal aspect of communication. But contradictory messages do not necessarily pose an either/or choice for the recipient; typically, they are reacted to in combination. In our example above, you were nonverbally rejecting, and you tempered your nonverbal rejection with a positive parting comment; this combination is what your visitor is likely to respond to.

Competition

The research on the nonverbal aspects of competition has concentrated mainly on gaze and seating arrangements. With regard to gaze, as noted in Chapter 4, Exline (1963) found that competition reduces the number of mutual glances between people who show a high need for affiliation but increases eye contact for those who have a low need for affiliation. This effect was especially pronounced for women, who, in the investigator's view, find the power struggle inherent in competition unpleasant.

Preferences in seating arrangements for different kinds of activities interested Sommer (1969), who asked people to mark on diagrams of rectangular tables where they would choose to sit with a friend of the same sex for different activities. The subjects were asked about seating preferences for a social conversation before class, for studying together for an exam, and for participating in a puzzle contest. The study revealed that people imagining themselves engaged in competition preferred seats across the table from each other, in contrast to the side-by-side seating chosen for cooperative tasks. This across-the-table preference for competitive activities has since been found to exist among school children (Norum, Russo, & Sommer, 1967) and among British university students and nonstudents (Cook, 1970). These findings have generated considerable confidence that such seating preferences serve some competitive function.

It is not clear from people's seating choices for competitive events whether the intent is to increase the distance from the other person (the across-the-table position affords more room than the side-by-side position) or to have greater visual access to what the other is doing. A study designed to sort out the relative importance of gaze and distance asked male pairs of students to play a game in which a cooperative or a competitive strategy could be used to win (Gardin, Kaplan, Firestone, & Cowan, 1973). Subjects sat either side by side or across the table from each other and could see the other player or not, depending on the placement of a visual barrier between them. Results showed that subjects cooperated most when they had visual access to and sat across from the partner. Apparently, in studies like those conducted by Sommer, when people choose seats on a diagram, they pick positions across from each other to get greater distance. If the subjects are actually seated in such positions, as in the Gardin et al. study, visual access becomes more salient, and the encounter becomes more personal.

More evidence on the intimacy inherent in being able to see the other person comes from experiments on bargaining under circumstances in which negotiators can and cannot see each other. In simulations of management/union bargaining in which one side was given a stronger case, the side with the stronger case was more likely to win when the negotiations took place by telephone than when they took place face to face (Morley & Stephenson, 1969). In a series of studies investigating telephone and face-to-face bargaining, Short (cited in Argyle & Cook, 1976, p. 159) consistently found that bargaining by telephone resulted in victory more often than face-to-face negotiation. In other words, Short found that it was easier, or quicker, to change the other's mind over the telephone than face to face. Another and more recent study comparing face-to-face with telephone negotiations found that in the face-to-face situation the interaction was more spontaneous and diversified. In contrast, the telephone situation was more formal and task-related (Stephenson, Ayling, & Rutter, 1976). What this means is that, when one has visual access to the other, the other becomes much more immediately present. It should be noted, however, that there appear to be sex differences in this regard; in problem solving tasks, males seem to be more efficient than females in a face-to-face situation and indicate greater satisfaction with it (Bell, Cheney, & Mayo, 1972). As we shall see in Chapter 13, women attend more to social interaction; this may impair women's competitive performance in a face-to-face situation. For both sexes, it appears that in these bargaining and problem-solving tasks, the mutual visual access inhibits the driving force of competition, perhaps by making the loser's feelings more inescapably evident to the winner. The more limited nonverbal information available in telephone negotiations may make the verbal argument and its logical properties more salient and/or reduce the mute appeal of the loser for mercy. So the next time you want a refund for a defective product, you might consider bargaining by phone rather than returning the product in person.

How is the aftermath of winning or losing (no matter how you've played the game) expressed by nonverbal behavior? Ryen and Kahn (1975) put male triads into cooperative and competitive situations and noted how far the men sat from members of their own triad and from members of another triad they had worked with. Predictably, cooperating triads sat close together and near members of the other group. Competing triads placed themselves farthest from members of the other group. When one group was told it had won and the other was told it had lost the competition, the members of the winning triads moved closer to the members of the losing triads (as compared to the groups who were not informed of the outcome). Losers, however, tried to sit as far from winners as possible. On the basis of information concerning how the subjects rated their own group versus the other one, the experimenters speculated that the winners' behavior (moving close to the losers) was a move to take the best, most prominent position rather than a friendly, propitiating move. The preference for a particular seating arrangement is clearly the result of the interaction of several elements, such as the prominence of the place, the visibility the place affords, and how the arrangement is seen by others. We shall return to this topic in Chapter 8, when we discuss leadership and seating arrangements.

The study we just described looked at the effects of competition and cooperation on proximity. Another study reversed this strategy by asking what effects greater or lesser proximity would have on performance under cooperative and competitive conditions (Seta, Paulus, & Schkade, 1976). Groups of two men and two women were seated 5 feet or 2 feet apart while working on mazes under individually competitive or group cooperative instructions. In the competitive situation, subjects spaced 5 feet apart performed better than subjects spaced 2 feet apart. The reverse held true for cooperation.

What emerges from all this research on competition is that you need room to compete. People seek farther distances from those with whom they've competed, and they compete more effectively when they are allowed greater interpersonal distance. People also perform better in competitive situations when psychological distance is achieved through blocking of the visual channel. This is not to say that gaze plays no role in competitive struggles, for staring down another is a device sometimes used to rattle an opponent or, at the very least, to indicate that one is not a pushover. The way the winner feels about "visual" confrontation was aptly described in a few words by Secretary of State Dean Rusk when, in discussing the United States' confrontation with Russia in the Cuban missile crisis, he said "Eyeball to eyeball, they blinked first" (Janis, 1972, p. 164). Short glances at the other are also often employed to serve a monitoring or surveillance function. In any case, these latter two gaze phenomena have not been studied for their role in competitive situations. The next time you're competing with someone, try to pay attention to your own visual behavior and that of your adversary. It isn't easy to be your own observer in the heat of a contest and it may impair your concentration, but you might discover some interesting things about nonverbal competitive strategies.

Spatial Invasion

You've entered an empty elevator, punched the controls for your floor, and taken a position near one of the corners, when another person gets in and moves over to stand beside you. What do you make of it? You're sitting in a nearly empty bus, when a stranger sits down right next to you. How do you feel about it? You walk into an airport waiting lounge and, although there are available seats next to occupied ones, you opt to stand against the wall instead of sitting down. Why? You scan the library looking for a private place, see two empty tables, but notice that there are a couple of books and a sweater on one of them. Which one do you head for?

All these situations have an element in common—interpersonal distance, which refers to how people arrange themselves when others are present. If you had been in the elevator or bus described earlier, your probable reaction could have ranged all the way from mild discomfort to real anxiety and perturbation. It appears that the source of your discomfort comes from the fact that there is a social rule that governs most situations involving strangers congregating in public places. The rule is that, if given a choice, one should take the position farthest away from the others present. When people elect to behave differently—for example, stand or sit close to a stranger when there is a lot of space available—the norm is violated and the violator's motives become suspect.

Because of this rule, you seek to avoid situations in which your own spatial behavior might be misconstrued. In the airport waiting room, for instance, you may avoid sitting next to someone; both of you know the social rules, and, if you violate those rules, you feel that you must "explain" the violation. As places fill and the waiting room becomes crowded, the choice of sitting or standing becomes moot, and people tolerate closer proximity without questioning each other's intentions. But what if others touch you or look at you in places like crowded elevators or buses? Then a whole new set of social rules about "maintaining one's distance" becomes operative. Finally, if you are looking for a quiet place to study, you probably would elect to sit at the empty table rather than at the one marked by someone else's possessions, thus respecting the interpersonal spacing of another who is not immediately present.

The interesting aspect about the rules of interpersonal spacing is that they are usually followed automatically, without a hitch, and hence remain outside of awareness. What brings these social rules home is any deviation from baselines, and deviation in the direction of closer proximity is especially notable. Researchers call it *spatial invasion.*

In work pioneered by Robert Sommer (1969), experimentally controlled spatial invasions were carried out in a variety of natural settings including hospitals and libraries. The procedure usually involved sitting down next to a person who was sitting alone and noting the person's responses. Typical reactions included turning the other way, putting an elbow between oneself and the other, building barriers with books, and, as a last resort, leaving the scene (Barash, 1973; Felipe & Sommer, 1966). In an effort to make spatial invasion even more notable, another research team had the invader ask the invaded subject about the availability of the seat he or she was about to take. Results showed that more people left when so addressed than when an invader just sat down without saying anything (Polit & LaFrance, 1977).

In a fascinating and detailed study, Baxter and Rozelle (1975) explored

This student discourages spatial invasion by building a barrier with posture and books.

the impact of spatial intrusion on people in a simulated police-citizen encounter. Male college students were asked to imagine that the interviewer was a police officer gathering information. In the experimental condition, the interviewer began an 8-minute session standing at a distance of 4 feet from the subject; after the first 2 minutes, he moved in to a distance of 2 feet; after 4 minutes, he moved in to a distance of 8 inches; and finally, for the last 2 minutes, he retreated to a distance of 2 feet. Another group of subjects went through the same procedure, except that the interviewer never came closer than 2 feet from the subject. The interviews were videotaped, and each subject's behavior was coded for a number of nonverbal cues, including speaking time; eye behavior; facial movements; head, neck, shoulder, arm, and hand motions; trunk, leg, and foot behaviors; and emotional signs. Analysis showed that the closest approach (8 inches) led to significant changes in a wide range of the subjects' nonverbal behavior. Specifically, speech became noticeably disrupted, eye movements increased (for example, blinking became excessive), gaze aversion intensified, head movements multiplied, and defensive arm and hand positions were adopted (such as a substantial increase of the hands-at-crotch position). The investigators argued that all these behaviors were a product of the invasion and were not due to unique personality characteristics of the subjects. The important implication of these findings is that interviewers—whether they be police officers or employment counselors—would be in error if they attributed the occurrence of this kind of behavior only to the internal state of the person being interviewed, without taking into account the interaction itself. In other words, it would be a mistake to conclude from such nonverbal cues that the individual is guilty, when the person may in fact be responding to pressure from the interviewer.

Similar signs of stress as a result of being spatially invaded have been found by another study, which took place in a men's lavatory (Middlemist, Knowles, & Matter, 1976). These investigators reasoned that the anxiety produced by invasion should become especially acute in a situation in which retreat is not immediately available. The findings supported this hypothesis. The pattern of urination (delay of onset and shorter duration) of those who found themselves closest to an experimental confederate showed the greatest amount of stress effects.

The most common reaction to spatial invasion clearly lies in the realm of withdrawal—for example, rapid departure from the situation. But when, for one reason or another, people choose to remain, they may use a variety of cues to ward off or repel the approach of others. One such signal is tongue showing. Observations of children and adults in different cultures, as well as of captive primates, indicate that showing the tongue signifies an unwillingness to interact, especially when one is engaged in some demanding activity (Smith, Chase, & Lieblich, 1974). Part of this study compared tongue showing by billiard players of varying ability when engaged in shots of varying difficulty. Good players showed their tongues more often on hard than on easy shots and, overall, showed the tongue less than did poor players, whose tongue showing did not change with the difficulty of the shot. In this context,

Tongue showing signals concentrated activity and wards off interruption.

showing the tongue signals the engagement and concentration of the player
and wards off interruptions. The differential use of this device by players of
differing abilities on different shots is a nice demonstration of the interaction
of individual and situational elements in nonverbal behavior.

Research has also shown that people stay away from those situations in
which they might potentially intrude upon another's space. People avoid a
small, although public, room in which another is already ensconced, or, at the
very least, it takes them longer to enter such a room than an empty one (Sommer & Becker, 1969). Also, it takes people much longer to occupy a vacant
table on which personal belongings, such as sweaters and books, have been
left than one that shows no signs of occupancy.

It also appears that people may desist from an intended activity if such activity can bring them too close to others. Presumably, if you're thirsty and there's a free water fountain nearby, you'll take a drink. Research indicates that this is not always the case. A study by Barefoot, Hoople, and McClay (1972) showed that fewer people drank at a public fountain and that those who did so drank for a shorter time when an experimental confederate was sitting close to the fountain (1 foot) than when the confederate was far from it (10 feet). This effect occurred, however, only when the experimenter was a woman.

When people cannot avoid invading another's space, they show nonverbal signs of distress and report feelings of discomfort and embarrassment (Efran & Cheyne, 1974). In one study, male students were required to walk from one room to another and, in so doing, had to walk between two people talking to each other (invasion), pass them but not walk between them (slight violation), or pass physical objects. Not only did the subjects report feeling very awkward when they had to walk between two people, but their discomfort was manifested in gaze aversion and negative mouth movements such as grimaces.

Although invasion has typically been defined in spatial terms and assessed literally by the physical distance between people, there are also other, metaphorical kinds of nonverbal invasion. Goffman (1971) has suggested that one can also invade when one is too loud, too noticeable because of odor, too meddling by use of intrusive questions, or too incursive through staring. In terms of this last modality, Rohner (1974) found that male university students are more likely to switch roommates when they share rooms furnished with twin beds than when they share a room with bunkbeds. Presumably, bunkbeds allow greater visual privacy and ward off visual invasion.

Rejection and Aggression

For certain people, rejection in social encounters is a sad and common experience. The blind, the crippled, and the old are among those who often encounter rejection. Since there is a social rule that inhibits verbal rejection of the handicapped, such rejection tends to be manifested through nonverbal channels. Especially on first encounter, many people keep their distance from and won't look at, talk to, or touch a handicapped person.

Stigma

Goffman (1963) has emphasized the extent to which the management of stigma is a two-way process. The more obvious and obtrusive the deviance, the more of a problem it presents both for those who bear the burden and for those who interact with them. A person in a wheelchair has a handicap that is easier to ignore in a conversation than is a stutter. The same handicap, however, would be harder to ignore during a walk in the country. The nonverbal behavior of the handicapped themselves can ease or hamper others' interaction with them. For example, a blind person who fails to show by turning his head toward the speaker that he is aware of the shifts in conversation from one speaker to another makes it hard for others to realize that he is listening.

Robert Kleck and his associates (Kleck, Buck, Goller, London, Pfeiffer, & Vukcevic, 1968) conducted two studies on nonverbal reactions to stigma. Male students were asked to place a small rectangle representing themselves on a line with another rectangle representing people identified by various labels. Some of these labels referred to conditions that carry some kind of stigma, such as epileptic, amputee, mental patient, and blind person. With the exception of the blind person, the students consistently placed themselves farther away from these stigmatized others (especially the epileptic and the mental patient) than from a liked professor or friend. Verbal statements concerning how they felt about the handicapped bore little relation to the figure placement, perhaps because of inhibitions about making such negative verbal statements.

The second study looked at distance and eye contact in actual interaction with an experimental confederate who presented himself to some subjects as an epileptic and to others as a "normal" person. The subjects were asked to place their chairs for a conversation with the confederate (measure of distance). Later, the experimenter moved the subjects to within 3 feet of the confederate and recorded their gaze at the confederate, who looked steadily at the subjects. Although the subjects sat farther from the confederate labeled epileptic, no significant differences in eye contact were recorded. That there were no differences in eye contact may have been due to the fact that at least two conflicting patterns were operating. A student interacting with a handicapped person may wish not to look at that person as part of the desire to distance oneself from the stigmatized. But the handicapped person may also seem unpredictable or unusual and thus may draw more visual attention than a "normal" person. Such a pattern is shown in the study discussed below.

Langer and her colleagues (Langer, Fiske, Taylor, & Chanowitz, 1976) postulated the existence of competing forces in the reactions to stigmatized others. On the one hand, the appearance of the handicapped constitutes a novel stimulus, to which people might wish to respond by staring; on the other hand, there are social rules that call for politely ignoring the stigmatized difference. In the Langer et al. study, students stared more at photographs of crippled people than at photographs of physically normal people, but only when they believed themselves to be unobserved. Apparently, it is the novelty that wins out when people believe that no one will notice their staring. Moreover, these investigators found that, when subjects had the opportunity to see a "novel" person through a one-way mirror, they later sat closer to him or her in social interaction than did subjects who had had no prior exposure. With no prior exposure, subjects sat farthest from a crippled person and closest to a normal person.

Goffman's (1963) suggestions concerning the special problems that the handicapped encounter when they first meet someone have been examined experimentally. Males with leg disabilities requiring the use of a wheelchair were interviewed by an experimental confederate who presented himself as either similarly handicapped or normal (Comer & Piliavin, 1972). Differences in the nonverbal behavior of the handicapped emerged in response to the different roles played by the interviewer. When the interviewer presented himself as handicapped, the handicapped men talked longer, smiled more, and made more hand and head movements—all nonverbal signs of attraction. Somewhat unexpectedly, the subjects positioned their wheelchairs farther from the handicapped interviewer. As the researchers point out, this may not be so much a sign of rejection as a result of the practical problem of arranging two wheelchairs for conversation. The subjects also indicated that they liked the handicapped interviewer better and felt more comfortable with him. Presumably these results reflect the handicapped's greater comfort with and attraction for similar others. Goffman (1963) has noted that there is an in-group allegiance among the stigmatized and a considerable degree of effort on their part to handle and manage the out-group of normals. It is generally true that people feel attracted toward those who are similar to themselves on a number of dimensions (Byrne, Ervin, & Lamberth, 1970). The existence of some kind of stigma appears to provide such similarity; furthermore, it provides a common attribute that elicits rejection from the majority who do not share the handicap.

A similar pattern was found with regard to race. In simulated job interviews, White interviewers placed themselves farther from Blacks than from White job applicants. White interviewers were also less fluent in their speech and terminated the interview sooner with Black applicants (Word, Zanna, & Cooper, 1974). Also, White students were judged less vocally friendly when they were giving experimental instructions to listeners they believed to be Black than when they were giving the instructions to listeners they believed to be White (Weitz, 1972).

Glares and Stares

Another way to send a message of rejection is to stare or glare. This device is often used when there are constraints against a verbal reproof. For example, a spouse who wants his or her partner to stop telling an embarrassing anecdote may resort to a glare, and so might a parent who wants a child to stop doing something naughty when guests are present. In a series of interesting studies, Ellsworth and her associates have documented the role that the situational context plays in how the targets of direct gaze interpret the gaze. In Chapter 6, we described a study showing that frequent eye contact in conjunction with positive comments produces positive evaluation of the gazer but in conjunction with negative comments produces negative evaluation (Ellsworth & Carlsmith, 1968). Following up on this contextual difference, these researchers speculated that in an ambiguous situation the person who is being stared at cannot account for the look and, being unsettled by this ambiguity, is moved to escape from the situation.

In a series of field experiments (Ellsworth, Carlsmith, & Henson, 1972), a person on a street corner stared at some of the drivers of the cars that had stopped for a red light and not at others. An observer timed the speed with which the cars crossed the intersection after the light had turned green. Drivers who had been stared at crossed the intersection faster. The same results were obtained with pedestrians, both men and women, and it didn't make any difference whether the experimenter was a man or a woman and whether the experimenter was a pedestrian or the driver of a motor scooter. These findings are easy to understand. If you are a driver, you've probably found yourself a number of times making eye contact with the driver of a car stopped next to yours at a light or caught in a traffic jam. Recall how quickly you looked away and how you affected casualness by looking out the other window or adjusting your radio or lighting a cigarette. To be stared at in this situation is uncomfortable because there are no cues to help you understand what the stare means. Is it friendly or hostile? In the absence of contextual cues to provide the command aspect, people choose to escape from the situation.

But there are situations in which a stare is interpreted in such a way that it leads to approach rather than to escape. In a shopping mall, female shoppers were approached outside a department store by a young woman carrying a suitcase, who said she was hurrying to catch a train. Pointing to another woman about 25 feet away, she said to some shoppers that the woman had lost a contact lens and needed help (clear context); to others, that the woman looked unwell and needed help (ambiguous context). When the shopper looked at the "victim," the latter was either looking directly back at her or looking down (Ellsworth & Langer, 1976). The results were clear-cut. When the victim looked at the subject in a situation in which the plight and the appropriate response were clear-cut, 10 out of 12 subjects came over to help and look for the lost contact lens. When the victim was said to look unwell, only 3 of the 12 who were stared at came to her help. When the victim didn't look, fewer subjects came to her assistance even when the plight was clear. These findings indicate that in the right context a stare can be interpreted as a command to approach.

In this study, the stare by the victim was interpreted as an appeal for help and was responded to accordingly. But, since in this chapter we are concerned with negative relationships, we now turn to the question of whether a direct gaze from a victim can effectively check an aggressor's attack. For obvious reasons, aggression is difficult to produce and study in the social-psychology laboratory. But, typically, attempts are made to anger subjects by insulting them in some way, and the subjects are then allowed to express their anger by ostensibly giving electric shocks to someone in a learning context—that is, to signal mistakes on the part of a "learner" (in fact, an experimental confederate). Using this kind of procedure, Ellsworth and Carlsmith (1973) found that angered subjects gave fewer shocks to learners who always looked at them than to learners who always averted their gaze. Stares had no effect on subjects who were not angry. But when the learner alternated between looking at his aggressor and lowering his eyes, he received more shocks when he was looking than when he was not, and this held true whether the subject was angry or not. This situation apparently allows the subject to "punish" the learner for staring (which presumably the subject finds uncomfortable). The subject uses this strategy when the learner's *variable* gaze gives him some reason to think that he can use the shock to get rid of the unwanted stare. In the constant-stare situation, there is no reason to think that the shock will turn off the stare.

Other nonverbal cues can be used to ward off attack. In a similar experimental situation, subjects gave fewer electric shocks to their victims when instructed to maintain eye contact with an audience but not when they didn't have to look at the others present (Scheier, Fenigstein, & Buss, 1974). They also gave fewer shocks to victims who had dilated pupils than to those who had constricted pupils (Kidd, 1975) and to victims who had angry expressions than to those who were smiling (Savitsky, Izard, Kotsch, & Christy, 1974).

Aggression is apparently accompanied by a variety of nonverbal behaviors in both aggressor and victim, but how these are interpreted depends a great deal on the context. Ellsworth (1975) pointed out that direct sustained gaze has a high probability of being noticed and is therefore salient in any situation in which it occurs. Furthermore, gaze is involving and thereby demands interpretation. The interpretation centers on the interpersonal relationship between the two people engaged in the eye contact. As we have seen in Chapter 6, a direct gaze can be interpreted as attraction if the context is appropriate to that interpretation. It can also be interpreted more negatively if the context of the relationship at the time allows for that interpretation.

Inconsistent Messages

Galloway (1976) tells a poignant story about inconsistent communication. A teacher comes into a classroom and announces with great verbal enthusiasm how happy she is to be there, what a marvelous class this seems to be, and how good the students' behavior is—in other words, how great it is to be the teacher of these students. Her pupils sit quietly as she speaks, in what appears to be rapt attention, until one child stands up and says "If you're so happy to be here, why don't you tell your face?"

At one time or another, you probably felt the urge to ask this very question, but you didn't because you knew that it wasn't the proper thing to do. So, when you hear someone exclaim just how marvelous or how horrendous something is and you notice that the person's nonverbal behavior doesn't really correspond to the verbal statement, no matter how put on you feel, you are not likely to call attention to such contradiction. What is going on when contradictory messages are sent and received? Why would someone say one thing verbally and quite another nonverbally? And how is one to interpret this kind of message?

A debatable assumption that underlies much of the research on contradictory messages—and one to which we've alluded before—is that people always express their "real" feelings nonverbally and the more socially acceptable ones verbally. For example, Argyle (1975), taking an extreme position with regard to that assumption, has argued that "in animals interpersonal signals reflect the real attitude of the animals concerned. In human beings things are more complicated, and for strategic reasons signals are often sent which are not genuine" (p. 125). But let's look at the assumption a little more closely by examining Argyle's statement. First of all, how can animals send inter*personal* signals? Then, what *attitudes* are they expressing? Finally, how do we know that these are in fact the animals' *real* attitudes?

That people sometimes mask their emotions is not in dispute here, for humans are certainly quite capable of dissembling. What is at issue is the complexity of the human communication process. People do use words to lie, and they do say one thing when they mean quite another. But to recognize this is not to conclude that, if people were only to stop talking, truth would reign undisputed. In Chapter 3, you learned that people can dissemble nonverbally; they smile when they're feeling quite unhappy; they grimace to indicate pain when none is actually felt. These are all "lies" nonverbally told. Consequently, when you are the recipient of a message that you perceive to be contradictory, be wary of placing all your faith in the nonverbal part of the message.

Because of the common assumption we discussed earlier, research in which positive verbal messages were coupled with negative nonverbal ones showed that the nonverbal content was generally given more weight. Specifically, recipients rated a friendly message delivered in a hostile manner as insincere and a hostile message delivered in a friendly way as confusing (Argyle, Alkema, & Gilmour, 1972). It is interesting to note here that the interpretation these researchers gave to the recipients' ratings was that the nonverbal outweighed the verbal. But is that the best interpretation? A better one seems to be that perceivers *combine* information from both channels to reach a coherent interpretation of the message. Attributions of insincerity or hypocrisy are made not by attending only to the nonverbal negativity (which, taken alone, might be seen as hostility) but by simultaneously incorporating negative and positive messages.

Mehrabian and his associates, too, have addressed the question of how people decode inconsistent messages. One study found that, when there was contradiction between facial expression and verbal message, the facial expression predominated over the words to determine the impression formed (Mehrabian & Ferris, 1967). In a second study, results showed that the nonverbal component (in this case, vocal tone) influenced subjects' interpretations more than did verbal content when the two were combined in an inconsistent fashion (Mehrabian & Wiener, 1967). In another study, inconsistency itself had a strong effect on the interpersonal distance that students adopted with regard to a counselor, depending on whether the counselor had given them congruent or discrepant verbal and nonverbal cues (Graves & Robinson, 1976). Students came closer when they received consistently positive as well as consistently negative messages than when they received inconsistent messages. Here, too, it seems that the impression the person receives represents a combination of the inconsistent information coming from different channels. The end result may be simply that senders of inconsistent messages are puzzling, and, therefore, others feel that they should be approached cautiously.

One interesting suggestion with regard to message inconsistency was made by Mehrabian (1970), who said that inconsistency is more likely to occur in informal settings than in formal, structured ones. If you think about this suggestion for a minute, you may agree with Mehrabian. Are you more likely to kid someone or make sarcastic comments at home among friends and family or in a job interview or courtroom appearance? The answer is pretty obvious. Mehrabian argued that the reason for this is that formal situations actively inhibit the expression of feelings that are potentially embarrassing. But another way of looking at this difference is that, in an informal situation, people are much more concerned with interpersonal relationships than they are in a formal one. Therefore, they are more concerned with sending relationship-bound messages that say "This is how I see you" and "This is how I feel about how you see me." Sarcasm directed at a friend (positive content with negative tone) not only indicates displeasure but indicates it in a context of expected pleasure. It is this double-edged quality that is the message here and not simply a clear-cut negative comment. A lover kidding the loved one (negative content with positive tone) is not sending a message in which the nonverbal aspect reflects the true and only feeling. If the message contains criticism, it is criticism combined with affection.

The picture that emerges from the preceding discussion about inconsistent messages is that people pay attention to the combination of the verbal and nonverbal aspects of a message and not just to one aspect of it. Sometimes the nonverbal element is given a great deal of weight, but sometimes it is discounted. Bugental (1974), for example, found that, when a speaker conveys an inconsistent verbal-vocal message (that is, a message in which the words are in conflict with the tone of voice), but one in which the vocal tone is unconvincing because it comes across as slow, deliberate, and overpolished, the tone fails to have any effect on the interpretation of the message. If, however, the tone seems convincing and spontaneous, it is the vocal tone that is believed, no matter what the individual is actually saying.

Why has so much attention been focused on inconsistent messages? As our discussion of emotional blends in Chapter 3 indicates, people often experience and express more than one emotion at a time. Some psychologists believe that all people should be aware that they send multiple messages, including contradictory ones, at times. In psychotherapy, attempts are made to get clients to accept all their own feelings and not to deny some of the messages they send. But what about the recipients of such mixed messages? Clearly, inconsistent messages are more demanding than consistent ones. And sometimes they may be even stressful. The stress may come not so much from inconsistent *reports* per se but from inconsistent *commands*. To be the recipient of commands that say both "Go away" and "Come close" or "I care" and "Who, me involved?" can be an unnerving experience.

Summary

It is interesting how the nonverbal channels can both inhibit the expression of negative attitudes and allow them full reign. With regard to inhibition, research indicates that, when people can see each other (thus being senders and receivers of all kinds of cues from face and body), competitive tendencies are constrained. Face-to-face negotiation allows one to see the other side as a flesh-and-blood human being.

With regard to the expression of negativity, people are often likely to communicate nonverbally rejection and hostility that they would be disinclined to acknowledge verbally. Deviant others encounter nonverbal rejection; such rejection makes it possible to avoid one's having to take responsibility for the rejection or even to admit any negative feelings at all.

The work on inconsistent verbal/nonverbal messages demonstrates once again the patterned and multichanneled nature of communication and our capacity to express negative and positive feelings at the same time. When the nonverbal cues prevail, it is because other contextual cues indicate that the nonverbal is the truer expression. In and of itself, the nonverbal message is not necessarily truer than the verbal one.

The research on spatial invasion highlights the importance of social rules and indicates how aware people are of one another, even of strangers. Transgressions of these social rules is discomfiting. People don't like to be invaded, and generally they'll try to avoid invading the space of others.

Moving Up and Looking Down: Status Effects

It's your first day on a new job, and you're being introduced to the people you'll be working with. Typically, many of the introductions are by first names: "Joe, this is Sue, Tom, Mary, and Ben." The next room brings you to "Joe, this is Bertha Brown, who is in charge of our section." And finally you hear "Joe, Mr. Jones isn't in yet, but you'll get to meet him later." A clear status hierarchy has been laid out before you, one that you understand because you have learned the status distinctions reflected in the forms of address used in our culture. Generally, first names are used between people of equal status, and titles and last names for those of higher status (Brown, 1965).

You start to work on the job and, with time, you get to know your co-workers better. You chat during coffee breaks, have lunch with some, and gradually establish your place in the organization. Then you are picked to work on a special project with Mr. Jones, and the two of you spend a lot of time together. You travel with him to a meeting out of town and spend more than just working time together. That poses a problem for you. With more time (especially more informal time) spent together and increased liking on both sides, you begin to feel that calling him "Mr. Jones" is becoming inappropriate. Your assumptions about the forms of address that go with friendship collide with what you know about forms of address and status differences.

The English language and social custom provide a temporary way out of this dilemma. In everyday interaction, you can avoid using any title for quite some time. That is how most of us resolve the ambiguity of a changing social relationship; we stick to the pronoun "you" and let time pass. Notice that this is a problem only for the person of lower status in the relationship. Mr. Jones has been calling you "Joe" all along. It is a problem for you because mistakes are likely to cause some discomfort. If you address Mr. Jones by his first name too soon, he may think you presumptuous and ill-mannered (also because, strictly speaking, it is up to him to invite you to call him by his first name).

So let's assume you finally take the risk and call Mr. Jones "Ralph." As you have seen, all social interactions involve the nonverbal realm as well. Even after you've adopted the more intimate first-name form of address, your nonverbal behavior is still likely to reflect your struggle with the changing nature of the relationship with Ralph Jones. On entering his office, for example, you're likely to pause in the doorway before approaching and take a seat farther from him than you would with a colleague. He sprawls back in his chair and puts his feet up; you wouldn't dream of doing the same. Nonverbal behaviors may continue to echo the status differences between the two of you even after you have mastered enough courage to call him by his first name.

Gaze

Let's now consider the nonverbal cues that signal and maintain status differences. The most extensive work on the relation between gaze and status has been carried out by Ralph Exline and his colleagues (Exline, 1972; Exline, Ellyson, & Long, 1975). For the most part, they have studied visual behavior in the social-psychological laboratory, where status was manipulated by giving one person power over the monetary rewards derived by the other person from the experiment. Visual behavior during conversation was then recorded. In one study, greater legitimacy was given to this manipulation by always assigning the high-power role to an ROTC officer and the low-power role to an ROTC basic cadet (note that both men were in uniform). In all instances, the person with low power looked more at the other than did the high-power person.

But high-power people, too, look at others, and what is of interest here is *when* they look. Exline and his colleagues identified a pattern, which they called *visual dominance behavior,* that is characteristic of those in high-power positions. Specifically, people in roles of high power look more at the other when they speak than when they listen. Furthermore, at a training camp, those ROTC officers who showed a visual-dominance pattern were given higher leadership ratings than those officers who didn't show such pattern. This means either that people who have developed the visual-dominance pattern in association with a personality trait of dominance (recall our discussion of this point in Chapter 4) come to be selected as leaders or that people placed in high-power positions develop a "look of command." As we have seen, behavior is usually a product of both personal and environmental forces; hence, the visual-dominance pattern is likely a product of both these forces.

Although these studies represent the most comprehensive attempt to specify how higher status is visually cued, aspects of the process have been known for some time. In examining eye contact in small groups, for instance, Hearn (1957) found that the least eye contact was established with low-status others in the group and the most contact with those of moderate status. With those of highest status, the amount of eye contact was intermediate. These results become clearer if you recall that eye contact requires that both parties sustain mutual gaze. Low-status members of a group are probably rarely talked to; thus, while they may be dutifully listening and looking, they establish little eye contact simply because they are not looked at. When high-status members are addressed by others, their withholding of the attentive gaze while listening results in relatively little eye contact. That eye contact is greater for high-status people than for low-status people is probably a function of the fact that, when high-status people talk, they show the visual-dominance pattern. But, being high-status people, they encounter the gazing of attentive listeners, and eye contact results. Moderate-status people have the highest amount of eye contact because they are looked at by lower-status listeners as well as by higher-status talkers.

One explanation for these visual patterns is suggested by research with primates, among whom visual attention is directed toward the more dominant animals. Field studies of primates have noted that submissive animals constantly watch the more dominant ones. Subordinates are said to watch the dominant animals both to see which way they lead the group and to stay out of a dominant animal's way, thereby avoiding aggressive confrontations. It is suggested that attention thus directed at the most dominant animals serves to maintain dominance hierarchies; less dominant animals follow the leaders and do not fight with them (Chance, 1967).

Another curious aspect about gaze behavior among primates is that, even though lower-status animals are constantly vigilant, when eye contact occurs as the result of the dominant animal's looking, the submissive animal breaks contact by looking away. Although a great deal of caution should be exercised in extending explanations drawn from animal research to human social behavior, it is not unlikely that the visual attention given by lower-status people to higher-status ones may serve somewhat analogous functions. Recall some staring matches you have had in your life. In a study of gaze behavior in student conversations (Strongman & Champness, 1968), a dominance hierarchy was derived by noting each time one of the pair broke eye contact with the other. Since each person was paired with every other participant in the experiment, it was possible to construct a dominance hierarchy for the entire group, led by the individual who least often broke gaze with all the others with whom he or she was conversing and ending with the person who broke gaze with everyone. In other words, the breaking of eye contact is not done randomly, and, when pairs of people are "tested" against each other, a systematic hierarchy for their gaze breaking emerges. Some people break gaze from no one; others break away from everyone.

Another manifestation of status in visual interaction is that it is within the prerogatives of the more powerful to tell others how and where to look and not look; that is, the higher-status person can control the gaze of the lower-status one (Argyle & Cook, 1976). Officers can order soldiers to keep their eyes straight ahead; teachers can tell students to give visual attention when being spoken to. To reiterate, then, lower-status people generally look more at higher-status people than higher-status people do in relation to lower-status people, especially in the listening role. However, when high-status people talk with someone, they look more at the other when they're speaking than when they're listening. Lastly, status does affect the circumstances under which people look away. Incidentally, if a lower-status person were asked why he looked away when a person of higher status looked at him, the person would probably say that he noticed someone coming into the room or that he was distracted by something—clearly, a less than accurate account.

Posture and Orientation

Just as higher-status people can direct the gaze behavior of those of lower status, so, too, can they direct other nonverbal behavior, such as posture. For example, an officer orders lower-status others to stand at attention, and a teacher tells a slumping first grader to sit straight.

Mehrabian (1968a) identified a cluster of postural behaviors related to status differences. Recall that Mehrabian's research strategy involved noting the nonverbal behavior that people adopt toward *imagined* others (see Chapter 6). He always asked subjects to seat themselves (or to stand) as if they were conversing with a liked or disliked other of higher or lower status. The dimension that, by its presence or absence, seemed to best describe the postural behavior characteristic of a situation involving people of different status was *relaxation*. Specifically, Mehrabian (1972) found that, in interaction with each other, higher-status people adopt relatively relaxed positions whereas lower-status people adopt more "at attention" positions.

The most important component of relaxation has been found to be asymmetry in the position of the arms. People of higher status sit or stand with their arms in different positions—for example, one arm in the lap and the other hooked over the back of the chair. In contrast, those of lower status tend to keep hands together or both arms straight down at their sides. Other aspects of a relaxed posture include sideways lean, leg-position asymmetry, hand and neck relaxation, and reclining angle. Thus, the posture of the individual with higher status is marked by a sideward and backward tilt of the torso, crossed legs, loosely extended fingers, and the head resting on the back of a chair or couch. The lower-status member of the encounter sits upright, with both feet flat on the floor and hands clasping some object or clenched together. Goffman (1961), for instance, observed psychiatric-staff meetings and noted that psychiatrists sat in looser, more relaxed postures than did staff members of lesser status. Try to recall your posture the last time you went to a teacher to inquire about your grades. Were you comfortably sprawled as you usually are when you chat with a friend? Quite unlikely.

Proximity and Seating Arrangements

Status is conveyed not only by how people sit or stan[d]
they position themselves. Imagine a meeting of a corpor[a]
tors. As you picture the members gathered around the r[o]

(Ward, 1968) fulfills both of these requirements.

As noted in our discussion of competition in Chapter 7, winners head for the favored seats, whereas losers withdraw from them. The same process is operative in interactions among higher- and lower-status people. When, during a week-long training conference, mental-health professionals were asked to name "the true leader," their choices correlated positively with where the leading people chose to sit in the dining room at mealtimes (Heckel, 1973)—a location that allowed the person sitting there to be at the center of things. Access to desirable space by powerful people was also illustrated in a study that took place at a residential facility for juvenile offenders (Sundstrom & Altman, 1974). Boys were asked to rank one another in terms of who was "strong, tough, and able to tell others what to do." Boys so described were found to use the desirable areas more often than members low in the dominance hierarchy of the group. This selective space use was most pronounced when the group composition was stable and for long-term members of the group. Presumably the reason for this is that, in groups of long standing, the battles for group leadership have long since been fought and won. In addition, "desirable social areas" may be desirable not just in terms of their objective characteristics but also because they have taken on the symbolism of such desirability and everyone belonging to the group shares that view. The oldest, shabbiest chair may be the most valuable one precisely because it has been around the longest.

Next time you are in a small discussion group, look at the seating arrangement and observe how the interaction is going. You may want to tackle a problem that has long puzzled the researchers in this field—namely, how to separate status and seating arrangement enough to get a sense of how they affect each other. The two seem to be so intertwined in our culture that it is hard to know whether people are accorded more status when they sit in what are considered the best places or whether people with leadership skills gravitate to these spots. In extreme cases, we can make fairly confident judgments, of course. Someone who sits at the head of a table but makes stupid comments and behaves in other ways that are unbecoming of a leader is not likely to be picked as leader by the others. Similarly, an able individual (especially one who gives off other high-status cues) may be recognized as "in charge" even when he or she is seated in an out-of-the-way place. But, in general, you expect status and spatial position to go together. If at a meeting (or in a class) someone makes an authoritative statement in commanding tones from the far back of the room, people turn around to look at the speaker—something they will not do for other comments made from that locale in a less authoritative manner.

Interpersonal spacing, too, carries status implications, as was demonstrated by the following studies. Lott and Sommer (1967) manipulated status by selecting students on the basis of the year they were in and found that upper-class students sat nearer their peers (other upper-class students) than to others they were told were professors or freshmen. In a military setting (where status cues are clearly very pronounced), similar results were obtained

(Dean, Willis, & Hewitt, 1975). Conversations between naval personnel were observed in a variety of military-post locations. Since the men were in uniform, status differences were evident. Naval personnel stood farther away when they *initiated* a conversation with a superior than when they initiated a conversation with a peer, and the distance increased with increased difference in rank. A seaman initiating conversation with a navy captain stood farther away from him than he did when he was conversing with a petty officer. There was no difference in distance in the course of conversations initiated by superiors and in conversations between peers. These findings were interpreted in terms of the unilateral freedom that the superior has to stand close to a subordinate. In contrast, if someone initiates a conversation with a higher-status person, he or she must be careful not to offend the other by coming too close.

Another study (Jorgenson, 1975) that looked at distance as a function of status didn't find the differences in distance that the studies above revealed. But, when the investigator looked at another nonverbal cue—namely, body orientation—he did notice status differences. The subjects of this study were the employees of a utility company, and they were observed as they conversed during coffee breaks. While it was noted that pairs of equal status (where both men were either supervisors or nonsupervisory employees) stood no closer to each other than pairs of discrepant status, their body orientations varied. People of equal status faced each other at a more direct angle of body orientation than did discrepant-status pairs. This finding is another demonstration of the degree to which different nonverbal behaviors interact.

In interpersonal distance, not only is status encoded (in the sense that people arrange themselves spatially in ways that indicate their respective social status), but some spatial arrangements are also decoded (in the sense that such arrangements reflect status). In a study manipulating status by means of age and dress, high-status pairs who engaged in conversation in a university hallway were less intruded upon by passersby than were lower-status pairs (Knowles, 1973). Apparently, the boundaries surrounding such pairs were perceived as more inviolable than the boundaries of pairs who looked younger and were more casually dressed. It was the impression of observers in this study that those few people who did walk through the boundaries of the informal interaction taking place between higher-status people were themselves of higher status, like college faculty and administrators.

Vocal Cues

As our example about the use of first names and titles suggests, status differences are often signaled by the use of language. But the whole voice, rather than the words alone, provides considerable information about social status. Certainly, many verbal and vocal clues to status are present in everyday interaction. Both these cues were available in a study in which nine speakers responded briefly to a few standard questions such as "How are you?" On the basis of the few words exchanged, listeners were able to make very accurate guesses concerning the social class of the speakers (Harms, 1961). In fact, they made these judgments very quickly, after hearing only ten seconds or so of the recording.

That the ear is finely tuned to the nuances of status cues was also demonstrated by a study in which people were asked to fake an upper-class accent. Listeners were able to identify the real social-class standing of the speakers despite their efforts to disguise it (Ellis, 1967). According to Argyle (1975), the vocal characteristics of higher social class include clearer articulation, sharper enunciation of consonants, and more vocal intonation. These particular characteristics were derived from studies of British speech, but they may have greater generality, since it is likely that, in all cultures, the more educated urge their children to speak clearly and enunciate carefully.

In the nonverbal behaviors reviewed thus far—gaze, body orientation, and interpersonal distance—the particular behavior signaled the status relationship of two or more interactants. For example, we stressed that, in a given encounter, the lower-status person looks more at the higher-status person. If, on the other hand, in another encounter that same individual occupies the higher-status position with regard to someone else, he or she will be looking less at the other person. Vocal cues don't appear to be so variable, but this remains an unresearched, and therefore unanswered, question. It would be interesting to find out whether a higher-class accent is as sharply articulated and intonated when the person is speaking to a lower-status other as it is when the same person is addressing a peer.

In our discussion of gaze and status differences, we suggested that most of the time higher-status people tend to "have the floor" more than lower-status people. It is important to note, however, that floor time is important not in an absolute sense but only in relation to someone else's time. This very point was made clear in a study (Stang, 1973) in which female subjects listened to the tape recording of a discussion in which one of the participants had a lot to say, another a medium amount, and the third very little. The subjects were asked to rate the speakers in terms of how much they liked them, how important each speaker appeared to be in leading the group, and how much general leadership ability each showed. Although the listeners liked best the speaker who talked a medium amount, the speaker who spoke the most was rated as showing the most leadership. Not only do people of higher status talk more in groups (Stephan, 1952) but people who talk more are seen as showing more leadership.

Touch

The status connotations of touch have been described by Henley (1973, 1977), who, observing people in a variety of settings, noted that, in an interaction between two people of different status, the higher-status person is always freer to touch the other than is the lower-status person. If you think of pairs made up of people of unequal status—for example, teacher/student, doctor/patient, and foreman/worker—you'll have little trouble deciding

Nonreciprocal touching is a prerogative of higher-status people.

which of the two is more likely to take the arm of the other or to tap the other on the shoulder. When Henley (1973) categorized status by social class and age, she found that the person of higher standing and the older person touched more and were touched less in return. Henley (1973) also found that males and females didn't seem to be equally free to touch a person of the opposite sex. When age and social class were equal, sex differences elicited a striking pattern of more touching on the part of men toward women. Since people of higher status were found to touch people of lower status (and not the reverse) and since men were observed to touch women more than women touched men, Henley argued that this latter pattern reflected the fact that, in our culture, men are afforded more status than women. In other words, Henley argued against the more conventional interpretation that touching by men conveys sexual attraction or friendliness. She reasoned that attraction and warmth are experienced by both men and women. Therefore, if touch were reflective of only these feelings, men and women should touch each other about equally. Consequently, some explanation other than attraction should be sought for the fact that women are rarely observed in public either to initiate touch toward men or to reciprocate it. It is likely, then, that the same status differential that underlies the nonreciprocal touch patterns governing class and age relationships is at work in heterosexual pairs.

Summary

The role of nonverbal behavior in status-bound relationships presents several interesting features. First of all, there is the fact that status and its nonverbal concomitants are always relative things. A college junior has higher status than a freshman but lower status than a professor. Because of this relativity, the nonverbal cues are very much a function of the relationship one is in at that particular moment and not permanent baggage that the individual carries with him or her wherever he or she goes. In this sense, the *other* is a very important aspect of the environment.

Second, relationships between and among peers are characterized by nonverbal behavior that is different from that observable in relationships between or among people of unequal status. In status-discrepant relationships, the lower-status member looks more but breaks gaze first if looked at, stands or sits in an "at attention" posture, keeps a respectful distance from the other, until or unless the higher-status person approaches or even unilaterally touches the lower-status one. In equal-status relationships, gazes are more equally exchanged, postures are more relaxed, distance is jointly negotiated, and touch is more likely to be reciprocal. Presumably, when these nonverbal behaviors start being negotiated, albeit very much out of awareness, they reflect the fact that changes in relative status are occurring as well.

Third, we have seen that the multichanneled nature of communication operates here, too. Even though one behavior (such as distance) at one point in time may not indicate status distinctions, when other nonverbal behaviors (such as body orientation) are taken into account, status once again becomes visible.

Chapter 9

Influential Moves

Think about the expression "How to win friends and influence people." No doubt you have heard it before and in a variety of contexts. Although it can be said casually or even cynically, humorously or bitterly, it seems nevertheless to reflect a truly basic concern most people have. You want to have impact on others. You seek approval and respect. You try to convince others of the goodness or reasonableness of your opinions or suggestions. Conversely, you are constantly the focus of similar attempts on the part of others.

This chapter reviews some of the nonverbal manifestations of influence, ranging from prototypic attitude-change attempts, through the more subtle maneuvers to elicit another's approval and the apparently inadvertent efforts to alter someone's behavior, to deliberate attempts to deceive, and, finally, to endeavors not usually regarded as influence, such as striving to help people improve their performance.

Attitude Change

As you'll soon see, much of the nonverbal behavior associated with persuasion is remarkably similar to that associated with attraction, which was described in Chapter 6. There is a relatively straightforward explanation for such similarity. Basically, researchers have begun with the assumption that interpersonal influence succeeds to the extent that the influencer is well regarded by those he or she is attempting to influence.

Using an encoding research technique, Mehrabian and Williams (1969) asked male and female college students to present an argument with three different degrees of persuasiveness: in a highly persuasive manner, in a moderately persuasive manner, and in a neutral manner. Topics included getting free parking permits for university students and obtaining an extra week to prepare for examinations. Note that, in the highly persuasive condition, the subjects were instructed to be enthusiastic and not to hide or in any way disguise their intent to persuade. The researchers found that a greater intent to persuade was accompanied by a significant increase in the amount of eye contact; head nodding, gesticulation, and facial activity; faster speech rate, louder speech volume, more intonation, and less halting quality of speech; and smaller postural reclining angles.

When Mehrabian and Williams (1969) used, instead, a decoding technique, they found that raters could discriminate between convincing and not-so-convincing persuasion attempts. In this study, the raters saw videotapes that showed different kinds and amounts of various nonverbal behaviors related to intention to persuade. The results indicated that smaller distances and an indirect postural orientation by a male persuader enhanced perceived persuasiveness. In contrast, postural orientation by females didn't seem to have any effect. With eye contact as well, perceived persuasiveness varied with the sex of the persuader. For males, more eye contact coupled with increased distance produced less persuasiveness; for females, more eye contact at increased distance was regarded as more convincing. Finally, the researchers found that relaxation affected convincingness ratings. For females, the effect was clear-cut: the greater the body relaxation, the less the persuasiveness. For males, however, the least relaxed posture was regarded as less convincing than the slightly relaxed position.

Here, too, the results should be taken in context; the meaning of nonverbal behavior depends not on specific cues in and of themselves but on accompanying contextual features, such as sex of sender, the kinds of nonverbal behaviors that are operating together, and who is interpreting the meaning.

Notice that, when males were asked not to hide their intention, they looked a great deal, which ended up by making their entreaty less convincing. When males were communicating maximum intention to persuade, they were apparently conforming to the conventional wisdom that, in order to persuade, one engages the other in the most direct way possible. Strangely enough, however, perceivers found the males who looked less to be more persuasive. Something very complicated seems to be at work here. Perhaps males who don't hide their intentions to persuade look more and, by so doing, come across as less convincing. A male's ability to convince another may thus entail subduing the obviousness of a persuasion attempt, at least as far as gaze is concerned. Notice also that, in the encoding study, the focus was on the individual. Subjects were asked to attend only to their own behavior and to appear enthusiastic. In the decoding study, however, the focus became more interactional, with judges being asked to attend to the other person. Once again, we see that the meaning changes with the level of magnification that is being used.

The two studies described above were concerned with what people do nonverbally when they attempt to persuade and with whether others find this nonverbal behavior convincing. Neither study measured whether the persuasion was effective—namely, whether listeners actually changed their views. A study that took actual persuasion into account found that more persuasion occurred as the distance between speaker and listener increased (Albert & Dabbs, 1970). With regard to perceived persuasiveness, listeners paid more attention to the content of the argument and saw the speaker as being more expert at the middle distance (4 to 5 feet) than at the far distance (14 to

15 feet). And, yet, there was more actual attitude change at this greater distance. The researchers reasoned that subjects were reacting less defensively at the farther distance than at the closer distance and hence were more susceptible to change efforts. This study, too, as well as the work described above, seems to indicate that a persuasion effort that is not offset by some reduction in intensity is less effective than one that is.

Think about this the next time you try to persuade a reluctant person about what he or she should do. Your natural tendency at a time like that would be to move in on the person to make your case intensely. But research suggests that a little more constraint on your part will elicit less resistance on the other person's part.

Distance is not the only thing to take into account in a discussion of nonverbal behavior and attitude change. Your body posture can also influence how effective you are at changing someone's mind. In one study (McGinley, LeFevre, & McGinley, 1975), female students were shown photographs of another female, ostensibly taken while she was discussing her beliefs. The photographs differed only in the openness of the body position. In the closed position, the woman was shown with elbows held next to the body, arms crossed, and knees and feet together; in the open position, she was pictured as leaning back, legs stretched out, knees apart or with one ankle crossed over the other knee, and arms and hands held outward from the body. Subjects were given two sorts of information about this woman: a set of her responses to a questionnaire and the pictured openness or closeness of her body posi-

In an open-body position (right), a person is more influential than in a closed-body position (left).

tion while talking about her views. Subjects were asked to fill out their own attitude questionnaires a second time to see if the woman's views (as expressed in her answers to the questionnaire) had influenced their own opinions. Results showed that the subjects changed their attitudes in the direction of the woman's views when they had seen that woman in an open-body position. No opinion change followed their viewing her in a neutral or a closed-body position. What does the description of this open-body position remind you of? In Chapter 8, higher-status people were described as taking relaxed positions very similar to this open position. Perhaps, then, more opinion change occurred here because the stimulus person conveyed a sense of power and status. As you will see in the next study, the credibility of a communicator is a powerful determinant of attitude change.

Subjects in this study (Miller, Maruyama, Beaber, & Valone, 1976) were approached in public areas, such as shopping centers, by interviewers who introduced themselves as being from a radio station and as being interested in the subjects' reactions to various topics. The subjects then heard a tape recording about the "danger of drinking coffee." Some heard the speech read fast, and others heard it read slowly; some heard the speaker identified as a highly credible person, and others as a less credible communicator. Subjects were asked to indicate their agreement with the main argument heard in the tape. Results showed that the fast-talking communicator was more persuasive than the person who talked slowly. Furthermore, results showed that rapid speech served as a credibility cue and that this cue enhanced the persuasion.

That nonverbally credible communicators are more effective in changing attitudes was also the assumption in a study on the effectiveness of accented versus standard speech (Giles, 1973). The researcher believed that credibility and expertise are signaled by the use of respected language forms, as opposed to regional speech variations. The results, however, did not bear him out. Although the subjects regarded the argument presented in the standard-language form more favorably, only the less prestigious, regional accents were effective in eliciting opinion shifts. These results are similar to the distance findings in the Albert and Dabbs (1970) study mentioned above. There, speakers were judged as more expert at a middle distance, but persuasion occurred only at the far distance. It may be that expertise and its attendant high status can sometimes be too much to take. If the discrepancy between the speaker and the listener is too great, it may generate resistance to the persuasion attempt.

Approval Seeking

Think about the times when you wanted something from someone else—let's say, from a parent hesitant to give permission, a teacher who could grant you an extension for an overdue assignment, a maitre d' who had the power to give you or refuse you a table in your favorite restaurant, a job interviewer with an overabundance of applicants, or even someone with whom you just wanted to spend more time. What strategies did you employ in such situations? And how effective were they? Most of the research to date has addressed the first of these two questions. Specifically, what are the verbal and nonverbal behaviors that come into play when one person is seeking the approval of another?

In an early study (Rosenfeld, 1965), subjects were asked to try to gain or fail to gain the approval of an experimental confederate. The approval-seeking behavior under observation was the distance at which the subject placed her chair from the confederate. Rosenfeld found that women seeking approval from another woman placed their chairs significantly closer than those avoiding such approval.

In a more detailed second study, Rosenfeld (1966) found that both male and female approval seekers engaged in greater verbal and nonverbal responsiveness. They smiled more, made fewer negative head movements, and talked longer during their speaking turns. In addition, male approval seekers made more positive head nods, while women approval seekers gestured more. Rosenfeld also found that, in general, approval seekers were evaluated more positively by those whose approval they had tried to get than by those whose approval they had tried to avoid. Similarly, it was found that applicants for a loan who, during the loan interview, gestured, gazed, and smiled, were judged more suitable than those who did not (Wexley, Fugita, & Malone, 1975).

But approval seeking, like persuasion attempts, is not a straightforward, up-front process; rather, it entails some delicate balancing. Approval seekers, like persuaders, want to convey enough of a positive image so that the other will like them and then presumably give them the approval they want. But too much positive responsiveness can elicit suspicion instead of high regard, withholding instead of generosity. For example, another study, which also found that approval seekers engaged in a higher percentage of smiles and gazes, disclosed other interesting features as well (Lefebvre, 1975). After seeing videotapes of ingratiators and noningratiators, viewers rated ingratiators as more charming, warm, and intimate; but they also saw them doing precisely what they were doing—that is, ingratiating themselves and seeking to be liked. In other words, perceivers saw the behavior not just in its own terms but also as a strategy designed to get something. What we're reminded of again here is that a communication is a game that one person alone cannot play. An interpersonal strategy that ignores, disregards, or is in other ways nonresponsive to the other is usually a doomed strategy.

Experimenter Bias

Throughout this book, we've given you not only details of what social scientists know about nonverbal communication but glimpses as well into how they go about exploring it. You've heard about videotaping, role playing, standardized situations, and experimental confederates, and perhaps you have wondered whether all these paraphernalia are really necessary. Yes, they are, because all the particulars of a research are arranged precisely so that experimental researchers can say "All else being equal, this behavior differs from that one."

So a basic guideline of research is to make everything comparable save for that in which one is interested. But recent studies have indicated that, although research subjects were being exposed to the same conditions and given the same instructions, they were not always getting the same nonverbal messages. In fact, there is now considerable evidence suggesting that, along with the presentation of standard instructions, experimenters also send presumably unintended and unprogrammed nonverbal directives to their subjects (Rosenthal, 1966).

One channel containing such covert directives is the vocal one. In a typical study, the vocal behavior of interest was that of experimenters whose task was to show to subjects some photographs that had been pretested to convey neutrality and to obtain from the subjects ratings of the degree of success or failure shown on the faces portrayed in the photographs. Some experimenters were led to believe that certain pictures would get ratings of success—the same pictures that other experimenters were led to believe would get failure ratings. Analyses of sound films of the experimenters reading the instructions to the subjects revealed that the experimenters conveyed to the subjects the expected "correct response" by subtle changes in vocal stress. Specifically, experimenters who gave differential vocal loudness to one alternative over another apparently suggested to the subjects that the stressed alternative was the right one (Duncan & Rosenthal, 1968).

In a follow-up study, results again showed that slight shifts in an experimenter's paralanguage could systematically bias subjects' responses. More specifically, this study showed that subjects were influenced by the experimenter's vocal emphasis to the degree to which they were anxious about their own performance. In other words, subjects who strove to do well on the task because not to do so would reflect personally on them were more susceptible to subtle changes in the researcher's presentation (Duncan, Rosenberg, & Finkelstein, 1969). Using essentially the same procedure, another study (Burkhart, 1976) found that this susceptibility doesn't always lead precisely where the experimenter directs. When given positive, negative, or neutral vocal cues, subjects high in evaluation apprehension (that is, those who thought that the picture-judging task involved in the experiment measured their emotional health) responded to the experimenter's vocal cues in the opposite way. Given positive cues, they gave negative ratings to the pictures, and, given negative cues, they gave positive ratings. It appears, then, that nonverbal cues are particularly influential with people who are concerned about coming across in the best possible light. Sometimes that means going along with the "true path," and at other times that means resisting the suggested course and taking the opposite direction.

Unintended influence is not a concern of researchers alone. It can have great significance in the real world as well. One such applied context is represented by police and legal work involving eyewitness identification of suspects. One procedure commonly used involves essentially the same task as the experiments described above; people are shown a set of pictures and asked to pick the perpetrator of the crime from this array.

In a study to test the legal ramifications of nonverbal influence, subjects watched a simulated crime on film (Fanselow, 1976). They were then shown six photographs of innocent suspects (that is, people not present in the original film clip) and were asked to pick the guilty party. In some presentations of the photos, the interviewer emitted positive nonverbal behaviors (such as eye contact, smiling, and forward lean) when one picture came up. In another presentation, a particular photo was accompanied by negative nonverbal behaviors (such as frowning, gaze aversion, and fidgeting). In a final condition, neutral nonverbal behaviors were used for all the pictures. Results showed that subjects picked the photograph that had been paired with *either* negative *or* positive nonverbal behavior more often than any photograph presented neutrally. Witnesses, in fact, refused more often to make any identification in the condition in which all photographs were accompanied by neutral nonverbal behavior.

From all these studies, it would appear that people are sensitive to the nonverbal behavior of others who seek to influence them, but whether people are in fact influenced as directed is a more doubtful point. People seem to react to changes from baselines of "neutral" behavior, but, once alerted, they may react either in or against the implied direction.

Deception

The act of deception is a relevant instance of interpersonal influence, although perhaps not its most shining example. While it is certainly possible to deceive oneself, our focus here is on deception directed at others. We look at primarily conscious and intentional attempts to foster in another a belief that the deceiver knows to be untrue.

Perhaps because everyone is at some time deceiver and deceived, there is considerable interest in knowing whether nonverbal cues can be used to detect deception. Was Freud (1905/1959) correct when he said about the deceiver "If his lips are silent, he chatters with his fingertips; betrayal oozes out of him at every pore"?

One popular notion holds that the act of deception is usually accompanied by stress on the part of the deceiver. If this is so, perhaps the deceiver can be identified by the nonverbal cues that signal this distress. There is some research support for this idea. Mehrabian (1971a) found that subjects who were asked to lie about their real attitudes toward abortion made more speech errors. Similarly, a number of studies have found that, when people lie about their feelings or about matters of import to them, they engage in more self-manipulations, such as touching the face with the hand (Ekman & Friesen, 1974; Knapp, Hart, & Dennis, 1974; McClintock & Hunt, 1975). Finally, it appears that the voice leaks stress. Two studies have found that people pitch their voices higher when they are lying than when they are telling the truth (Ekman, Friesen, & Scherer, 1977; Krauss, Geller, & Olson, 1976).

Are people more likely to smile or show negative facial expressions while lying? Presumably, if one is feeling guilty about lying, the guilt will show it-self in negative or, at least, less positive facial expressions. McClintock and Hunt (1975) found that people smiled less while lying, but Mehrabian (1971a) found just the opposite. The weight of the evidence seems to be that facial expression is not a clue in one direction or the other (Ekman & Friesen, 1974). The reason is that, since deceivers are more aware of what their faces are displaying, they are also more able to control what messages their faces transmit. In addition, there is little clear-cut support for the homespun apho-rism that liars won't look you in the eye (Knapp et al., 1974; Mehrabian, 1971a). Therefore, facial cues don't seem to be too helpful in detecting deceit.

Another notion that has been tested is whether deceivers do too little or too much of what most people do when telling the truth. Again, there is re-search support for this idea. Deceivers have been found to talk less than truthful people (Knapp et al., 1974; Mehrabian, 1971a) and to gesture less (Ekman & Friesen, 1974; Mehrabian, 1971a).

The essential interactional nature of deception is particularly obvious when one focuses on a deceiver who is not visible to his or her target. When judges looked at a videotape taken secretly of a person lying to another over an intercom, they were able to detect the deceit. But when the judges looked at a videotape of this same person lying in a face-to-face interaction, they were unable to detect the deceit. Apparently, then, nonverbal cues to decep-tion are available when the deceiver is not on guard. However, in the pres-ence of the target, these cues are kept very much in check by the deceiver (Krauss et al., 1976).

Improving Performance

A recurring concern for those interested in the study of nonverbal com-munication is the use to which knowledge about it could be put—for example, to influence people, through nonverbal persuasion, to do things they wouldn't otherwise do. On the optimistic side are those who believe that knowledge about nonverbal processes can contribute to better teaching, counseling, therapy, and interpersonal performance. It is this second type of influence, presumably producing positive outcomes, that we now address.

In an early study, Reece and Whitman (1962) showed that a person con-veying warmth through direct postural orientation, smiling, and eye contact coupled with verbal reinforcers such as "mm-hmm" could increase the amount of talking another person did. Such increased talking on the part of the normally reticent is an outcome that teachers, parents, and therapists of-ten seek.

Something that most teachers would like to see is more attentive behav-ior in their students. How does one go about increasing a desirable behavior? For one, it was shown that retarded elementary-school children became con-siderably more attentive when the teacher smiled at them and touched them (Kazdin & Klock, 1973). Similarly, Kleinfeld (1973) showed that those Es-kimo and Indian students who were smiled at and kept at a reasonably close distance from their counselor performed better on intelligence tests than those who received no smiles and were kept far away. Incidentally, the counselor deliberately avoided eye contact with the children, because in both their cultures eye contact signifies anger.

Another study, which took place in a therapeutic context, showed that increased touching of a client by a counselor, expressed by shaking hands on entry, guiding the client in and out by keeping a hand on his back, and touching his hand and arm occasionally during the session, increased self-exploration by the client (Pattison, 1973). When counselors smiled and nodded, they were judged by other counselors to be interpersonally skilled and to have empathic understanding (D'Augelli, 1974). In a related setting, interviewer enthusiasm—demonstrated by a considerable amount of smiling, gesturing, and gazing—elicited better performance from interviewees in a simulated employment interview (Washburn & Hakel, 1973).

An optimistic view of the possible application of these results, however, must be tempered by the consideration of some realities involved in the communication process. One of these is the sequence and timing of nonverbal behavior. Birdwhistell (1970) has suggested that instructing novice teachers and counselors only about the nonverbal behaviors (for example, telling them to nod, smile, and the like), without imparting to them the attendant knowledge of where such behavior is appropriate, can lead to no positive effects or even to some detrimental results. He has described one example in which counselors were taught that positive head nods are a "good." The counselors did in fact nod, but to express their own anxiety rather than to respond to something coming from the client.

Summary

With this chapter on influence and nonverbal communication, we conclude the section of the book that deals with the interactional level of analysis. As you have seen, the nonverbal elements involved in influence are very much a part of relationships between people. A well-planned, thoroughly rehearsed, highly perfected presentation designed to change someone's mind but performed without taking into account the other's reactions, both verbal and nonverbal, may come across quite accurately as a beautiful presentation, which doesn't produce any noticeable change. You have seen how powerful an influence nonverbal cues can be in suggesting what choices to make. Some people may not intend to influence, and others may rail against the idea that they can be so influenced, but the evidence suggests otherwise, at least sometimes.

You have also seen that people occasionally become resistant to influence—a resistance generated by too much nonverbal intensity directed at them. But note that, although people are not always predictably malleable, the nonverbal behavior has, nonetheless, its impact.

Deception is an especially intriguing interactional phenomenon because, for the most part, people take what others tell them to be the truth. The governing social rule is to take and be taken at face value. Deception is a transgression of this rule. Some liars emit cues of tension and stress, but you are not likely to be watching for such cues. When you do begin paying attention to the nonverbal signs of deception, your own signs of increased vigilance are likely to put the liar on guard. The liar increases his or her self-monitoring of the nonverbal behavior that he or she has learned from past experience to be revealing to others. Deceiver and deceived are suddenly consciously trafficking in the realm of the nonverbal.

Rules and Rituals
for Moving Bodies

The study of human communication is, by its very nature, a study of social inter*action.* Thus, the researcher of communication is interested in interdependence more than in independence, in movement more than in stillness. He or she is interested in nonverbal behavior not only for the understanding it provides about individuals but for the light it sheds on the dynamics of interpersonal interaction per se. To put it in social-psychological terms, as Kendon (1975) did, "the focus is upon systems of behavior rather than upon systems of motivation, intent, or effect" (p. 5). The title of this book, by its very emphasis on movement—on the dynamics of human interaction—reflects this approach.

The questions we pose in this and the next three chapters are quite different from those we asked earlier. We take now the role of the musicologist rather than that of the parent. As you recall from our analogy in Chapter 2, the musicologist is tuned to the score and how the parts combine. The written score for a symphony shows the contribution of each instrument over time to produce the total musical work. Instrumental parts enter and leave, combine with others, and are heard alone to form one coherent composition. In this chapter, we ask how the different modes of communication come together to create a meaningful process. We consider the relation between moving and speaking and the way in which pauses and conversational rules make people intelligible to each other. We also discuss the social rules by which people enter and leave social occasions. In Chapters 11, 12, and 13, we describe the nonverbal behavior that results from being of a certain age, sex, and culture. These chapters tell you what nonverbal behaviors people have in common and what they share as members of a group.

The Relation between Moving and Speaking

The body is capable of moving in an incredible number of ways, and nonverbal researchers have tried for a long time to find some way of describing and classifying human motion in all its complexity. It has not been an easy task.

The Linguistic-Kinesic Analogy

The scheme worked out by Ray Birdwhistell (1965, 1967, 1968, 1970) is one of the few systematic and exhaustive treatments of body motion. His approach describes body movement using labels analogous to those used by linguists. In linguistics, language behavior occurs in standard units called *phonemes* (roughly equivalent to syllables). Such units are in turn made up of *phones,* which are categories of sounds. For example, the *p* sound in *pit* is a phone that includes all the slight possible variations of that sound. The *p* sounds in *pit* and *pat* are two different ways of making the *p* sound; that is, they are the phones of the phoneme /p/. All the phones combine to make up a phoneme. Phonemes then further combine into larger units called *morphemes* (roughly equivalent to words), which are, in turn, integrated into still larger units, called *syntactic sentences.* In sum, phones, phonemes, morphemes, and syntactic sentences are increasingly larger and more inclusive linguistic units hierarchically arranged.

So, where is the analogy between linguistics and kinesics? Birdwhistell (1965) has subdivided body motion into units that he has termed *kines, kinemes,* and *kinemorphs* and that are analogous to phones, phonemes, and morphemes, respectively. And just as the linguist has discovered that it is not particular sounds but classes of sounds (phonemes) that are of significance, so, too, has the body-motion expert (the kinesicist) found that it is not individual movements but classes of body movements (kinemes) that are important.

On the basis of his extensive observations, Birdwhistell has come to the conclusion that movement among natives of the United States consists of approximately 50 to 60 kinemes. For example, within the head area, there are four kinemes of brow behavior: lifted brow, lowered brow, knit brow, and single brow movement. The four eyelid kinemes are: over-open, slit, closed, and squeezed.

Just as phonemes are rarely found in isolation, so, too, are kinemes. A movement generally occurs as a part of several movements combined in meaningful sequences. So a lifted brow with over-open eyes and over-open mouth is a very different combination from that of a lifted brow with over-open eyes and compressed lips. This line of reasoning led Birdwhistell to posit that gestures are partial acts, like stem forms in language, and hence are meaningless in the absence of other known movement features. For example, just as the stem form *part* changes meaning with the addition of *im* or *de* (that is, *impart,* and *depart* have different meanings), so, too, does the meaning of a movement change in combination with a lifted brow or crossed arms.

Birdwhistell's analyses suggest more than the mere existence of similarities between the structures of kinesics and those of linguistics; they also indicate that there is an actual correlation between gestures and words. One example is represented by the notion of *kinesic markers,* which are particular movements that serve to illustrate or elaborate what is being said and that occur regularly in association with or in substitution for certain syntactic arrangements. Examples of kinesic markers are the slight downward motion of the head, eyelids, and hands at the end of a declarative statement and the slight upward tilt of the head at the end of a question.

While there is research support for the notion of kinesic markers, there is less support for the absolute comparability of kinesics and linguistics. In a review of Birdwhistell's work, Dittmann (1971) argued convincingly that there are some problems with Birdwhistell's model. In particular, he noted that, while some movements are discrete (that is, individually distinct) enough to be regarded as kinemes, there are many others that are continuous and hence not easily categorized as separate units—for example, changes in body orientation and distance or increases in eye contact. In other words, Dittmann argued that it is difficult to see how small changes in the *amount* of a nonverbal behavior can be regarded in the same way as a distinct change *from one sound to another.* As we've noted previously, whether any change is noticed at all depends in part on the amount of the behavior already present.

Nonverbal Escorts

One of the most obvious functions of nonverbal behavior is that of accompanying verbal behavior. As Ekman and Friesen (1972) have shown, there are several ways in which hand movements can illustrate speech. These *illustrators* include: batons, which are movements accenting particular words; ideographs, which are motions describing the direction of a thought; deictic movements, which involve pointing; spatial movements, which describe shape; rhythmic movements, which convey tempo; kinetographs, which show a bodily action; and pictographs, which are movements that draw a picture.

As you might expect, illustrators make complicated explanations more comprehensible. Try, for example, to explain to a stranger, without using your hands, how to find some out-of-the-way place in the middle of a downtown area. If that is not enough to make you speechless, try to explain to someone—again, without using your hands—how to hit a tennis forehand shot with top spin. In fact, without illustrators, instruction can become very convoluted and long-winded. One study found that, when students were asked to describe abstract line drawings without the aid of gestures, they used more words, spoke longer, and paused longer (Graham & Heywood, 1975). The interesting thing about illustrators is their interactional quality. When male college students were asked to give directions to an experimental confederate, the students used significantly more hand illustrators when they were in a face-to-face situation than when they were communicating through an intercom (Cohen & Harrison, 1973).

The usual assumption is that the verbal channel is helped along by this additional nonverbal activity. In other words, the verbal channel is regarded as the primary source of communication and the nonverbal channel as an auxiliary channel, which provides supplementary, although probably not absolutely essential, material. But the verbal/nonverbal relation can probably

This man is using one type of illustrator to indicate the shape of what he's describing.

be looked at in another way. As you recall from our discussion of self-syn-chrony in Chapter 5, Condon has noted that, when a person is speaking, the changes in the person's speech sounds and those in his or her body move-ments occur simultaneously. Speech doesn't occur first and then is modified by movement; each is coordinated with the other (Condon & Ogston, 1966, 1967). Furthermore, another study has found not only that speaking is ac-companied by more frequent hand and arm movements than nonspeaking activity but that it is mostly the right arm moving (Kimura, 1973). Since such movements are made predominantly by the hand opposite the speech hemisphere of the brain, one might then conclude that there is some system that is common to illustrators and speaking. Such data "raise the suspicion that the left hemisphere may be especially well adapted, not for symbolic function *per se,* but for the execution of some classes of motor acts, to which symbolic meaning can be attached" (Kimura, 1973, p. 49). In fact, developmental theorists have speculated that the illustrator type of gesture is primary in the development of the symbolic expressive system of the child (Werner & Kaplan, 1963). Piaget (1963) has given the example of a child who, in order to represent a matchbox containing a desired object, opened and closed her mouth.

For Birdwhistell (1965) the relevant question is not how the nonverbal affects the verbal but, rather, how both the verbal and the nonverbal contribute to communication. How highly interdependent the two modes are was illustrated by a study that required subjects to talk while observing or performing a gesture prescribed for them by the experimenter (Wolff & Gutstein, 1972). The gestures were either circular movements or linear movements that involved a repeated up-and-down motion of the arms. Results showed that the movements, whether observed in another while talking or produced while talking, altered the content of the talk. For example, circular gestures elicited circular themes, such as buses being "rolled over."

But even with movements that are less specifically pictorial in nature, the relation between speech and body movement is an intricate and interactive one. Several researchers have suggested that body movement plays a very important role in providing rhythm to speech so that listeners can hear it in clusters rather than as a monotonous one-word-at-a-time sequence (Dittmann & Llewellyn, 1969; Kendon, 1970b). Similarly, another study found that larger body movements in the form of postural shifts do not occur randomly in conversation or just when someone has apparently become physically uncomfortable; rather, they occur regularly when there are changes in the interaction itself, such as changes in topic (Erickson, 1975b). As a matter of fact, there are even times when you use movement change in an attempt to change the topic of conversation. Have you ever got up from a conversation that was becoming too heavy or tense to get a refill of coffee in a nonverbal attempt to change the subject of conversation?

As our discussion indicates, body movement, whether small or large, can be regarded as providing structure and pacing to human interaction. Scheflen (1964) maintained that there are three units of movement size, which he calls the *point,* the *position,* and the *presentation.* The point is the hand illustrator that accompanies the verbal point made in a discussion. When several points or gestures are combined, the result is a position, both postural and topical. Finally, the presentation "consists of the totality of one person's positions in a given interaction. Presentations have a duration from several minutes to several hours, and the terminals are a complete change in location" (Scheflen, 1964, p. 323).

When people observe the movements of others, they see them as grouped in clusters. *Changes* in movements are the signal to the observer that a new phase of activity has begun (Newtson, 1976). When students were shown videotapes of everyday activities, such as making a phone call, and were asked to press a button whenever they thought a meaningful action occurred, they divided the activity at breakpoints where change of movement occurred.

In summary, it is clear that communication comprises both movement and speech and that it is inappropriate to talk about the nonverbal as subsidiary or secondary to the verbal. It appears also that it is the *change* in nonverbal behavior that is noticed and that sets the boundaries in communication. When a friend asks you about some event he or she has missed, the questions repeatedly take the form of "And then what happened?" For most people, events occur in units marked by time and place; you tend to become more conscious of this when you're asked to tell about a sequence of events than when you're actually living it. But even when you're not aware of these clusters of movement, you're creating them as well as being influenced by those of others.

The Structure of Pauses

One important difference between the written and the spoken language is the presence of pauses. Punctuation marks are used in written matter to separate structural units, and it is at those places that pauses occur when the material is read aloud. Spontaneous speech contains many more pauses and nonfluencies than the reading of a prepared script. These prosodic features of speech have a structure and regularity that have received some attention from researchers. Consider the following speech from Shakespeare's *Romeo and Juliet* as a real-life Romeo might have delivered it.

> But [*pause*], soft! [*pause*] wha—what light [*brief pause*]
> through yonder window breaks? [*longer pause*]
> It—it is [ah] the east, [*pause*] and [uhm]
> Juliet is—is [ah] the sun! [*pause*]

When a real suitor, rather than an actor, says these words, he delivers them with a number of hesitations. First, there are silences, called *unfilled pauses,* that help mark the grammatical structure of the speech. Fairly long unfilled pauses occur at the ends of sentences and clauses. But there are also shorter unfilled pauses that occasionally occur in the middle of a sentence. A second category of pauses are the *filled pauses,* during which some vocalization occurs. Filled pauses include vowel sounds (such as "ah" and "uhm"), repetitions of words, and false starts, in which the first letter or syllable of a word recurs.

At first, the meaning and function of all these pauses were sought in attributes of the speaker—that is, at the individual level of analysis. It was thought that they were perhaps signs of a speaker's nervousness or anxiety (recall our discussion in Chapter 5) or that maybe they were part of a speaker's attempt to convey a difficult idea. In order to investigate this latter possibility, subjects were asked to describe or to explain a number of cartoons (Goldman-Eisler, 1961, 1968; replicated with children by Levin, Silverman, & Ford, 1967). The assumption here was that explaining a cartoon requires more thinking than just describing it; therefore, explaining should involve more pauses and hesitations. Such was the case; more pauses occurred during explanations than during descriptions.

But the speaker is only one part of any communication, and the question of what function pauses serve in the decoding of speech was posed. In other words, did Romeo's hesitations represent only his creative struggles to express his feelings, or did they in some way aid Juliet's understanding? It was found that the different lengths of unfilled pauses serve different functions and that the placement of shorter and longer unfilled pauses is anything but random. Longer pauses (from half a second to a second) occur *between* clauses in speech, whereas shorter pauses (about a fourth of a second) occur *within* clauses (Boomer & Dittmann, 1962). The longer pauses are called *juncture* pauses (because of their placement), and the shorter ones *hesitation* pauses. Boomer (1965) argued that hesitation pauses are the ones that relate to the speaker's thought processes. Juncture pauses are functionally different and help the listener get the message. For example, speaker pauses occurring at the juncture points between sentences help listeners to memorize orally presented nonsense passages, whereas speaker hesitation pauses do not (Suci, 1967).

When the length of hesitation and juncture pauses was experimentally varied, listeners were more aware of changes in the length of the hesitation pauses (Boomer & Dittmann, 1962). Listeners reported that sentences with hesitation pauses of varying lengths differed more from a standard sentence than did sentences with juncture pauses of varying length. This greater awareness of the hesitation pauses may provide indirect, additional evidence that the nonverbal behavior we really notice is the unexpected. Juncture pauses are a regular feature of talking, since they must occur for speech to be intelligible to the listener. Presumably, their absence would be noticed. On the other hand, hesitation pauses are rarer; hence, it is their presence that strikes the listener. The norm is smooth-flowing speech without nonfluencies. Therefore the "uhms" and "ahs" of filled pauses are also likely to be noticed and perhaps attributed to the speaker's personal characteristics. So, if Juliet reached the conclusion that her Romeo was shy and nervous, such a conclusion may have been due more to his hesitation pauses than to his juncture pauses.

Since juncture pauses are instrumental to listener comprehension, they occur at more predictable points than hesitation pauses. Because of the rhythm with which speech flows, juncture pauses occur at the end of sentences, before conjunctions, before interrogatives (*who, which, what*), before adverbial clauses of time and place (introduced, for example, by *when* and *where*), and around parenthetical comments (Henderson, Goldman-Eisler, & Starbek, 1965). During spontaneous speech, about two-thirds of the breaths taken occur at juncture points, and virtually all breaths taken during reading aloud occur then. It is also known that listener responses such as "oh," "I see," nods, and smiles are more likely to occur at juncture pauses (Dittmann & Llewellyn, 1967, 1968).

Further evidence that juncture pauses function to make speech more comprehensible can be drawn from research on pauses in mothers' speech to children of different ages. Broen (1972) found that, when mothers speak to 2-year-olds, virtually all the pauses come after well-formed sentences. With 5-year-olds, almost 90% of the pauses in mothers' speech come at such points. In contrast, only half the pauses in speech directed to adults occur after sentences. Presumably, in an effort to help children decode speech, mothers automatically stress the separations between sentences.

What seems clear is that pauses in speech serve different functions for speaker and listener; they help the speaker express his or her thoughts, and they help the listener make sense of what he or she hears. Longer unfilled juncture pauses help package the speech stream into manageable units so that the listener can understand it. Shorter unfilled pauses and filled pauses are rightly called hesitation pauses, because hesitating is exactly what, for one reason or another, the speaker is doing. When strangers meet, conversation is sometimes awkward as each searches for appropriate expressions to offer the other. In relatively short order, however, their task becomes easier, as indicated by fewer filled pauses and faster speaking rates (Lalljee & Cook, 1973).

Conversational Rules

The next time you are walking down a relatively busy street, try going a whole block at the same speed, without straying from a straight-line course. In other words, your task is to proceed down the street as though no one else were there. Do you think you could do it? How would it make you feel? And what would be the likely reaction of others to your steamroller approach?

If you are like most of us, walking "as if" no one else were there—when in fact there are a great number of people around—would be a very difficult, if not impossible, task. The reason is that you have learned to take others into account. You may not be aware of it. You may not intend to. You may even think that with strangers it's not necessary. But you subtly and continuously adjust your behavior to others, as they adjust their behavior to you. Stated in another way, you know the *social rules* for walking down a busy street just as you know the rules for a myriad of other everyday events involving other people. In fact, it is now being argued that the basis of many research findings involving nonverbal behavior between people resides largely in the social-rules domain. Other terms for the rules we are talking about are *rituals* (Goffman, 1971), *conventions* (Lewis, 1969), *programs* (Scheflen, 1968), *customs* (Malinowski, 1944), and *social norms* (Sherif, 1936). Whatever the word, it appears that much of our social behavior follows social rules of various kinds, including such things as how to greet a friend, what position to take in an elevator, and how to avoid colliding on a sidewalk. These are the kinds of behaviors about which Goffman (1967) said "Most actions which are guided by rules of conduct are performed unthinkingly, the questioned actor saying he performs 'for no reason' or because he 'felt like doing so' " (p. 49).

Turn Taking

Another example of this kind of social rule is what has been termed *state of talk* (Goffman, 1964) or *floor apportionment* (Kendon, 1967) and refers to the way people manage to carry on conversations without "colliding" with each other all the time. More specifically, it refers to the verbal and nonverbal mechanisms by which participants manage the smooth exchange of speaker and listener roles in a conversation.

Kendon (1967) was one of the first to show that participants in an interchange tend to take turns speaking and listening. At face value, this may not appear to be a particularly surprising finding; what is surprising is that this apparently simple procedure is managed by a fine and subtle coordination of nonverbal behavior. In particular, Kendon (1967) found that *where* a person is looking may function as a signal regulating the exchange of the speaker role. At those points in the interaction in which speaker and listener exchange roles, the speaker characteristically ends his or her utterance by looking directly at the listener with a sustained gaze, and the listener characteristically looks away as he or she begins to speak. Kendon also noted that speakers look away as they begin long utterances, perhaps in an attempt to tune the listener out so that they can gather their thoughts. They look again at the listener toward the end of these utterances, perhaps to check the listener's reaction.

One important point here is the sequence and timing of gaze direction. Speaker gaze can regulate the behavior of the listener. Thus, a speaker can forestall a response from a listener by not looking at him or her or can increase the demand for some response by looking directly at the listener. The same function is served by *speaker gesticulation signals*—hand movements by the speaker that can appear to almost literally hold off entry by the listener (Duncan, 1973).

There are some other nonverbal cues that in one way or another control turn taking in conversations. Duncan (1972) coded a number of behaviors he examined on videotape and concluded that a listener may begin his or her speaking turn when the speaker gives a turn-yielding signal. This turn-yielding signal is the display of at least one of a set of six nonverbal and verbal cues. Among the cues described are the termination of a hand gesticulation, a rise or fall of pitch away from the mid-range, and a vocal stretching out of the final syllable (a drawl). Duncan (1972) also noted that disruption (in the form of simultaneous talk) results if the listener begins to speak before receiving a yielding signal. Yielding cues also occur in entering a social situation in which one might become a speaker. For example, when an outsider approaches a group of people who are interacting, he or she will wait at a little

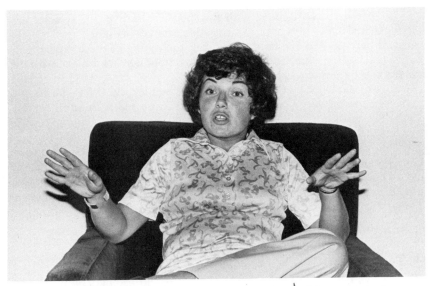

Hand gesticulations by speakers keep listeners from taking a turn in the conversation.

distance from the group until a member of the group looks at and gestures the outsider in (Kendon, 1976). Check the validity of Kendon's suggestions next time you try to join a group at a party, when you are sure they know you're there and somehow you are not finding a way to get in. You will probably agree that, in the absence of some yielding by the group, joining is a very hard thing to do.

Speaker/Listener Coordination

Kendon (1976) also noted that, when entry begins, there is a finely coordinated display of movements by the person entering the group and by the insider yielding to that approach. This precise coordination of speaker and listener was first noted by Condon (Condon & Ogston, 1966, 1967) and termed *interactional synchrony.* His method involved exhaustive analyses of filmed records of interaction by means of a time-motion analyzer. This machine allows one to look at a film in slow motion or even at one film frame at a time. (With standard filming of 24 frames per second, one frame lasts 1/24 of a second.)

Using this projector, Condon mapped every movement of the human body on graph paper, so that a flow chart of body motion over time results. As we mentioned earlier, Condon found that a speaker's body movements and speech sounds are rhythmically coordinated (Condon & Ogston, 1966, 1967). But even more fascinating was the finding that the body movements of a listener are precisely coordinated with the speech sounds of the speaker addressing that listener. Listeners, as a rule, don't move very much—just a slight head nod here and an eye blink there—but the timing of these movements (that is, their starts, stops, and changes of direction) is synchronized with the changes in the speaker's speech stream.

More recent work by Condon (Condon & Sander, 1974) has shown that the movements of very young infants are synchronized with adult human speech. The most intriguing finding here is that infants, even when they are just a few days old, will "sync" with any human speech, regardless of the language being spoken. Apparently, as time goes by, through constant exposure to one language instead of another, the child becomes habituated to some kinds of speech rhythms and not to others. We address the issue of nonverbal differences among people socialized into different languages and cultures in Chapter 13.

Listener Responses

We have been talking about what speakers and listeners do in unison. There are, however, additional, separate cues emitted by listeners that can regulate the speaker's behavior. These cues, which tend to control and manage conversation, are called *regulators* (Ekman & Friesen, 1969b; Wiener, Devoe, Rubinow, & Geller, 1972). They are not idiosyncratic to the people who use them and are meaningful only as social rules.

Several investigators have noted that listeners spend a great deal of time looking at the person who is talking to them (Exline & Winters, 1965; Kendon, 1967; Nielsen, 1964); that is, one way listeners indicate their attention is by looking at the speaker. Another way is represented by properly timed, although brief, accompaniment signals, such as head nods and "m-hms." Called *back channels* by Duncan (1973), these listener responses were found to occur at the end of a speaker's longer clauses and sentences or when the speaker turned his head toward the listener. Although seldom conscious of back channels when they do occur, speakers respond with alarm to their absence as well as to their unusual placement. If listener responses are absent, a speaker may be inclined to stop talking and ask the listener whether he or she is still there (Fries, 1952). In a study in which adult interviewers withheld smiles, head nods, and verbal listener responses, the teenagers who were being interviewed smiled and nodded less in turn, touched their own bodies more, and talked less frequently (Rosenfeld, in press).

If back channels are unexpectedly placed, a speaker may feel that the listener is responding automatically and without interest. And, finally, if a listener makes a number of single head nods in rapid succession in the middle of a speaker's utterance, the effect is to cause the speaker to hesitate and even to stop talking altogether (Birdwhistell, 1970). Note again that the crucial thing is not just the nonverbal behavior itself but its timing and sequence as well. Consequently, social rules direct not only *what* to do but *when* to do it. In order to communicate successfully, an interactant must subscribe to the social rules of his or her culture.

Rituals

Preceding sections of this chapter have been concerned with the organization of nonverbal behavior into ever-larger and more complex sequences and routines. Looks, smiles, and gestures are part of sequenced patterns; they don't appear in the stream of behavior according only to the individual's mood or the interactants' relationship. This final section is concerned with the larger of these sequences—with rituals such as greetings and farewells that prescribe fairly complex and lengthy themes of mutual nonverbal coordination.

Remedial Interchanges

Goffman (1971) has described the "norms of co-mingling" that enable social encounters to take place. These norms provide you with the baselines of behaviors on which your expectations for yourself and others are based. When infractions occur, the person who has committed the violation tries to make amends by involving the other in repair rituals. Goffman calls dialogues that transform the offensive into the acceptable *remedial interchanges.* Repairs can be made by trying to give a good account of oneself. For example, a person can make believe that he or she did not in fact commit the infraction, as in the case of someone who has noisily knocked over a wastebasket in a public place and keeps walking while indignantly looking around at others as if in search of the offender.

Remedial interchanges can also take the form of apologies, most often verbal, but with nonverbal enactments as well. Goffman gives the example of the bustling manner in which a middle-class person gets up from his bus seat when an undesirable passenger occupies a seat beside him. The purposeful air is offered to the other person in apology for the potential insult of getting up and serves to indicate to all the other passengers that one is in fact getting ready to leave the bus. Such postures and gestures, called *body gloss,* are often directed to the world at large as well as to a specific other. They are exaggerated displays designed to give an acceptable definition of self. In fact, body gloss can be seen as a deliberate command to take the definition of self that is being offered.

The third form of remedial interchange involves requests, which typically occur before the violation. Someone who suspects that he or she might give offense by taking a seat adjacent to another may try to catch the other's eye and, by a hand gesture, request permission to sit down. The other's smile and nod grant the request. All these interchanges involve fairly lengthy sequences in which the moves and countermoves are so well programmed that they hardly need any conscious planning on anyone's part.

Greetings and Farewells

In addition to remedial interchanges, Goffman (1971) also described *supportive interchanges* that regulate social interaction. Central among these positive rituals are greetings and farewells. Goffman described mutual approach and orientation, eye contact, smiling, and hand waving or hat tipping as part of the greeting ritual. He noted also that greetings sometimes culminate in touch, as in handshakes and embraces. A more precise description of the greeting ritual has been offered by Kendon and Ferber (1973). On the basis of their careful analysis of greetings that were filmed at several social gatherings, these researchers distinguished four steps in the greeting process: a prephase of sighting and announcement, a distance salutation, an approach phase, and a close salutation.

Careful coordination is required at all stages of the greeting ritual, because miscueing at any point can produce embarrassment and disruption. The *sighting phase* is exemplified by synchronization of movements between two people before they give any obvious sign of greeting or by a hostess turning her face and looking steadily toward an arriving guest. The *distance salutation* always precedes a closer interaction, although it need not necessarily lead to it. People who meet for a second time during the same event may offer only a distance salutation, which is marked by a head toss (that is, the head is rapidly tilted back and brought forward) and may also include a nod and a hand wave.

After exchanging the distance salutation, the greeters *approach*. How far each moves is quite significant. In the host/guest relationships observed by Kendon and Ferber, the further the host moved from the center of activities to greet the guest, the greater the show of respect for the guest. Conversely, the freer the guest was to penetrate the center of the action, the more intimate that person's relationship with the host. Clearly a subtle negotiation is involved in mutual approach. It was also noted that the duration of the party affected the location of the greeting encounters. Early in the event, the host and hostess were available to all arrivals at the edge of the party space; later, guests, regardless of relationship, came further into the gathering before being greeted. During the approach, the guest holds one or both hands in front of the body and engages in some grooming (such as straightening of hair and clothing). At the end of the approach, eye contact is reestablished, smiles appear, and a hand with palm toward the other is displayed.

The *close salutation* terminates the greeting ritual. The greeters come to a stop (usually about 5 feet apart) and, facing each other, engage in what is conventionally called a greeting. A handshake, a verbal greeting, or an embrace occurs. The conclusion of the greeting invariably involves a further change of location even if the two continue in conversation. Handshakes are often accompanied by head nods and, between men and women, by a kiss initiated by the woman offering her cheek. Male/female greetings sometimes involve a combination of kiss and embrace: the man lifts his arms outward and places them around the woman, who puts her hands on the man's chest or waist or reaches with her forearms to put her hands on the man's back. In the social gatherings observed by Kendon and Ferber (1973), most male-to-male greetings involved handshakes, female-to-female salutations usually had no physical contact, and male-to-female greetings were evenly distributed with regard to absence of contact, handshakes, and embraces.

Less is known about the nature of farewells. Goffman (1971) called greetings and farewells the "punctuation marks" of conversation and noted that farewells signal an interval during which the participants will have less access to each other for some time to come. It is Goffman's view that farewells can be marked by greater enthusiasm and warmth than greetings because the participants need not immediately live up to the expectations that these mutual commitments create. One might expect, then, to find some differences between farewells in situations in which people expect to see each other again soon and farewells in situations in which longer separations are anticipated.

Bakken (1977) compared farewells in a situation of early future access (a college student-union corridor) and in a situation of limited future access (airport departure gate). Farewells in the student union involved a synchrony of body movements in which shifts in orientation (face-to-face to side-by-side) were combined with movement to produce a mutual rotation permitting separation in different directions. Typically, one person begins a weight shift that, when mirrored by the other, results in mutual rotation around an axis drawn between the two parties. When this shift was not mirrored, the farewell was delayed. This oscillation has been noted also by Laver (1975), who pointed out that conversations can be terminated only by mutual consent. The person who wishes to leave signals his or her intention to the other by making departure moves in various nonverbal ways. Only when these moves are acknowledged and matched can leave taking be accomplished. The head toss noted in Kendon and Ferber's (1973) description of the distance salutation was seen here after the position shift; when combined with mutual gaze and a wave, it usually preceded the verbal goodbye.

Farewells at the airport were different mostly from the point of view of the frequency of touching. Only one embrace was noted in the student union, but virtually all farewells at the airport involved some physical contact. Handshakes were common in male-to-male farewells, embraces in heterosexual goodbyes, and both kinds of contact in female-to-female goodbyes. Virtually all airport farewells included the relinquishing by those remaining behind of some object belonging to the departing one. Verbal goodbyes preceded the last physical contact, and gaze was maintained during increased distancing. Often only the departing passenger moved away, with others remaining stationary until visual access was lost. These findings indicate that ease of future access may indeed shape the farewell ritual. It is also likely, however, that the different nature of the farewells was due to the more intimate relationship that, in comparison to that between student-union patrons, existed between the participants in the airport farewells. The greater amount of physical contact observed at the airport might result from either circumstance. The latter possibility was investigated by Heslin and Boss

The four stages that greetings go through are illustrated in these four photographs: sighting, in which the woman sees the man; distance salutation, in which she waves; approach, in which both people look, smile, and reach out; and close salutation, which involves an embrace.

(1976), who noted that in 85% of airport departures some touching occurred and 40% of the touching included kisses. When questioned, over half of these people said they were spouses, lovers, or relatives of the departing person, and the rest said they were close friends.

In farewells, as in greetings, timing is important. Another observation of departures noted that the nonverbal behaviors of smiling, nodding, and forward leaning all increased as leave taking approached. Fifteen seconds before leaving, all these behaviors peaked when one interactant stood up and left (Knapp, Hart, Friedrich, & Schulman, 1973).

By now you may be wondering why greetings and farewells seem to be such elaborate, time-consuming rituals. When people are ready to leave, why don't they just get up and go? The answer is quite simple: because farewells always involve at least two people, and the leave taking must be negotiated between them step by step. Even when the two people face a relatively long separation, the farewell itself is but one move in an extended sequence of moves. The farewell is part of a larger sequence—which is the relationship itself.

Summary

It appears that people really do talk with their hands—and eyes and heads. And they do it according to an intricate choreography, or, as Edward Sapir once put it, "an elaborate and secret code that is written nowhere, known by none, and understood by all."

In fact, the code has begun to be written. As bodies move, they provide cues that, often in conjunction with the verbal stream, make us intelligible to others as well as to ourselves. Movement can illustrate, elaborate, modify, and provide rhythm and pacing to verbal talk. Paralanguage, through elements such as pausing and tempo, provides cadence as well.

Bodies move in synchrony while conversation is exchanged, as in a carefully rehearsed dance. Conversational turn taking, greetings, and farewells are also part of this elaborate choreography and, as such, obey a set of rules and guidelines. You know the rules even if you cannot articulate them, for you know when they have been broken.

Chapter 11

Growing Up Moving

"They all look alike to me!" Proud parents notwithstanding, newborns really look remarkably alike. And then, in no time at all, they begin to look and move and sound like the individuals they're becoming. It's practically impossible to look at an infant wrapped in a blanket and tell its gender, but soon there will be no doubt whether it's a boy or a girl. Costumes aside, young infants show little sign of being of one nationality or another, but to the trained eye they begin before long to evidence their cultural ties; they start to look and sound French or British or whatever. And then there is that difficult-to-describe, although significant, progress toward an individual style—a style made of movement and sound and expression that is every bit as unique as a fingerprint. When do these developments occur? How does an infant become a person with a characteristic verbal and nonverbal behavior?

This chapter is concerned with the developmental aspects of nonverbal behavior. Throughout the book, we have been talking about the importance of context and social rules in understanding nonverbal behavior. Therefore, when we turn our attention to the issue of how children develop nonverbally, we must consider two related issues. First is the question of when and how children develop the requisite nonverbal repertoire that makes the report aspect of human nonverbal communication possible. Second, we need to know when and how they acquire the sense of context, the knowledge of when to use what they know and what it means when they do—that is, the command aspect of communication. The plan of the chapter follows the overall plan of the book; we begin with a discussion of the expression and reception of emotion, and then we turn to children's nonverbal interactions. When do they learn to behave toward friends and foes as adults do? Finally, we review material on how children learn the rules of conversation.

The Child as an Individual

Becoming Expressive

It has been said that in the first few weeks of life infants probably experience their world as a booming, buzzing confusion. It is probably also true that adults find it difficult to differentiate among the first emotional expressions of an infant. When babies are aroused, they are motion incarnate. Arms, legs, and faces are in excited animation all at the same time. An early study of emotional expression in children showed that excitement is, in fact, the first emotion to appear and it is only later that excitement becomes differentiated into positive and negative forms—that is, distress and delight (Bridges, 1932). Through detailed observations of infants from birth to 2 years of age, Bridges also found that emotional expression becomes even further differentiated: distress begins to take on different forms, such as fear, disgust, and anger, while delight develops into elation and affection. The primary finding here, then, is that, although children can be said to be "emotional" right from birth, it takes some time (about two years) before they demonstrate some of the range of emotional expressions evidenced by adults. By the time they are 2 years of age, they communicate nearly a dozen different emotions.

That the basics of the human emotional repertoire are present from the very beginning of life has received additional support by work done with children born blind or blind and deaf (Eibl-Eibesfeldt, 1974). Blind-and-deaf children laugh, smile, cry, frown, and stomp their feet in anger much like normal children. It cannot be argued that they have learned these expressions by imitation. Furthermore, Eibl-Eibesfeldt (1974) showed that children born blind cover their faces with their hands when embarrassed and that blind infants "stare" toward familiar voices. Because of these behaviors, it would seem reasonable to accept the hypothesis of some sort of inborn basis for many facial expressions of emotion.

There is agreement that infants in every culture smile and frown (Birdwhistell, 1970). But with development also comes differentiated responsiveness to particular environments. An early study found that indiscriminate smiling in infants ceased when they reached their fifth or sixth month (Spitz & Wolf, 1946). Similarly, it has been shown that smiling becomes increasingly social (that is, associated with other persons) in the first five years of life. Perhaps the more discriminating social smile—one that is triggered by other humans—emerges from the raw, undiscriminating form of smiling, which has a biological base. Context begins to determine the rules by which the developing person smiles in some social situations and not in others. More generally, as children become socialized, they learn to become expressive in some situations and inhibited in others.

In like fashion, it has been shown that, while the frequency of the *broad smile* (in which the corners of the mouth are drawn up and back, exposing both upper and lower teeth) does not change between the ages of 2 and 4 years, the frequency of the *upper smile* (in which only the upper teeth are exposed) increases dramatically over the same period. In addition, the incidence of the upper smile becomes increasingly selective. Boys by the age of 4 are reserving the "sociable" upper smile almost exclusively for other boys (Cheyne, 1976).

We've mentioned that all children express emotion and that their expressions become more differentiated and complex as they get older. There are, however, significant individual differences in children's ability to send accurate information to others about their emotional states. A recent study (Buck, 1975) has shown that some children are really good senders and others are not. In Buck's experiment, both the child's mother and unacquainted undergraduate students who had access only to a TV image of the child could tell what kind of emotionally loaded slide the child had just seen. In contrast, other children were poor senders, not only with regard to the students participating in the experiment but with regard to their own mothers as well.

Another series of studies also found considerable differences in the expressive ability of children in different age groups—more specifically, children in nursery school, and in second and fifth grades (Hamilton, 1972, 1973). Furthermore, it has been found that children's ability to produce facial expressions through either straight imitation or imaginative role playing does *not* improve with age after nursery school (Odom & Lemond, 1972). Given that a whole host of childhood activities improves with age, why would the ability to produce emotional expressions not do likewise? One possibility is that emotional expression may be reduced by socialization training; that is, parents may pressure the growing child to inhibit emotional expressiveness. Although very young children can convey a range of emotions, they may learn soon after age 2 that it is often inappropriate to do so. Furthermore, in the school and experimental context of being asked to role-play or imitate, social constraints may be especially pronounced for the growing child.

Inhibition (as well as expression) of emotional responsiveness is also tied to specific contexts. For example, Buck (1977) found that, when TV images of 4- to 6-year-old boys and girls looking at emotionally loaded slides were shown to their mothers, sex differences in emotional expressivity were found. Boys became less expressive as they got older, whereas girls did not. Buck speculated that the slides elicited the kinds of emotions (such as pleasure and disgust) that boys are socialized to mask; it is possible that in a different context calling for an aggressive response, girls would hide their reactions, because aggression is an emotion girls are not supposed to show.

The fact that children come to suppress their emotional expressiveness as they get older has received some anecdotal support from descriptions of children's behavior in classrooms. Galloway (1976) has directed attention to the changes that take place over time in the way a child "raises his hand" in class in order to be called on. In the first grade, a child remains barely seated, and his whole body seems to be waving at the teacher. The raised arm reaches, stretches, circles, and flaps in ways that cannot possibly be missed. Two years later, significant changes have occurred. Now, when the child raises his hand, the raised arm is supported by a prop under the elbow supplied by the other arm. Some energy has gone out of the act. By the fifth grade, the raised hand, when it does infrequently appear, seems to have lost all muscle tonus as it rests almost entirely on the top of the head, so that it's now difficult to tell whether the hand landed there by accident or whether it is really a signal to the teacher that the child wishes to be called on.

Becoming Sensitive

Some say that children are like barometers of the changing emotional climate around them. However, there hasn't been a great deal of research on emotional receptivity in children. Early studies indicated that 6-month-old babies respond to differences in tone of voice (Buhler & Hetzer, 1935; Lewis, 1936) and that sensitivity to facial expressions of feelings increases with age (Dashiell, 1927; Gates, 1923). More recently, a systematic study of receptivity to emotion expressed via vocal cues on the part of children ranging in age from 5 to 12 years showed a gradual and steadily progressive increase in the ability to identify the emotional meaning of the sounds (Dimitrovsky, 1964). Furthermore, this study found that, regardless of the stimulus presented, children of all ages more frequently picked the "sad" and "angry" labels than the "loving" or "happy" ones. Just why they should respond more often in negative terms to any expressed emotion is not altogether clear. One possibility was suggested by a replication in which children provided no more negative labels than did adults (Fenster & Goldstein, 1971). This replication was done with middle-class children (who are similar in social class to the adults used in most research), whereas the Dimitrovsky study was done with working-class children. It is possible that lower-class children expect more negative emotions in general or in the specific testing situation than do middle-class children.

Instead of taking one nonverbal channel (like sound) and asking children of different ages to describe what emotion was being expressed through that channel, a series of studies asked instead how children respond to messages conveyed simultaneously through several channels. Taking verbal and vocal channels separately, there were no differences between children's and adults' perceptions of emotional meaning. However, a developmental trend was in evidence for the *visual* channel. For young children, how the speaker looked was of less importance than what he said or how he said it (Bugental, Kaswan, Love, & Fox, 1970). In a follow-up study, similar results were reported (Bugental, Kaswan, & Love, 1970). It was found that, when children were presented with a "joking" message (that is, one in which the verbal content and voice tone were negative but the visual image was positive), they tended to see it much more negatively than did adults. This effect was particularly pronounced when the sender was a female. Children didn't see a woman's smile as offsetting a negative message, whereas they did see a man's smile as counterbalancing the negativity of the message. It has been suggested that joking messages that depend on channel incongruity may be lost on young children or even experienced badly by them because they don't integrate material from *all* channels. Hence the command that says "I'm only kidding" may be missed by the child, leaving behind only the bare hostility. Another interpretation may be that children have not yet learned to see the pattern created by all the channels operating at the same time. They don't see the various channels cross-referencing or commenting on the reports coming from other channels.

Acquiring Gender

A female human body moves very differently from a male human body. Many factors, such as skeletal structure and musculature, contribute to such differences, but many of the differences are learned. We develop a gender signature, so to speak. While much of our discussion on gender differences in nonverbal behavior is reserved for Chapter 12, we do need to mention here some developmental aspects of gender identity.

The most common question with respect to the study of developing sex differences is how these differences come about. Three factors are frequently cited: (1) genetic factors, (2) "shaping" of boy-like and girl-like behaviors by parents and other socializing agents, and (3) the child's spontaneous learning of behavior appropriate to his or her gender through imitation (Maccoby & Jacklin, 1974). With regard to the first of these factors, there is some indication that there are real sex differences in infant facial features, with female infants having more open eyes and higher brows than male infants (Haviland, 1976).

Birdwhistell (1970) has argued that the second and third of these factors are those that have the greatest impact. Observations in a variety of cultural settings convinced him that each culture has its own ideas of appropriate masculine and feminine behaviors and that children grow into these behaviors as they grow older; after a certain point, adults seem to "grow out of them" again. For example, Birdwhistell (1970) has shown that, in the United States, male children learn how to cross their legs, carry their bodies, and blink their eyes differently from female children. Specifically, they cross their legs at a greater angle apart than females, roll their pelvises back, and blink faster and more regularly than females. The intriguing observation here is that these gender cues become increasingly visible as the child moves toward early adulthood and thereafter decline. Even at the point of maximal gender display in early adulthood, context affects what gets displayed. Students in the authors' courses, when asked when they are most and least nonverbally feminine and masculine, reveal an interesting sex difference. Women report being most feminine in encounters with men and least feminine in encounters with women. Men, on the other hand, report the opposite; that is, they are most masculine with other men and least masculine with women.

Lastly, the role of socialization in gender development becomes apparent when we look at adults observing an infant. If they believe that the infant is a boy, they tend to label the baby's expression as anger; if, however, they believe that the infant is a girl, they label the same expression as fear (Condry & Condry, 1976). Perhaps, then, differentiation of facial expressions is influenced by expectations; given the same initial distress reaction, girl infants begin to show more fear expressions and boy infants more anger expressions.

The Child in Interaction

The early stages of life see not only the beginning of a child's nonverbal individuality, but also many forms of interaction between the child and those around him. Infants smile when smiled at, hug when hugged, and hit and bite when others try to control them. Children relate to people both affectionately and aggressively, and, at first, virtually all this communication is nonverbal, at least on the child's part.

Positive Interaction with Adults

Becoming communicative involves attending to others, responding to them, and knowing how, in turn, one's own responses affect others. Gaze is instrumental in all these processes. The exchange of looks between mother and child has received considerable research attention (Robson, 1967). When the baby is 3 months old, the mother looks at the infant more than the infant looks at her (Peery & Stern, 1975). This seems to be due to the fact that mothers' visual interest in their babies continues to remain high, while, as time goes by, babies begin to look around the room in search of more novel stimulation than the mother's face. The same is true with 6-month-old infants; they, too, look at their mothers less than their mothers look at them (Collis & Schaffer, 1975). Furthermore, mothers show a marked tendency to follow their infants' gaze toward toys. In the study above, when a baby looked at a toy, the mother also looked, thus indicating that the infant's behavior exerts influence on the adult. Conversely, children between the ages of 2 and 14 months showed an increasing tendency to follow the mother's, as well as an experimenter's, gaze to the left and right (Scaife & Bruner, 1975), thereby demonstrating their increasing appreciation of another's perspective.

Not only do mothers look more at their infants than the infants look at them, but mothers communicate more across the entire range of nonverbal modalities (Ling & Ling, 1974). During the infant's first few months of life, mothers use posture and touch a lot, but they also look and talk and make faces and noises at their babies. Particularly during the first year, children direct less communication at the mother, and, when they do communicate, they use one nonverbal channel at a time. This suggests that the integration of the nonverbal system may emerge as part of a developmental process. As children mature, they develop the skills needed to combine and coordinate the different nonverbal channels in more differentiated and hierarchically integrated ways.

Babies babble and coo when they are alone in their cribs. Most parents know that these infant vocalizations increase when someone leans over and smiles, touches, or talks to the baby. Research has shown that eye contact between adult and child is needed to produce an increase in the child's vocal response (Bloom, 1975). Neither the presence of an unresponsive adult nor the presence of one who just smiled or touched or vocalized to the baby succeeded in getting a vocal response when the baby couldn't see the adult's eyes, which were concealed with opaque eye glasses. In filmed interactions between a sighted infant and a blind mother, it was noted that the infant's cooing and smiling, which at 8 weeks of age occurred in rhythmic interaction with sighted adults, did not follow this pattern with the blind mother (Brazelton, Tronick, Adamson, Als, & Wise, 1975). Instead, the infant looked longer at the mother's motionless face and sightless eyes and then looked away without engaging in the cooing and smiling that characterized the baby's interaction with sighted others.

Such interactions establish early on patterns of mutuality between infants and adults. In a study of 3-month-old infants' interactions with their mothers, patterns of mutual cycling of involvement were noted (Tronick, Als,

Expression, gaze, and posture indicate a moment of high mutual involvement for mother and child.

& Brazelton, 1977). Coding facial expression, gaze, vocalizations, and body position and movement, these researchers found that mothers and infants engaged in periods of interaction marked by an almost perfect match of affective involvement. In other words, when the mother was looking, smiling, leaning, holding, and talking, the infant was similarly engaged—a pattern that indicated high mutual involvement. Such periods alternated in a cyclic fashion with periods of low involvement.

But sometimes the nonverbal interaction between mother and child can be troublesome. In a British study, a group of children were identified by their mothers as "noncuddlers." Although these infants didn't mind contact in the form of stroking or touch, they resisted strenuously any contact involving restraint (Schaffer & Emerson, 1964). Problems were noted when a "noncuddler" had a mother who wanted to hold and cuddle her child and conversely, when a "cuddler" had a mother who didn't often pick up and hold the baby.

This child is a "noncuddler" who resists touch when it involves restraint.

Infants interact from birth with adults other than their mothers, and very soon their behavior varies depending on who the other interactant is. Careful analyses of videotaped play interactions between infants and their mothers, fathers, and unfamiliar adults revealed that infants acted very differently with these different people and that adults acted differently with them (Yogman, Dixon, Tronick, Adamson, Als, & Brazelton, 1976). Seen weekly from ages 2 to 24 weeks, these infants differentiated their behavior toward mother, father, and stranger as early as 4 weeks, an age younger than most of the previous research had suggested. For example, infants frowned at strangers about four times as much as they did at either mothers or fathers. Infants consistently showed more positive expressions with mothers and fathers than with strangers. Moreover, these differential behaviors were reciprocal; slow-motion analyses showed infant and mother engaged in reciprocal limb movement toward and away from each other, with gradual accelerations and decelerations that established a mutual rhythm. Infant and father, on the other hand, were seen engaged in larger, more abrupt, and staccato movements with each other. With a stranger, the interaction was marked by cautious approaches and withdrawals; the stranger engaged in long silences and occasional tentative touches as if confused by the infant's cues and was noticed sending confusing cues in turn.

Somewhat in contrast to findings that show the mother's predominance in the nonverbal interaction between mother and child, an observational study of 8-month-old infants at home and in the laboratory found a clear-cut preference on the part of the babies for their fathers; they smiled at, vocalized to, looked at, reached toward, and touched their fathers much more than their mothers and strangers (Lamb, 1975). It was also noted that touch on the part of the mothers served primarily a caretaking and disciplinary function, whereas touch by the father most often occurred in the context of play. Preference for the father was explained by this contextual difference.

As the preceding discussion indicates, infants are engaged in communication with their mothers and with other people from the moment they are born. From these interactions children learn mutuality and differentiation; that is, they learn to match their responses to those of others and to vary their responses from person to person. And, finally, they begin to be active and important environmental influences on the responses of others. For example, Bates (1976) found that, when 11-year-old boys smiled at their teacher, they received positive nonverbal behavior in return.

Positive Interaction with Peers

Just as infants respond differentially to adults earlier than was previously thought, so, too, is there more peer interaction among very young children than was once thought. Where peer interaction was formerly believed to be negligible until the preschool years, it has recently been found to exist at a much younger age. Videotapes of a play group revealed the development of dyadic interchanges between 1-year-old boys (Mueller & Lucas,

1975). The interchanges were found to progress from imitation to more mutual interactions involving give and take that required reciprocity and timing on the part of both children.

The nonverbal modalities considered to be of central importance in the development of these early peer interactions are gaze and distance (Mueller & Rich, 1976). A child must be looking at another and must be close enough in space (and time) to exert influence on the other. It is interesting to note this early emergence of the critical role that gaze and distance play in social interactions throughout life.

The child's appreciation of distance and gaze as cues to attraction and liking become well established in the preschool years. Shown pictures of a man and a woman close to or far apart from each other and with or without eye contact, 4-year-old boys and girls used the distance cue to decide which pair liked each other best; gaze, on the other hand, didn't seem to play a similarly relevant role in the children's judgments (Post & Hetherington, 1974). The same study revealed that, by age 6, girls had improved in their use of the proximity cue and were using eye contact with better-than-chance accuracy as an attraction cue, whereas boys did not. When distance and eye-contact cues conflicted (that is, close distance with no looking or looking at far distance), all children made more inconsistent judgments and neither cue was favored over the other one.

Similar results (Guardo, 1969) were obtained with sixth graders who were shown pairs of same-sex children placed at different distances and who were asked how much the members of the pair liked each other. Both boys and girls inferred liking from the distance at which people stood from each other; the children agreed that those pairs who stood closer to each other knew each other better and liked each other more. Asked to place silhouettes representing a friend, an acquaintance, and a stranger in relation to one representing themselves, girls placed their "best friend" and "someone they liked very much" closer to themselves than did boys. Sixth graders also placed themselves closer to peers described as outgoing, happy-go-lucky, intelligent, or forthright—all regarded as interpersonally attractive characteristics (Guardo, 1976).

When the same procedure was used with boys and girls in third through tenth grades, the findings concerning liking and distance were consistently replicated (Meisels & Guardo, 1969). Although closer distances were generally used to represent liking, younger children placed opposite-sex pairs of friends farther apart than did older children. Similar results were also obtained in several studies using real interpersonal distances rather than silhouette placement (Whalen, Flowers, Fuller, & Jernigan, 1975). But in these studies, which used sixth to eighth graders, only girls stood close to boys they liked—a finding explained by girls' earlier social and physical maturation. This explanation is supported by the finding of another study that, by the time boys were in ninth grade, they stood close to girls they liked (Meisels & Guardo, 1969). In observations of eighth graders talking to classmates they had identified as least liked and best liked, those who liked each other better conversed at closer distances than those who liked each other less (Aiello & Cooper, 1972).

Observations of nursery-school behavior bear out the closer spacing that friends, as compared to strangers, like to maintain. For example, when eight 4-year-old newcomers joined all at once an existing nursery-school group, these newcomers maintained more interpersonal distance than did the children who were already part of the group and who, presumably, were closer friends (McGrew & McGrew, 1975). When newcomers to nursery school joined the group one at a time, within a day of their arrival they showed interpersonal-spacing patterns like those of established group members (McGrew & McGrew, 1972).

Very little research exists on later developmental differences in interpersonal spacing between friends. A study of people of different ages visiting the zoo found that pairs of children stood closer to each other than adolescents and that adolescents stood closer than adults, even when ethnic, sex, and environmental differences were taken into account (Baxter, 1970). In another study, pairs observed in conversation on London streets were later asked their ages and relationships (Heshka & Nelson, 1972). This study found that middle-aged people stood farther apart than either children or old people. The age differences were interpreted in terms of the dependence on others that characterizes both childhood and old age.

Negative Interaction with Others

Children can be quite nasty and aggressive, as anyone who has ever lived with a child well knows. Researchers have been reluctant to put children into experimental situations calling for aggression, but they have been able to glean considerable information about children's nonverbal behavior in negative interactions by observing children in natural settings, such as playgrounds.

As we saw in Chapter 7, the nonverbal aspects of adult competition are relatively subtle; the loser is supposed to appear good-natured about the loss, and the winner is expected to be modest and self-effacing. Children haven't yet learned these social rules. The reddening of the face, often noted in angry encounters between children, is unmistakable and, quite predictably, is characteristic of the child who is losing the contest and not of the one who is winning (Blurton Jones, 1967). Adult losers have learned to suppress their tears; children not only cry about their losses but sometimes work to produce tears. Each of the various forms of crying has its own unique display. Genuine distress is signaled by sobs, tears, a sad frown, mouth corners back, and reddening of the face. The display of crying that results from a deliberate intent is distinguished by an angry frown and few or no tears (Brannigan & Humphries, 1972). Do you remember when, as a child, you were desperately trying to produce tears in the aftermath of a dispute, so you would convince your mother or father of the depth and anguish of your distress? One might speculate that the moment children begin to intentionally present their feelings, they are showing that they've begun to learn the command aspect of communication.

In hand-to-hand combat among children, winners and losers look different. When children hit, the lips are forward, the chin is thrust out, and the face wears an angry frown. This offensive beating posture is marked by the arm raised, with elbow out to the side and the hand some distance from the head. The hand is usually open, with palm forward and fingers extended (Brannigan & Humphries, 1972). In contrast, there is also a defensive beating posture (Grant, 1969) characterized by a sad frown, oblong mouth, and chin in. The hand is held closer to the head and not as high as in the offensive posture. The defensive posture has been noted in a defeated child still under attack by another and as yet undecided or unable to escape.

These postures seem to undergo changes around age 5, when the child is taught to regard the offensive beating posture as inappropriate to the resolution of conflict. But traces of the posture remain. It has been suggested, for example, that, when adults place a hand on the back of the neck, they are showing a residual cue from the preschooler's beating posture (Brannigan & Humphries, 1972).

Despite the forthrightness of children's aggression, their negative interactions are more often characterized by avoidance than by attack. At 6 months, infants show avoidance of strangers by aversion of gaze and worried facial expressions and do not smile if touched by unfamiliar persons. These outward negative expressions have been correlated with physiological signs of distress such as acceleration of heart rate (Waters, Matas, & Sroufe, 1975). When children between 3 and 5 years of age were rated for friendliness or unfriendliness toward others in a play group, later testing in pairs showed that unfriendly pairs kept at a greater distance from each other than friendly pairs (King, 1966). In fact, avoidance of some children by other children can be extreme. A study investigating "omega children" (that is, children who are always chosen last for any team or activity) found that these children were kept at significantly large distances by the others. Consequently, they engaged in very little physical interaction with nonomega children (Ginsburg, Wauson, & Easley, 1977). The investigators also noted that the stream of ongoing activity usually completely bypassed omega children, who remained motionless while the entire group ran past them. Omega children are perhaps the stigmatized young.

The material on children's interpersonal spacing, as reviewed above for positive relationships, shows that there is a mirror image with regard to negative relationships. From third grade on, children place themselves farther from disliked, feared, or strange others than they do from friends (Meisels & Guardo, 1969). Children of this age also place themselves at greater distance from those fathers (although not from mothers) who are described as reproving or scolding (Guardo & Meisels, 1971).

In Chapter 7, you learned that spatial invasion is a powerful phenomenon. Among adults, strangers who approach too closely are reacted to with rejection or withdrawal. Do adults respond the same way when the stranger is a child? In a study in which 5-, 8-, and 10-year-olds approached adults wait-ing in line and stood as closely behind them as they could without making actual contact, the children received very different reactions depending on their age (Fry & Willis, 1971). Adults smiled at and turned toward the 5-year-olds. Adults, however, leaned or moved away more often from the 10-year-olds, thus indicating a change, perhaps as a function of the child's size, in the interpersonal distances that are regarded as intrusive by the adult. From the adult's reaction, the child quite likely learns that he or she is no longer a child and therefore must abide by the rules that govern distancing among and be-tween strangers in public places.

The Child in Conversation

Listen to the sounds very young children make. Suspend for the moment the effort of trying to make out what words they're uttering. When you ob-serve or interact with an infant, you're often waiting so eagerly for that "first word" that you may miss the rather extraordinary development in children's communication. They begin to *sound* as though they were having real conver-sations long before the words become comprehensible.

By the age of 4 years, children have picked up an incredible range of sound variations. Their manner of speaking, loudness level, inflections, tim-ing, tempo, and pitch variations all combine to give a sense of a fast-devel-oping conversational competence. You may recall that, in Chapter 10, we discussed the vocal elements of pitch, pause, loudness, and tempo; these are called *prosodic features*. Their function is to combine with verbal elements to produce sound variations that are related to meaning. For example, the pro-sodic feature of a rising pitch pattern at the end of a sentence changes the content of the sentence from a statement to a question.

Prosodic features are obviously so intertwined with verbal elements that the distinction between verbal and nonverbal becomes very fine. In this sec-tion, we take a look at some prosodic features in children's speech, because, although our emphasis is primarily on the nonverbal channels, we see com-munication as a multichanneled phenomenon. Nonverbal behavior, in-cluding vocal aspects, serves many functions; as we said earlier, one of these is to make speech comprehensible.

Pitch in Children's Communication

A very important prosodic feature is pitch change—that is, a rising or falling contour at the end of sentences. There is now some evidence to suggest that some pitch contours are present in infant cries (Lieberman, 1966). Chil-dren learning English typically employ downward pitch contours at the end of sentences. Observations of graphs of vocal variations in infant cries (pro-duced by pinching them) showed that the fundamental frequency of the cry gradually rose to a high level and then dropped abruptly at the end of the cry. It is Lieberman's contention that, when infants cry, they are "practicing" the intonation contours later necessary to make their adult English speech comprehensible.

Other research by Lieberman (1966) has shown that pitch begins to play a role in communication very early in life. He observed two infants (one a 10-month-old boy and the other a 13-month-old girl) as they interacted with one parent and then with the other. Their babblings were recorded and then analyzed for the fundamental frequencies they displayed. The results again point to the important role that the nature of the interaction plays in any one individual's nonverbal behavior, regardless of age. Lieberman found that the pitch in the infant's voice varied with the sex of the parent with whom the baby was interacting. With the father, the pitch level was lower than with the mother. In addition, Lieberman called attention to the fact that the pitch levels used by the infants in "conversation" with their parents were lower than the pitch levels they used in solitary babbling or when they were crying. Apparently, the infants not only were able to discriminate the pitch they were hearing but were able to respond to it in like fashion. The basic interactional character of these results indicates that, had Lieberman not noted with whom the infant was interacting or that the infant's behavior changed as the interactional partner changed, he might have attributed the differences in the pitch levels to the child alone rather than to the relationship between child and adult.

Pauses in Children's Communication

Everyday adult speech contains silence in the form of pausing, as well as sound in the form of words. As you recall from Chapter 10, pauses are not randomly distributed in the speech stream; they are placed so as to aid the speaker in expressing his or her thoughts and to help the listener understand what is being said.

When do children show the pausing characteristics of adult speech? Little is known about the development of pausal patterns, although there is general agreement that pauses are a well-established feature of children's communication by the time they enter school. In fact, even the babbling of an infant illustrates the pausal features of language. Again, if one listens closely to the sounds an infant produces, the rhythm and intonation are so well established that one receives the impression that a conversation is going on, albeit in an unfamiliar tongue.

There are, however, some significant differences in the use of pauses by children and by adults. When describing something, young children use more and longer pauses than do older children and adolescents (Kowal, O'Connell, & Sabin, 1975). In this study, children at seven age levels from kindergarten through high school were shown some Snoopy cartoons and asked to tell a story about them. The younger the child, the more frequently and longer he or she paused. Apparently, younger children cannot both think and talk at the same time—something that becomes easier to accomplish with age.

When children first display the ability to string several words together, they often rely on pauses as substitutes for words. For example, the child may say "Here [pause] big doggie," where at a latter stage the sentence will become "Here is a big doggie." Young children also use *filled pauses* like "um" or "ah" very early in the speech-acquisition process. One knows that a 4-year-old is well on his way into the speech community when his explanation of—let's say—why something got broken sounds like "Well, *um,* I don't know."

Learning Conversational Rules

To become a full-fledged participant in human communication, a child needs to learn about the give and take of conversations. Apparently, this learning takes place very early. Research has shown an alternating vocal style between mothers and young infants similar to that of conversing adults (Bateson, 1975; Stern, Jaffe, Beebe, & Bennett, 1975). Some interchange training also occurs through mothers' monologues with their babies. Observations have shown that mothers of very young infants often engage in serious, continuous monologues with the baby, asking the infant a question, pausing, then answering for the infant (Bateson, 1975; Stern et al., 1975). It's interesting that, when people do the same thing to you as an adult, the impression you get is that you're "being treated like a child."

To converse is in part to attribute meaning to what the other says. Infants get introduced to this facet of conversation by their mothers giving meaning to any gurgle or babble produced by the baby. Apparently, by so doing, the mother conveys the idea that vocal behavior is socially important. The infant thus learns that his or her sounds affect the other person (Hinde, 1976).

Infants and mothers also engage in a great deal of simultaneous vocalization; they do so when they are highly involved with each other. Research shows that this vocalization in unison usually terminates with the infant shifting to a listener role and that mothers try to prolong such periods of vocal synchrony when they do occur (Stern, 1974). Reciprocity may originate, then, from a single shared base.

Recall the phenomenon of vocal convergence discussed in Chapter 6; adults in conversation come to match various vocal features of each other's speech. Children, too, do this. A study of conversations between pairs of 5½- and 6½-year-olds found signs of mutuality in pause lengths in both groups (Welkowitz, Cariffe, & Feldstein, 1974). Of special interest is the fact that turn taking or switching pauses showed convergence earlier, whereas convergence in the length of pauses within a speaker's utterance occurred only between older children.

Although children get introduced to the nonverbal mechanisms of successful conversational management very early and although nursery-school children do display systematic turn-yielding cues (DeLong, 1977), their conversational behavior also shows signs of immaturity. For example, Dittmann (1972b) found that children's responses as listeners (like head nods and smiling) were very infrequent and, when they did occur, were either so slight as to be practically undetectable or so poorly timed as to be confusing. Similarly, in another study in which 4-year-olds and 7-year-olds were given facial cues by an experimenter indicating noncomprehension of what the child had said, neither group responded by repeating or rewording the communication (Peterson, Danner, & Flavell, 1972).

Blunders in communication are sometimes the result not of doing the wrong thing but of not doing the right thing at the right time. Timing is crucial in nonverbal behavior, and, to get it right, children must learn some of the larger contexts of social behavior. One study found that children begin to become aware of social contexts quite early (Fein, 1975). Infants at 18 months stayed farthest away from their mother when she was engaged in social conversation, came closer when she was not talking, and came closest when she and other adults were playing cards. Furthermore, the infants vocalized most when the adults were silent and least when the adults were conversing, thus indicating some sensitivity to interactions of which they were not directly a part. But another study found considerable variability in such sensitivity (Weeks, 1971). For example, some children learn to whisper at the same time they learn to talk, but others do not learn to whisper until later. Those who can whisper use the whisper appropriately—for example, when their parents are talking on the telephone. They appear to have acquired the social-usage rule along with the vocal variation.

Summary

Part of growing up is being able to say more, both verbally and nonverbally, as well as being able to hear more. From the very beginning, all children smile and frown and move their bodies and their vocal cords. Also, they become increasingly aware of how their own moving bodies affect others and are affected in return.

The repertoire of emotional expressiveness expands from birth to 2 years of age and thereafter becomes increasingly tied to context. Sometimes the contexts demand no expressiveness at all; the task then is to learn how to not do something.

The wonder of communication is its mutuality. Children, at first islands unto themselves, begin to take note of others and to react to the expressiveness of others. They begin to read distance and gaze as cues as to the effects they have on other people. Children link their nonverbal rhythms to those of others, at first with a little help from their mothers. They vary sounds and silences to match those of the person with whom they're interacting. But there are bugs to be worked out of these systems of communication. A child's timing is sometimes off, and his or her ability to alter a communicative course is still somewhat rigid.

Chapter 12

Gender Gestures

Assumptions about Sex Differences

Sex Roles: Proactivity and Reactivity

Are Women More Expressive than Men?

> *Facial Expression*
> *Vocal Expression*

Men and Women Tuning In and Tuning Out

Communication between the Sexes

> *Smiling*
> *Personal Space*
> *Touch*
> *Talk*

A Move toward Androgyny

Summary

You're in the library searching for a book in the stacks. As you enter a narrow row, someone comes toward you. You give way to let the other pass. Are you more likely to be a male or a female? You're in a restaurant watching a conversation at another table. One person is listening and looking at the other, with head tilted and a smiling expression. Is the listener a man or a woman? Near a bus stop, there's someone giving directions, pointing down the street and touching the arm of the stranger who's lost. Is the person giving directions a man or a woman? and the stranger? You notice two friends of the same sex walking down the street close enough so that their arms practically touch, occasionally brushing each other. Is this more likely to be a pair of males or a pair of females?

The answers to these questions are not arbitrary. Men and women differ systematically in their nonverbal behavior. Women are more likely than men to give way in an impending collision, and they are more likely to be listening in an attentive, unchallenging way. Women also receive more touching than men. So, in the example above, a man giving directions is more likely to touch and guide a woman, even if she is a stranger to him. This chapter examines how men and women differ in the extent to which they express themselves, tune in to the cues emitted by others, and are treated in nonverbal ways.

Assumptions about Sex Differences

One of the most important functions of nonverbal behavior is to provide, to others as well as to yourself, continuing cues about your social memberships. You use the whole catalogue of nonverbal behavior to signal culture, class, age, and gender—especially gender.

The sexes do differ in their nonverbal behaviors. But what are you to make of the differences? How do you interpret them? Why are they important, anyway? To enter into a discussion of sex differences is to address, at the same time, a host of implicit assumptions on the meaning of those differences. Jessie Bernard (1968) describes reactions to sex differences as falling into two camps: the "What difference?" contingent and the "Vive la différence!" contingent. The former group, although comprising several different views, essentially argues that sex differences are illusory, fortuitous, and unimportant. In other words, the similarities between the sexes are more basic and real than the differences.

The "Vive la difference!" school, on the other hand, highlights the differences to emphasize that the sexes differ through and through and that it shouldn't be any other way. While they don't explicitly refer to the superiority of some sex-related aspects over others, many of those who belong to this camp are likely to slide from "Vive la difference!" to "Please, God, let it be a boy!"

In the next several pages, we present what is known about male/female differences in nonverbal behavior. The plan is to describe what is known, while attempting to avoid exaggeration or minimization of the differences. Our other aim is to tackle the difficult question of why such differences exist.

Sex Roles: Proactivity and Reactivity

If we want to know why there are differences in the styles of communication of males and females, we must first ask what are the role expectations that people hold for men and women. In general, men are expected to show *proactivity;* that is, they are expected to be active, independent, self-confident, objective, and decisive. In contrast, women are supposed to be characterized by *reactivity.* It is society's conviction that women are expected to respond to the contributions of others and to do this by being sensitive, emotionally expressive, and interpersonally supportive (Broverman, Vogel, Broverman, Clarkson, & Rosenkrantz, 1972).

But why the need for proactivity and reactivity in the first place? It has been postulated that two forces operate in all living forms: *agency* and *communion* (Bakan, 1966). Agency is concerned with the individual as individual and is manifested through self-protection and self-assertion. Communion relates to the organism as a part of a community. Agency and communion must both be present in the individual, as well as in social groups. Each human being, in order to survive, needs to be both proactive and reactive. In most Western societies, the two modalities have become arbitrarily linked with gender: males demonstrate agency, and females communion.

To say that proactivity has been assigned to men does not mean, however, that it is their exclusive prerogative. Some women are also proactive, among themselves and with men as well. In addition, some women eschew the expressive role. Neither role is genetically given or necessarily superior to the other. The proactive role has to do with getting on with the task at hand; the reactive role complements the former by emphasizing solidarity and providing support.

Concretely, what does this mean for male/female differences in nonverbal style? As you will see, it means that, when the focus is on nonverbal behavior as it relates particularly to emotional messages at the interpersonal level, the sex differences are substantial. Community is a woman's world. More specifically, Western societal norms have it that communality is woman's work. Women are, in Bernard's (1968) terms, to "stroke" others. They do this through such acts as "reassuring smiles and silent applause."

So there are sex differences. But what do they mean, and how do you find out? As we have indicated a number of times elsewhere in this book, understanding nonverbal behaviors comes in part from increasing the magnification and not from reducing it. In other words, the meaning of sex differences becomes more apparent if you look at the wider context, at the relationships between the sexes, and at what other (that is, not linked to sex) nonverbal behaviors are operating. The fact is that sex differences do not stand alone; they cannot be understood in isolation. They are always shaped, modified, given meaning by other identification signals. What age is this man? From what culture comes this woman? Sex differences become differentially manifest and differentially meaningful at different ages and in different cultures.

Perhaps more importantly, sex differences exist within a larger societal structure. And within that structure, particularly in the United States, agency and communion are not only sex-role related; they are valued differently. The agency function is held to be more valuable, more important, and inherently more consequential. Accordingly, those who demonstrate a concern with communality (who, for the most part, happen to be women) are seen as being engaged in matters of triviality and inconsequence.

And, finally, the two functions, so differently valued, are related to each other. It is true that women sometimes reach the height of the stroking function precisely by putting themselves in a one-down position vis-à-vis men as men perform their agency function. Somewhat paradoxically, women who perform the communality function by nonverbally saying to men "You are strong, you are valuable, you are splendid—and so am I" are devalued. They are judged less feminine than women who express the communality and reactivity by nonverbal statements that say "You are strong (and I am not); you are valuable (and I am not)." It appears to be part of the cultural belief system that communality and agency cannot go together, and hence any indication that a woman or man lays claim to both is suspect.

We begin this chapter with a consideration of gender differences in emotional expression. As noted in Chapter 3, such expression includes both the sending and the receiving roles in emotional communication. The remainder of the chapter is concerned specifically with differences in the nonverbal behavior of men and women that result from gender-linked distinctions between proactive and reactive functions.

Are Women More Expressive than Men?

It is virtually a cliché of this culture that women are naturally more expressive than men and that "showing" emotions is something that the model male should not do. Among those concerned with mental health, nonexpressivity in men is currently viewed with some regret. The problem is not that men are intrinsically incapable of expressing their feelings but that, having been trained not to do so, they are no longer able to be expressive. Such sex-role barriers to expressivity have been linked to a variety of psychological woes in males (Jourard, 1964; Pleck & Sawyer, 1974).

Facial Expression

Studies that ask men and women to express specific emotions (such as those described in Chapter 3) generally find that women have a greater capacity than men to produce facial expressions that viewers can interpret correctly. One procedure had women and men look at photographic slides of emotionally arousing material and other men and women look at the faces of the viewers to guess what emotion they were "sending" (Buck, Miller, & Caul, 1974). The results indicated that women were more successful at communicating the emotions evoked by the slides. This particular study found no sex differences in decoding ability; that is, men and women were equally effective at reading the facial expressions of women senders.

There is some tentative indication that the more limited capacity of men as senders does not apply to all emotions. In one study, sex differences were found in the communication of positive and negative states (Zaidel & Mehrabian, 1969). Men were somewhat better communicators of positive feelings of liking than were women; women were considerably better communicators of dislike and negativity than were men. These findings may relate to the existence of baselines about expressions normally found on male and female faces. Given that women generally smile more, when they do convey dislike (at the experimenter's request), the expression may be more notable and therefore better decoded. Similarly, the smiling male, being a relatively rarer occurrence, is more likely to be noticed and his expression interpreted as really positive. As we indicated earlier, rarity elicits attention followed by greater confidence that the behavior is genuinely reflective of some underlying state.

Some preliminary findings also suggest that there are individual differences in expressiveness among men. Men who were asked about their sex-role attitudes and who were found to hold liberal views were rated as being nonverbally warm when interacting with both men and women. In contrast, men holding more traditional sex-role attitudes were judged to be less warm in such interactions (Weitz, 1976). It appears that rigid adherence to sex-role stereotypes is associated in men with constriction of emotional expression. Although, overall, women were not rated as nonverbally warmer than men, their conversational partners of either sex were rated as nonverbally warmer when they were conversing with women than when they were conversing with men.

Vocal Expression

Second only to the expressiveness credited to women's faces is the emotional range that women's voices are supposed to have. The vocal aspect most often singled out as reflecting sex differences is that of pitch, because of the fact that men's vocal output becomes lower-pitched in adolescence. These pitch differences were long attributed purely to anatomical changes associated with puberty, when male vocal cords become longer and thicker. It appears now that such differences are also due to the way men and women articulate the sounds they make in order to produce a culturally recognizable male or female voice. Speech samples from preadolescent boys and girls, who were selected by matching height and weight so as to have larynxes of the same size, were reliably identified as male and female by adult listeners (Sachs, Lieberman, & Erickson, 1973). Since the anatomical structures were the same, the difference in sound was more likely produced by the way boys and girls formed words. In particular, the investigators noted that spreading the lips shortens the vocal tract; women's tendency to smile while speaking has the effect of shortening the vocal cords in this way, thus producing a higher-pitched sound.

Given that male and female speakers sound different, how do these vocal differences strike a listener? Listeners turn out to have very different reactions to the same vocal characteristics in a male and in a female speaker. Changes in voice quality brought about by making the voice more breathy, thin, flat, throaty, nasal, and the like affected judgments of female speakers' personalities more than did comparable changes in a male voice (Addington, 1968). For example, thinness of voice in women led to attributions of immaturity and sensitivity but had no effect on judgments of male speakers' traits. Males with throatier voices were described as mature, sophisticated, and well adjusted, whereas deep-voiced women were seen as boorish, ugly, lazy, and sickly.

The research described above assessed the different meanings that listeners ascribe to the same sound when they encounter it in a man or in a woman. A different research strategy is to find out what different aspects of the voice are used in arriving at impressions of what men and women are like. In assessing the personality of a woman, listeners are influenced by *how much* she talks and how loud and high she speaks on the average. In judging the personality of a man, listeners attend to *how variable* the man's voice is in pitch and loudness. If one credits the cultural sex-role stereotype that men are stable and women variable, one will expect male and female voices to reflect these characteristics. Therefore, when a woman's voice sounds stable in loudness and pitch and a man's voice sounds variable, these unusual vocal characteristics are interpreted as providing more information about the speaker's personality—*because* they are unexpected. It is also clear from the above studies that the meaning of particular nonverbal cues, whether they be smiles or fast talking, depends on gender as an extremely important contextual feature.

Some intonation patterns have been noted to occur in the speech of women in this culture but not in that of men (Brend, 1975). For example, almost exclusive to women is the use of what is described as a "high/low downglide" of surprise, as in the intonation with which such expressions as "Oh, how awful!" are uttered. Other female patterns include a request-confirmation pattern ("You do?"), a hesitation pattern ("Well, I studied . . ."), and a polite cheerful one ("Are you coming?"). In fact, the hesitant questioning stance in most women's speech has been noted before (Lakoff, 1973). Women often answer questions with declarative statements that end with the rising inflection typical, in English, of questions. This makes female speakers sound unsure of themselves. Their answers sound as if the speaker were seeking the listener's confirmation that the answer is correct or even that it is all right to state an opinion at all. So, even when they are talking, women are reacting.

Men and Women Tuning In and Tuning Out

A natural partner to the question of emotional expressiveness is that of sensitivity. Is there a difference between men and women in their capacity to sense what other people are feeling? Considering the fact that this society assigns the responsive role to women, you might well expect that women are better at tuning in to others' emotional states. Research consistently bears this out. In order to be responsive and reactive to others, it is necessary to sense what the other person is feeling. This sensitivity is perhaps less important if your stance is proactive, and that may be why men don't show as much decoding skill.

Most studies find women to be better decoders than men. On one test of nonverbal sensitivity (the PONS test described in Chapter 3), women are typically found to be more accurate than men (Rosenthal, Hall, DiMatteo, Rogers, & Archer, 1977). As you may recall, the PONS test uses one young woman as the stimulus person acting out various emotional situations. A study using many different encoders of emotion, both male and female, also found women to be more sensitive judges than men of what the encoders were enacting (Zuckerman, Lipets, Koivumaki, and Rosenthal, 1975). In addition, this study found that same-sex judgments were more accurate than opposite-sex judgments. Another interesting finding was that the sex difference in accuracy was greater with pictures than with vocal samples of emotional expression. Research consistently shows that women look more at others than do men (Argyle & Cook, 1976). Given that women look more at others and given their greater accuracy in the visual channel, it is quite possible that women use the visual channel as a primary source of information about others.

This assumption was borne out in a study in which, in a conversation between two people, one of the participants was increasingly obscured from the other by dark glasses, a slotted screen, and a one-way mirror. More women than men found conversation more difficult when they couldn't see the other person; when invisible themselves, women decreased their amount of talk (Argyle, Lalljee, & Cook, 1968). In a study of spatial invasions in libraries, when men and women were intruded upon by a stranger sitting across from them or beside them, women reacted more negatively to the latter form of invasion, regardless of the sex of the intruder (Fisher & Byrne, 1975). The investigators explained this finding by suggesting that, since adjacent seating is generally preferred for social or cooperative ventures, women may regard a stranger's taking a seat next to them as an inappropriate demand for social interaction. As you may recall from Chapter 7, when visual access was available, people did not pick the adjacent seating for cooperative endeavors. Therefore, an alternative interpretation of the above findings is that women reacted more negatively to a stranger sitting beside them because this position offered them low visual access to the person so seated.

The research presented thus far has been directed at one aspect of the reactive function—namely, being able to detect what is going on in the other person (sensitivity). But there is a second, and very important, aspect to reactivity; and that is to be able to respond to what the other person is feeling (responsiveness). This aspect was shown in a study by Weitz (1976). The first minute of videotaped encounters between unacquainted men and women was coded by raters who saw only one of the interactants and therefore didn't know the sex of the other person in the conversation. This was done so that the raters' expectations of what *should* be happening wouldn't affect their coding. In male/female conversations, the nonverbal behavior of women was inversely related to the male partner's dominant or affiliative behavior. Women were found to be nonverbally more submissive with more dominant men and more dominant with submissive men. Weitz posited a monitoring process by which women adjust their nonverbal behavior to produce a comfortable interpersonal encounter for men. No such adjustments were noted for female/female encounters, nor were there adaptive moves by men in either same-sex or opposite-sex encounters. Considering that all this occurs in the first 60 seconds of interaction, the findings suggest a vigilant sensitivity and immediate responsiveness on the part of women with regard to men. Gender-linked reactivity is particularly evident in cross-sex encounters. As mentioned in Chapter 11, women report feeling less feminine in encounters with women and hence may feel less pressure to perform the reactive function. Since responsiveness is not expected by men from themselves or other men, it is rarely seen in male/male encounters.

A theme underlying all these studies is that responsiveness engenders more variable nonverbal behavior. Women do not behave the same way regardless of the person with whom they are interacting. One observational study of conversational distances, for instance, found that pairs of women stood closer to each other than pairs of men (Heshka & Nelson, 1972). This difference, however, was largely accounted for by the fact that women friends stood very close and women strangers quite far apart. Men did not change their conversational distance in response to different degrees of acquaintance. Female responsiveness, then, likely involves both the capacity to tune in to the feelings and wishes of the other and a behavioral adaptation to this information.

Communication between the Sexes

Smiling

A colleague of ours found that, during departmental discussion of her promotion, a great deal of importance was attached to her "overseriousness," perhaps even "glumness." Students and colleagues alike pointed to the fact that she seldom smiled. Without getting into the question of whether smiling behavior or lack of it should be a professional credential, it is significant that the *absence* of the behavior was noted. How can you notice the lack of something? You can notice it because you know what the baselines are. As stated earlier, women are socialized into smiling more than are men. Therefore, the occasion of a nonsmiling woman is a significant event. And therein lies a bind for many women. The absence of smiling generates concern about her humanity; the presence of smiling in a "professional" capacity engenders comparable concern about her proactive competence.

Apparently women smile more than men when they are alone, and they also increase their smiling when another person enters the picture (Mackey, 1976). This increase in smiling while interacting on the part of women and not on the part of men lends support to the notion that women are more responsive than men to social stimuli. In fact, it might be argued that a man's smile has meaning in terms of his own private state, while a woman's smile is essentially an interactional phenomenon. Furthermore, it has been found that smiles elicit smiles (Mackey, 1976). Given that women smile more and hence elicit more smiling, it is possible to see how this nonverbal behavior operates in the creation and maintenance of cohesion and solidarity. Seen in a more defensive light, this same behavior can be interpreted as an appeasement gesture, a sign of nonthreat (van Hooff, 1972).

Personal Space

The term *personal space,* as coined by Robert Sommer (1959), refers to that invisible boundary around each one of us through which others are not to come. The idea as first articulated had tremendous, almost tangible, appeal. The strange thing is that most people can "visualize" themselves and others housed in what are essentially invisible bubbles. Furthermore, Sommer (1959) suggested that the size of these bubbles varies as a function of different social contexts.

Try to picture the kinds of bubbles that would surround men and women. Are they the same size? What about the boundaries themselves? Are they thicker, denser, stronger around one sex than around the other? Place the bubbles in different situations, such as work and social contexts. Do the bubbles change shape or size or permeability more for one sex than for the other as the context changes?

Research in general seems to show that the bubbles surrounding women are smaller than those surrounding men (Evans & Howard, 1973). For example, a study using unobtrusive observation of people in a public setting found that female pairs stood closer to each other than did male pairs (Baxter, 1970). In addition, this study found that male/female pairs stood closest of all. Similarly, another study found that male and female pairs who were unacquainted differed in their interpersonal distance. Specifically, it was noted that, in a waiting-room situation, female pairs sat closer to each other than male pairs (Mehrabian & Diamond, 1971). Unequal space zones were also noted by Willis (1966). In studying the initial speaking distance set by an approaching person, he found that women were approached more closely than men by both men and women.

The most popular explanation for these particular sex differences is that women are more affiliative and generally more friendly and positive toward others than are men (Mehrabian, 1972). This explanation is based on the argument that people who like each other seek closer interpersonal distances than people who don't feel as friendly—a point we discussed at length in Chapter 6.

The greater affiliation attributed to women is certainly compatible with an explanation offered by Freedman and his associates (Freedman, O'Hanlon, Oltman, & Witkin, 1972) to account for sex differences in reaction to crowding. In a number of studies using same-sex groups, they found that females were more cooperative and less aggressive than males under conditions of high density. Their explanation was that density intensifies the typical response to or expectation for a given situation. Apparently, women expect encounters with other women to be sociable and friendly, while men expect more competitive and possibly aggressive interactions with other men. High density accentuates these sex-role expectations.

Do you, then, need to seek no further explanation for the smaller space zones attributed to women? In a study in which a male and a female experimenter approached students of both sexes until told to stop, women allowed a closer approach from both experimenters than did men (Hartnett, Bailey, & Gibson, 1970). But it is doubtful whether this can be interpreted to mean that women prefer closer interpersonal distances, for, when the subjects in this study were asked to walk toward the experimenters until they (the subjects) wanted to stop, women stopped at a greater distance. It made no difference to men whether they were approached or approaching. An interpretation that represents an alternative to the unqualified affiliative one is that, when women are put in a position in which the reactive dimension is most salient (that is, when another is approaching), they are more "giving." But when the proactive dimension is being emphasized, women react differently by taking more space.

It may also be true that women tolerate more spatial intrusion as a result of a socialization process that inhibits the assertiveness associated with defense of territory. A recent spatial-invasion experiment in libraries found that females responded to someone's sitting down in the chair next to them differently than males, particularly when the invader's presence could not be ignored. Specifically, they fled the scene; males were more likely to "hold the fort" (Polit & LaFrance, 1977). Just where giving *to* others becomes giving *in* to others is a moot question.

We've already suggested that women sometimes show their reactive side best when they not only tune in to another's emotional state but respond by submitting to others' wishes and by backing off in order to accede to others' demands. In the nonverbal realm, this has quite literal manifestations. Silveira (1972) reports that a study of who gets out of the other's way when passing on the sidewalk revealed that the woman moved out of the man's way in 12 of the 19 observed mixed-sex near-collisions. In 4 of the remaining 7 cases, both the man and the woman moved to make room for the other, and in only 3 cases did the man alone move. The person who backs off affirms the other's higher status—that is, the right of the other person to proceed onward uninterrupted.

The close relation between women's responsiveness and submissiveness in their dealings with men is evident in another study. The question investigated was whether, in the simple matter of walking together, males would more often assume the position "in front of" their female partners. The researchers reasoned that the spatial positions *above* and *in front of* imply superiority and status and that men in this society are accorded more of both than women. Presumably, if sex were not linked to status, men and women would each be walking in front approximately half the time. Not so. Results showed that men were out in front significantly more often than women (Grady, Miransky, & Mulvey, 1976). The saying that "*Behind* every successful man, there is a woman" might have a more literal meaning than you had suspected.

It is clear from these studies that in heterosexual encounters the woman is often asked to demonstrate her responsiveness through submissiveness—a nonverbal response that is not in evidence in same-sex encounters. For example, Silveira (1972) found that, when women approached women or men approached men, the two people involved got out of each other's way about the same number of times.

It might also be argued that the different postures evidenced by men and women are in part a function of their social roles. For example, Mehrabian (1972) has shown that in general women take up less space than men as a direct result of the way in which they position themselves. It's not simply that women are generally physically smaller than men; it is also the fact that women compound this difference in size by sitting with arms close to their sides and legs crossed at very small angles. In contrast, men sprawl more, draping their arms over backs of chairs and either stretching their legs out in front or crossing them at larger angles. Expansive postures take up more space and thereby create larger personal-space zones.

It has also been found that male and female college students carry their books in consistently different ways. Women have been found to wrap one or both arms around books and to rest the short edges of the books in front of

Here are two examples of the different amounts of space taken up by men and women. Men sprawl more and use more space when carrying things, while women adopt compact postures and hold things close to their bodies.

the body, against the stomach and chest region. In contrast, men are more likely to support their books by one arm and hand at the side of the body, with the long edges approximately horizontal (Jenni & Jenni, 1976). The female carrying method results in positions that are more compact, while the male carrying method results in positions that are more expansive.

Touch

When behavior at the closest interpersonal distance is considered, sex differences become apparent here, too. Little systematic research has been done on touch, most likely because, in this "noncontact" culture, touch is a somewhat taboo topic. It is difficult to create experimental conditions in which touch between unacquainted adults can occur comfortably, and little touch occurs under naturally observable circumstances.

Yet, it has been argued that touch plays a fundamental part in human development (Frank, 1957; Montagu, 1971), and sex differences in touching behavior are presumed to arise in the early contacts between mother and child. Mothers of 6-month-old girls were observed to touch and handle their infants more than did mothers of 6-month-old boys. When the babies were 13 months old, girls tended to touch their mothers more than boys did (Goldberg & Lewis, 1969). The little girls' touching behavior at 13 months showed a curvilinear relation to their being touched and handled at 6 months: both the girls who had been handled a great deal and those who had been handled very little touched their mothers more than did the girls who had received a moderate amount of handling. For boys, the relation was linear: those who were touched, touched; those who were not, did not. Presumably, boys who don't receive much touching get the message during that first year of life that tactile contact is not to be sought, whereas girls who are not handled continue to try to get in tactile contact with their mothers. A study that compared the touching behaviors of children aged 3 to 11 in seven cultures disclosed sex differences among them (Whiting & Edwards, 1973). Girls sought and offered more nonaggressive contact than boys, particularly in the younger-age group. Nonaggressive touch decreased with age for all children, presumably as a reflection of socialization pressures on both sexes to reduce displays of affectionate touching.

With adults, sex differences in touching behavior have also been studied by questionnaires. Men and women have been asked to indicate on a diagram of the human body where they had touched or had been touched within the last year by their father, mother, closest same-sex friend, and closest opposite-sex friend (Jourard, 1966; Jourard & Rubin, 1968). Most touch was reported with opposite-sex friends. Women reported that the closest male friend touched them more than did their father, mother, or closest woman friend. Men, in contrast, reported that their closest woman friend touched them least. This difference reflects the stereotype of women's passivity in contrast to men's activity in what are most likely sexual relationships. It should be noted that questionnaire studies asking people to remember and report in which part of the body they have been touched during the last year can be subject to a great deal of distortion, because people tend to report what they think is consonant with what others deem proper.

Women's reports indicate that they receive much touching from men, and observations of actual touching support these reports. As you may recall from our discussion in Chapter 8 of the relation between status and touch, Henley (1973, 1977) reported that men touch women about twice as much as women touch men. This pattern was even more clear-cut when the women lacked certain status advantages such as age or social class. Henley interpreted this pattern as a status reminder by men rather than just a simple show of affection. In light of our discussion earlier in this chapter concerning gender differences in personal space, there seems to be at least some support for Henley's argument. When women are approached spatially, they allow people to come close, often even to touch. When they themselves are approaching, they stop farther away, out of touching range.

It seems, then, that women do not always elect to be touched. Further research shows that a male's touch is not always perceived as pleasant by a woman. In one study, some of the female subjects were verbally instructed and others were physically guided in a problem-solving task by a man. The subjects were least attracted to the man who had touched them when the task ended in failure (Touhey, 1974). Those who were physically guided to a successful outcome were more attracted to the man who so guided them.

Another study attempted to specify the meaning of touch between the sexes. When unmarried college students were asked what a pat, a squeeze, a brush, and a stroke meant when directed to different parts of the body by someone of the opposite sex, men and women differed considerably in their responses (Nguyen, Heslin, & Nguyen, 1975). Women discriminated among body parts more than men did. Men seemed to be tuned to the differences among patting, stroking, and squeezing but unconcerned about the body part involved. For women, love and friendliness were shown by touch on the hands, head, face, arms, and back but not by touch on the breasts or genital areas. In fact, women excluded touch that signaled sexual desire from touch indicating love and friendliness. For males, pleasantness, sexual desire, warmth, and love were all similar in meaning. It seems that women make more interpersonal distinctions on the meaning of nonverbal behavior; a touch is not a touch is not a touch.

Talk

Although cultural stereotypes characterize women as more talkative, research shows otherwise. In most encounters between women and men, the men do the talking and the women do the listening. Recording all spontaneous talk exchanged by a married couple at a summer resort, Soskin and John (1963) found that the husband's total share of talking time across all situations at the resort was just over 50%. When he was in conversation with his wife, however, he talked 79% of the time. When married couples were asked to reach joint decisions about questionnaire answers on which they individually disagreed, men outtalked women and won more of the contested decisions (Strodtbeck, 1951). In simulations of jury deliberations, this effect was magnified; men constituted only about two-thirds of the juries studied but took up 80% of the talking time (Strodtbeck & Mann, 1956). Even in one-way communication, men talk more than women. When asked to describe thoroughly three pictures by Albrecht Dürer, men talked about four times as long as women, and 3 of the 17 men in the study talked longer than the 30-minute cassette could record (Swacker, 1975).

In conversations between men and women, part of the male dominance in speaking time is achieved by interruptions (Argyle, Lalljee, & Cook, 1968). In a study comparing same-sex and cross-sex conversations, many more interruptions occurred in cross-sex conversations, and it was always the man who did the interrupting (Zimmerman & West, 1975). In same-sex conversations, interruptions, overlaps, and silences were evenly distributed between speakers. In conversations between women and men, however, women were silent for noticeable periods of time after being interrupted, and in no case was a woman noted to protest the interruption. In addition to interruptions and overlaps, women engaged in conversation with men also encountered mistimed responses from them. As you recall from Chapter 10, responses from listeners help sustain the speaker's flow and provide cues that the listener is attending. Three of the ten male/female conversations examined by Zimmerman and West contained mistimed responses on the part of male listeners—responses in which the "um" and "hmm" sounds were delayed by as much as ten seconds after the women stopped speaking. As a result, the female speakers dropped the topic of conversation.

A clear-cut way of indicating responsiveness to others is to be a good listener—and that is what women are good at. A recent study showed that, when pairs of unacquainted male and female college students were asked to talk about anything they wished, gender differences in listening emerged. Both males and females spoke more to a female partner than to a male partner (Markel, Long, & Saine, 1976).

A Move toward Androgyny

We began this chapter by suggesting that men are expected to be proactive and women reactive. Our review of the research on gender differences in nonverbal behavior bears this out. We also mentioned that proactivity and reactivity are not exclusive prerogatives of either gender, since there are considerable individual differences in the degree to which women and men stay within the prescribed sex-role boundaries. Some men do demonstrate sensitivity, warmth, and nurturance. And some women do radiate assertiveness, dominance, and independence. By going beyond the prescribed sex-role boundaries, these men and women show that they are capable of responding appropriately to the situations in which they find themselves. Stated somewhat differently, these people show greater adaptability across situations and engage in situationally effective behavior without regard for society's stereotypes about what one or the other sex "should" do. People who can be both instrumental and expressive, assertive and responsive, have been called psychologically *androgynous* (Bem, 1974).

Research by Bem (1975) has shown that androgynous males and androgynous females (that is, people who describe themselves as possessing both masculine *and* feminine characteristics) are more adaptive and situationally responsive than males and females subscribing to traditional roles for themselves. They can be both more reactive and more proactive in situations calling for these behaviors. Although there is little research to date relating specific nonverbal behavior to androgynous versus traditional males and females, one study is suggestive. When videotapes of androgynous males and females and of traditional males and females were presented to judges, strongly sex-typed males were perceived as both more masculine and less feminine than strongly sex-typed females. The androgynous persons were perceived as somewhere in between the other two groups (Lippa, in press).

Summary

Oscar Wilde said "A man's face is his autobiography; a woman's face is her work of fiction." The implication, of course, is that a man's face is truly reflective of his inner state whereas a woman's face is fabrication. Research supports the letter of Wilde's statement, if not the spirit.

A woman's face is reflective not so much of her inner state but of the inner states of others with whom she is interacting. Sex-role expectations call for women to be reactive and responsive, particularly with men. Women do this by being sensitive to others' nonverbal expressiveness, by varying their nonverbal behavior to complement that of their partners, by being good listeners, and by giving way and being there when others want to approach and touch.

A man's face may be his autobiography—or, at least, his current press release—because he is less tuned to the socioemotional side of human relationships and more concerned with getting the job done. Sex-role expectations call for him to be proactive; he does this by talking more (particularly to women), interrupting more, holding his spatial territory, and leading the way.

The display of gender-linked nonverbal behavior is neither permanent nor immutable. It is affected by various contexts, such as age, the company one keeps, and the amount of androgyny one has. But gender is itself a context for other nonverbal behaviors. It is difficult to think of communication in the absence of gender; it is nearly impossible to determine the meaning of nonverbal behavior without knowing the sex of the person who performed the behavior.

Chapter 13

Cultural Cues

What does it mean to take something for granted? Although this phrase certainly has a variety of connotations, the essential meaning seems to be that something has become so familiar, so reliable, so predictable, that you no longer need concern yourselves with it. It will in effect run by itself. The process of communication is taken for granted most of the time. Hence, the discovery that the process has somehow gone astray is a disconcerting one and one that leaves you in a state of bewildered helplessness. That which is supposed to work well has somehow unaccountably gone wrong; the reaction is often no more sophisticated than that of kicking the coffee machine that has taken your coin and failed to respond to that communication with a cup of coffee. This chapter addresses one very significant source of communication breakdown—that brought on by cultural or ethnic differences. An important assumption throughout our description of these differences is that awareness of the ways of others brings us to see our own ways that we take so much for granted.

One very positive outcome of taking something for granted is that it is then possible to go on with other things—for example, getting to know someone better. If you couldn't rest easy with the knowledge that you know how to communicate, it would be well nigh impossible for you to even begin a relationship. When you operate within your own culture, you can take communication for granted most of the time. You cannot, however, when you are involved in an intercultural interaction.

Report and Command in a Cultural Context

We said in Chapter 1 that communication has both a report and a command aspect; the former relates to the content of the message and the latter to how that content is to be taken. In other words, the report is in the behavior itself, and the command derives from the environment in which the behavior takes place. Culture is an important aspect of that environment. Therefore, while people from two different cultures may share the same nonverbal report—that is, they may engage in the same behavior (such as moving the head up and down)—the command aspect of that behavior may be entirely differ-ent in the two cultures. One culture may be signaling "Yes, I agree," while the other is, in effect, saying "Oh, is that so?" Similarly, the command may be the same, but the report may differ; two people from two different cultures may want to communicate the same thing, but they may do it in different ways. Let's say that an Indian and a North American want to signal agreement. The North American would do so by a downward nod of the head, whereas the Indian would be likely to tilt his head sideways—a motion quite similar to that which a North American would use to accompany negation.

In your own culture, the connections between the report and the com-mand aspects are so intimate and apparently self-evident that you can take for granted that you are communicating. This sense of security can lead you to believe (quite erroneously) that your own patterns are the "natural" ones and dissimilar patterns are therefore disruptive and wrong. When two people share the same culture, they share communication systems as well. They speak the same language, verbal and nonverbal, and in more or less the same way. They may not like each other, and they may not like what is being said, but both would probably agree more often than not with regard to what has been said. This kind of agreement may be more difficult to assume when the encounter is between two people of different cultures. They may share the same sentiments but express them with different words and—what concerns us here—different nonverbal acts. For example, each wants to communicate liking for the other, but one does this by a steady, frank look, while the other does it by a respectfully averted gaze. Despite the same intent and goodwill, the differences in report may contribute to the breakdown of communication, because each of the two people involved may misread what the other is trying to signal.

The same problem arises when the report is the same but the accom-panying commands are different. The two people are likely to think that they are communicating accurately, when in fact their interpretations of what was communicated differ. Both have shaken hands in greeting, but for one this cues a distant and formal relationship, while for the other it signals growing warmth and intimacy. The different meaning that each assigns to the same gesture may not cause an immediate breakdown in communication, because, after all, the gesture *is* the same; but the misunderstanding will soon become apparent. Identical gestures with different commands may be particularly troublesome when they occur quite early in the encounter; having one's ini-tial trust later disconfirmed can lead to very negative feelings. Language sys-tems are less susceptible to these potential problems, since people usually know when they don't speak the same language. Because of the out-of-awareness nature of nonverbal communication, however, the potential for unrecognized communicational misunderstanding is far greater.

At a time when the world has become so much smaller and encounters between people of diverse cultural backgrounds are an everyday occurrence, the issue of cultural differences and similarities is no longer just an academic or individual concern. In the following pages, we review some of the research on cultural aspects of nonverbal communication. We step back, look at what we have talked about in the preceding chapters, and ask how much of what we have said is culture specific. We conceive of the cultural aspects of nonverbal behavior as representing successive layers around a core of basic elements. Most of the time, bodies come clothed in successively revealing layers. Bodies can be attired very differently, in high fashion or weekend grubbies, with European tailoring or California flair. This is the outermost layer and the one that shows most cultural variability. Inside the clothing is a body; while every body has skin and hair, colors and textures vary. Hence, this middle layer shows both similarities and differences. Finally, inside the body are the internal organs—heart, lungs, nerves—that are nearly universal in appearance and function, as organ transplants have shown. At this innermost core, humans are most alike.

If we look at nonverbal behaviors as analogues of these layers, we identify as body organs those basic behaviors considered to be universal and innate. Facial expressions of happiness and distress, for example, are recognized the world over. Those nonverbal behaviors that show both uniformity and diversity can be seen as analogous to body appearances. Members of all cultures show emotion, express intimacy, and deal with status, but the particular manner in which they do it varies from culture to culture. Finally, there are the culture-bound cues—the clothing in our analogy—which show more dissimilarity across cultures. This chapter presents the cultural aspects of nonverbal communication in this layer-like fashion. We start with a core of similarities and proceed to examine the accruing differences stemming from varying experiences and environments. For the most part, the report aspect of communication lies in the similarities—that is, in the innermost core—and the command originates in the layers. Efforts to understand intercultural communication by focusing on the core alone, by attending only to the similarities, are limiting and often bound to failure. If we truly want to understand communication, we need to know both the report and the command; this requires knowing the cultural differences as well as the similarities.

Cross-Cultural Similarities

We begin our discussion of cultural nonverbal communication by looking at some elements that we all share. To identify a bit of nonverbal behavior as a product of the social rules of culture is difficult, because we tend to look at behavior as uniquely individual. In order to see cultural influence at work, we must in fact recognize another as a member of a group different from our own. Then we can begin to see someone's expansive conversational gestures as "typically" Italian or someone else's restrained seated posture as "typically" British. For now, we are going to consider cultural similarities in nonverbal behavior as they manifest themselves in a single channel of communication—facial expression of emotions.

Pure Affect Expression

In Chapter 3, we described Ekman's (1972) theory of emotional expression. As you may recall, each primary emotion is thought to be connected to a specific set of facial muscles by a particular set of neural impulses. It follows that, since all humans have similar nervous systems by virtue of their membership in the human race, there should be no cultural differences in the facial expression of basic emotions. In seeking support for this theory, Ekman and his colleagues (Ekman, Friesen, & Ellsworth, 1972) carried out a number of cross-cultural studies in which people from different countries were asked to match emotion labels (which had, of course, been translated into the subjects' own language) with pictures representing the facial expression for each primary emotion. The primary emotions included happiness, sadness, anger, disgust, surprise, and fear. Subjects from South American cultures were able to assign the labels correctly. It's interesting to note that similar results were obtained by Izard (1969) with citizens of various European countries.

Even more conclusive were Ekman and his colleagues' findings for members of a preliterate culture in New Guinea. These subjects, who had had little contact with Western cultures, were shown three photographs of Caucasian faces, each expressing a different emotion, and were presented with three stories. Their task was to match the photographed expression with the appropriate emotion conveyed in the story. Both children and adults matched facial expressions and emotions correctly, just as the Western subjects had done. The only exception was fear, which was often confused by New Guineans with surprise. Another research strategy employed by Ekman (Ekman et al., 1972) revealed cross-cultural similarities in the encoding of emotions in facial expressions. Videotapes were made of New Guinean subjects who had been asked to show the emotional expression their faces would have if they were the person described in a story. These videotapes were accurately decoded by college students in the United States; that is, students who had never seen a New Guinean before were able to tell by looking at the videotapes when a member of this culture was trying to look happy, angry, or sad. On the other hand, the students had difficulty recognizing fear or surprise. This difficulty is likely to be related to the difficulty New Guineans had in decoding these two emotions in North American faces.

The results of this study offer strong evidence that at least a few basic emotions are conveyed by the same facial expressions. It does not detract from the importance of this finding to realize that this panculturalism is confined to a very few emotional states. This limitation does, however, restrict the generalizations that can be drawn about cross-cultural encounters in real life. Only four of the six associations between facial expressions and primary emotions (happiness, anger, disgust, sadness, surprise, and fear) yielded high cross-cultural accuracy. It is true that, at the simplest and most basic levels of emotional experience, human beings are similar. But the emotional life of people is varied and rich and encompasses more than the so-called primary emotions. We might speculate that Dorothy Parker's criticism of an actress who ran "the emotional gamut from A to B" was prompted by someone who expressed only a very few emotions.

Some cultures appear to express more or less emotion than others. Orientals, for example, have been frequently called "inscrutable" because of their restraint in manifesting emotions. But research shows that the emotional reactions may be present even if they are not reflected in facial expressions (Ekman et al., 1972). People in the United States and Japan were videotaped, without their knowledge, as they were watching a neutral film about autumn leaves and a stress-inducing film about sinus surgery. People from both cultures showed essentially the *same* negative facial expressions when they were watching the stress film without knowing that they were observed. When, later on, the Japanese subjects described the stress-inducing film to a Japanese interviewer, they displayed less negative or more impassive expressions. United States subjects, instead, continued to show in the subsequent interview the surprise, disgust, and sadness they had expressed while viewing the film. Evidently, the cultural rules about appropriate emotional expression overrode the common experience shared by members of both groups. This indicates that, while clearly there exist fundamental cultural similarities in the reports of facial expressions, there are considerable differences with regard to how members of different cultures wish to be taken.

Some cultural similarities have also been found in social interactions. Ethological studies of natural situations have revealed cross-cultural similarities in some elements of social rituals. Using cameras with right-angled lenses, which keep persons unaware of being the object of focus, Eibl-Eibesfeldt (1972) found that in many cultures social greetings at a distance between friends involve an *eyebrow flash*. Europeans, Samoans, South American Indians, and Bushmen were noted to move their eyebrows, keeping them maximally raised for about one-sixth of a second, when greeting a friend. This signal seems to indicate a friendly willingness to interact and probably originates in the expression of surprise that entails a similar facial movement. Similarly, the hiding of the mouth or face in moments of embarrassment has been noted in a variety of cultures. Both the eyebrow flash and the covering gesture are small bits of behavior embedded in larger rituals of the kind discussed in Chapter 10.

Some sense of the relative weight of cultural similarities and differences can be derived from cross-cultural results based on the PONS test (described in Chapter 3). As you may recall, the PONS film shows brief samples of the multichanneled nonverbal behavior of a young North American woman, and viewers are asked to choose which of two situations better characterizes the behavior they have observed. The film was shown to viewers from 20 different countries (Rosenthal, Hall, DiMatteo, Rogers, & Archer, 1977). Accuracy was found to vary widely among national samples. College students in Australia scored highest and those in New Guinea lowest, but even this least-accurate group matched behavior with situations better than would be expected by chance. This seems to suggest that there are some elements of nonverbal behavior common to different cultures. When the foreign groups were ranked according to their cultural similarity to the United States, viewers from cultures very similar to that of the young woman in the film (that is, Canadian) were found to be more accurate in decoding her nonverbal behavior than viewers from more dissimilar cultures (such as New Guineans). The lower accuracy of those from dissimilar cultures cannot be construed as emotional insensitivity. Rather, the experiences of these people are simply not comparable to those of college-educated Americans; therefore, these people don't recognize some of the expressions used by Americans, nor do Americans recognize some of theirs.

Similar and Dissimilar Cultural Cues

Rules for Emotional Displays

In the experiment by Ekman and his colleagues (Ekman et al., 1972) described in the section above, the Japanese and Americans were alike in some ways and different in others. Their faces showed the same feelings of fear and disgust when they were watching the stress-inducing film, but, in talking with someone about the film, the Japanese showed the neutral expressions that many Westerners define as inscrutable. In the presence of others, the Japanese did not show their emotions. This means that, although the response to the film is the same, culture dictates what feelings one should reveal to whom under what circumstances, and people behave accordingly. Termed *display rules* (Ekman & Friesen, 1975), these ways of controlling the expression of feelings are learned early in life and become thoroughly automatic; with members of your own culture, you seldom notice their existence. But display rules differ from culture to culture and, in an intercultural encounter, they may cause problems. Suppose an American and a Japanese are watching the stress film together. The American who sneaks a look to see how the other is taking this disturbing film sees a controlled expression in the other's face. Thus, the American easily comes to the false conclusion that the Japanese is an uncaring, unfeeling, perhaps even cruel person. In this situation, cultural display rules that dictate what is shown to an observer can, when they go unrecognized as in fact being cultural, give rise to false impressions of the other person.

Cultures differ not only in their rules about what emotions should be revealed but also with regard to what objects and situations should give rise to different emotions. Food regarded as a great delicacy in one culture brings out expressions of disgust in another. The cultural rules about how to respond dictate when and how the disgust is to be displayed or concealed. Emotional expression can be managed in three different ways: by qualifying, by modulating, or by falsifying the emotion actually being experienced (Ekman & Friesen, 1975). When you *qualify* a facial expression, you try to limit the impact of that expression by adding another expression to the original one. A very common qualifier is the smile, which is frequently used to lessen the impact of a negative expression. The Japanese often greet annoying breaches of etiquette with a smile. The annoyance is qualified by a smile in part to command others to note the person's inner strength and control (Morsbach, 1973). In a study in which interviewers gazed steadily at the other person's face or at the other person's knees, Japanese smiled in both situations, although the gaze directed at the face was clearly more stressful, as indicated by increased self-manipulation (Bond & Komai, 1976).

Modulation changes the facial expression to increase or decrease the intensity of what is shown. The proverbial "stiff upper lip" of the Anglo-Saxon who is in pain or sorrow is quite a literal description of one means of modulating the intensity of the negative emotion expressed. By holding the lip still through deliberate effort, the person controls the trembling characteristic of the tearful face. So, too, with positive feelings, when the culture dictates that expressions of joy and happiness be muted. To laugh loudly, rocking one's entire body, is seen as very inappropriate in cultures where a slight smile is considered the proper way to indicate amusement or pleasure.

Falsification is clearly the most extreme of the expression-management devices, since it requires you to show something quite different from what you actually feel. This can involve expressing an emotion you don't feel or hiding one that you do. You can also try to falsify what you feel by neutralizing or blanking out the expression of what you do feel. But since it is much harder to show nothing (at least in Western cultures) than to show something, most falsifying is done either by simulating a different feeling or by masking the true one. In most cultures certain events (for example, weddings and funerals) call for the expression of specific emotions; if, for whatever reason, you don't happen to feel the right emotion, you will probably falsify the expression on your face. Most likely, you'll try to show the emotion that's expected or, at least, to disguise the inappropriate one. In our culture, the jilted suitor at the wedding is supposed to look happy; the politician at the funeral of a hated opponent is expected to look sad.

Managing Status Differences

In every culture, you meet and interact with people whose social standing is higher or lower than your own, and you learn the rules that regulate such interactions. Some cultures have very few status distinctions; in many so-called primitive societies, only the tribal chief is set apart from all the other members. Most complex societies have many status distinctions based on wealth, power, age, sex, family, occupation, and other reasons. Some cultures have evolved very elaborate nonverbal rules for monitoring and regulating status. In Japan, before a comfortable verbal interchange can begin, status cues of badge, costume, and business card must be exchanged (Morsbach, 1973). Only then can both parties be sure of the appropriate level of discourse for their interaction.

In encounters between Westerners and Japanese, postural cues can be misleading. Encounters between status equals among American men call for a moderately relaxed seated posture. As described in Chapter 8, the American of executive rank sits with arms and legs extended or crossed and the torso leaning back. No Japanese would adopt this posture in most social situations (Taylor, 1974). Instead, the comfortable Japanese will likely sit in an erect-from-the-hips posture, feet flat on the floor, and hands in the lap. This posture strikes the American as reflecting tension, disagreement, or antagonism—hardly the basis for a comfortable exchange between equals.

The nonverbal ways of expressing and acknowledging equal status across cultures are difficult to identify and use. Take speaking order, for example. In our culture, speaking order usually reflects the status hierarchy of those present, with higher-status people speaking first. In other cultures, the higher-status person often is among the last to speak—a custom that, in a cross-cultural encounter, can be very misleading. The same thing is true of silence. Silence is often a powerful status regulator, especially in non-Western cultures, yet its status meaning often goes unnoticed by Westerners. Where bowing is used to show deference, the depth and duration of the bow convey degrees of respect. The social inferior bows more deeply, and the social superior terminates the bowing ritual (Morsbach, 1973). Those who wish to indicate equality must therefore engage in a very complicated maneuver to get out of a sequence of mutual bows (Condon & Yousef, 1975).

Conveying Intimacy

Just as all cultures develop rules for the management of status differences, so, too, do they develop rules for conveying intimacy. As discussed in Chapter 6, gaze, distance, and touch all serve as nonverbal indicators of liking and attraction. Within any given culture, these cues are learned and understood. But in cross-cultural encounters, miscueing can occur.

The initial observation that people of different cultures interact at different interpersonal distances is credited to Hall (1959). A number of researchers have sought support for this observation, with somewhat mixed results. In an experiment involving conversations between friends, Arab foreign students sat closer, faced each other more directly, looked at each other more, and were more likely to touch than American students (Watson & Graves, 1966). Although Latin Americans are also considered members of a "contact culture," they were not found to differ in conversational distance from North Americans (Forston & Larson, 1968). This study's failure to show any difference may have to do with the controversial subject matter of the discussion (the Middle East crisis) and the fact that the conversants were not friends. The rules governing conversational distance may vary with topic and relationship in all cultures. Potentially conflictual topics call for a different spacing than social talk, particularly when strangers rather than friends are involved in the discussion.

A number of studies have looked at subcultural differences in interpersonal distance in public places. If people observed together in such settings can be assumed to be at least somewhat friendly, then some cultural differences in spacing between friends do appear to exist. For example, Aiello and Jones (1971) noted that, when conversing on the school playground, middle-class White children stood farther apart from each other than lower-class Black and Puerto Rican children. However, at the Houston zoo, Blacks were observed to stand farther from each other than did Mexican-Americans or Anglos (Baxter, 1970). Such differences in interpersonal spacing may reflect relative social-class differences, as indicated by observations of Black and White schoolchildren in Canadian schoolyards, which found that, regardless of race, middle-class children stood farther apart than lower-class children (Scherer, 1974). It is also possible that the Black children in Canadian schools were of Caribbean extraction, which those in Houston were not. One should be cautious in drawing conclusions about the nonverbal expression of intimacy in situations in which culture and status overlap.

When, instead of being observed, people are asked about their preferred interaction distances, clear cultural differences emerge. Members of Mediterranean cultures (for example, Greeks and Southern Italians) prefer closer distances than Northern Europeans, such as Scots and Swedes (Little, 1968). Interactions between friends are reported to take place at closer distances than those between strangers. The potential problems posed by these preferences are illustrated in a study of student immigrants from Argentina, Iraq, and Russia who had been in Israel less than one year (Lomranz, 1976). Students from all three cultures preferred closer distances with friends than with strangers and with a fellow countryman than with an Israeli. Argentinean students sought the greatest distance from strangers (a distance that was almost nine times greater than that they chose for friends). The Iraqis, on the other hand, preferred the smallest distance and made little distinction based on relationship. All cultures place friends closer than strangers, but the absolute distances for preferred interactions vary widely.

In a similar study of students in Hawaii (Engebretson & Fullmer, 1970), native Japanese indicated a preference for greater distances when interacting with a friend, their father, or a professor than did Hawaiians of Japanese extraction and Caucasian American students. There were no differences between the latter two groups, indicating that the Hawaiians of Japanese extraction had adapted to Caucasian preferences in interpersonal distancing. With regard to relationship, all three groups chose closer distances for friends than for fathers and professors, but the preferred distance between friends for the native Japanese students was still significantly greater than that for the other two groups. An observational study on the same campus (Sechrest, 1969) coded touch and distance between mixed-sex student couples and found that Oriental couples engaged in less touching than Caucasian couples. Mixed-culture couples kept touch and distance somewhere in between the extremes represented by their own cultural groups.

Physical contact is considered a very basic intimacy signal deriving from mother/infant communication. Yet, the amount of touching varies from culture to culture. Members of the English upper class maintain very distant relationships between parents and children (Montagu, 1971). English culture as a whole tends to regard physical touch quite negatively. Accidental contact, even between family members, calls for an apology, and public displays of affection are considered vulgar. In Chapter 12, we described the questionnaire technique that Jourard (1966) used to gather information about touching. We also reported that one of this study's findings was that in North America males are less accessible to touch than females. In contrast, Israeli male students report more overall touching than female students (Lomranz & Shapira, 1974). More touching between men is considered acceptable in Middle Eastern cultures as well as among Jews than among Anglo-Saxons. The same questionnaire technique applied to Japanese and North American students in Japan (Barnlund, 1975) found that in nearly every category the amount of physical contact reported by Japanese was half that reported by North Americans. In particular, North Americans reported nearly three times as much physical contact with their fathers as did Japanese. Even with a friend of the opposite sex, Japanese reported only half the contact reported by North Americans, and the contact was restricted to a much more limited area of the body.

The preceding discussion indicates the existence of cultural similarities and differences with regard to intimacy, status, and emotional displays. In other words, there is agreement across cultures that friends are to be treated differently than strangers. But actual differences do exist; the distance an Italian male may consider acceptable with regard to a friend is much smaller than the distance a German may choose when interacting with someone of similar intimacy. In these differences lie the roots of possible intercultural misunderstanding. All the verbal indications may be present to lead two interactants from different cultures to believe themselves to be on friendly terms, but the nonverbal expressions of such a relationship may still be absent or, worse yet, contradictory. Cross-cultural training in nonverbal communication can make a difference. When Collett (1971) trained Englishmen to behave nonverbally more like Arabs (for example, to stand closer, look more, smile more, and touch more), Arabs liked these Englishmen better than other Englishmen who had not been trained. English people who met both groups of fellow Englishmen seemed to like them about equally.

Cross-Cultural Dissimilarities

When you're getting ready for a trip abroad, you often prepare by reading guidebooks that tell you not only where to eat and sleep and what to see but also how to avoid offending the natives of the country. For instance, you are given examples of gestures that you ought not to make if you are to remain on friendly terms with the people you are going to visit. You read your guides, try to keep in mind the various tips they offer, and head off toward the new terrain with a feeling of confidence. And sometimes you return vowing never to go there again. What has happened? Why, in spite of goodwill on both sides, do relationships between people of different cultures sometimes end in frustration and bad feelings? Part of the reason may be that, although you expected some differences, you were unprepared for the depth and pervasiveness of these differences. You learned a few foreign cues and probably used them correctly, but perhaps you relied on them too heavily. So, when you are confronted with an array of differences, both subtle and obvious, that you cannot manage, you end up wondering why *they* can't learn to communicate better.

As discussed in the preceding section, display rules clearly vary from culture to culture. Furthermore, some expressions of emotion are unique to particular cultures. In other words, members of some cultures may feel and convey sentiments that members of other cultures neither know nor recognize. For example, Ekman (1977) found that New Guineans frequently show a blend of sad brows and angry mouth that viewers in the United States cannot recognize and therefore name. Similarly, the facial blend that North Americans call "smug" is not recognized in many cultures. A comparable blend, called the "wry smile," is a composite of two expressions resulting in a mouth with one corner down (indicating doubt) and the other corner up (indicating a partial smile) (Brannigan & Humphries, 1972). This wry smile is characteristically British and may not be understood elsewhere. Contrary to what you may think, facial expressions vary even from region to region within the same country. The United States is no exception. Seaford (1975) analyzed 10,000 high-school yearbook photographs and found a characteristic Southern United States facial expression. This expression is marked by a pursed mouth, two variants of tongue showing, and one or both lips drawn inward over the teeth. It is an expression rarely found in other regions; it does appear in Colonial portraits of Southerners and may thus be well established in Southern facial display.

Cultural differences become very apparent in the rules of conversation management. The differences are most evident in conventionalized gestures, in the movements that accompany speech to improve its intelligibility, and in the regulation of speaker and listener roles. Ekman and Friesen (1969b) have called these three categories of nonverbal behavior *emblems, illustrators,* and *regulators.*

Emblems

Emblems are conventional nonverbal gestures that are widely recognized and understood within the user's culture. According to Ekman and Friesen (1969b), their meaning is unambiguous and they are usually displayed deliberately in order to send a particular and specific message to someone else. Although emblems can be used alone without any verbal accompaniment, they could theoretically be replaced by a word or two. For example, the middle finger raised in the air or the index finger and middle finger raised in the form of a V have emblematic meanings. The cultural basis of emblems becomes evident when one traces an emblem's history. Harrison (1974) reported that the A-OK emblem (that is, a circle made by joining the index finger and thumb together) originated in the United States in the 1840 presidential elections, when the expression "O. K." was coined. Martin Van Buren, the Democratic candidate, was born in Old Kinderhook, New York, and the Democratic O. K. Club was formed to support him. The group gained such political influence that, in order to run for office, any candidate had to get its "O. K."

Other groups, not sharing the same North American history, would not attach the same meaning—or, perhaps, they would attach no meaning at all— to this nonverbal sign. In fact, this same O-shaped gesture has an entirely different, even obscene, meaning in other cultures (Saitz & Cervenka, 1972). The gesture represents the female genitalia; directed to a woman, it conveys the message of a seduction attempt; directed to a man, the gesture has insulting implications for his masculinity (Harrison, 1974). In Japan, the O-shaped gesture has still another meaning—money.

Condon and Yousef (1975) have described another emblem, which, because of the different meanings it has in the two countries, can create misunderstanding between Russians and citizens of the United States. Russians will clasp their hands over their heads when receiving a tribute. For a North American, this gesture not only doesn't represent gracious acknowledgement but can in fact convey triumphant superiority.

Other emblems clearly reveal their cultural specificity. Ask yourself how you would interpret the following gestures: the little finger pointed straight up, a rapid crossing of the index fingers, and the drawing of the index finger over an eyebrow after the finger has been briefly licked. Morsbach (1973) reports that in Japan the first of these three gestures can refer to a girlfriend, wife, or mistress; the second alludes to a fight; and the third is an indirect way of suggesting that someone is a liar.

A visit to France reveals immediately that the French have gestures all their own. For example, disbelief is signaled by the mouth drooping in utter contempt while the index finger of the right hand tugs down on the lower eyelid of the right eye (Brault, 1962). And there is the characteristic French way of communicating exquisiteness: the fingers of the right hand are pinched together, pointed toward and then raised to the lips, kissed and softly tossed into the air; the chin is held high; and the eyes squint briefly. Brault cautions, however, that, although this gesture is well known, it is frequently misused by Americans imitating Frenchmen. The French reserve it for expressing only the more subtle and refined emotions and display it very gently.

If you were in Colombia, would you know what to do if someone gestured to you, hand extended, palm down, and index finger moving back and forth? This is the Colombian emblem for "Come here" (Saitz & Cervenka, 1972). In this culture, when the hand is cupped palm up about six inches below the chin, it indicates disbelief. The emblem is thought to have originated as the description of a goiter, a symbol of stupidity. A Colombian male who wants to indicate strength may take hold of his trouser belt and move it up

This classic French emblem conveys exquisiteness. For people in other cultures, it is easier to recognize than to imitate.

and down several times. This gesture is not likely to be recognized, and therefore understood, by a North American.

In the Middle East, emblems are very specific to the sexes; that is, the gestures used by men and by women differ (Hamelian, 1965). Even when the gesture is the same—such as lifting the chin upward to indicate negation—women use the gesture with a wider range of nuances than men. Friendship in Jordan is indicated by placing both index fingers side by side or by inviting the other to lock little fingers. The same gesture, but also involving the third finger, conveys hostility. Hamelian (1965) indicates that in Syria and Lebanon the meanings of these two locking gestures are reversed. It seems that, even in similar cultures, similar gestures can have different meanings; when the meanings are clearly opposite in command, an attempt at communication can be hazardous indeed. In Iran, too, hand gestures convey a multitude of meanings (Sparhawk, 1976). When, in an interaction, one of the two people places his right index finger beside his nose, he's saying to the other "You have lost face." It is a gesture that originates in the allusion to burning the nose. The hand held palm down in front of the chest and moved horizontally with fingers extended signifies equality between conversants, whereas enmity is conveyed by the hand held vertically, palm out, with the index and second finger apart. These examples represent but a very few of the emblems commonly used in some cultures; the study of Iranian emblems identified nearly 300 emblems, many of which are culture specific and others are, instead, more accessible to foreigners.

In order to find out what emblems are used in the United States, Ekman and his colleagues (Ekman, 1976; Johnson, Ekman, & Friesen, 1975) used an encoding/decoding procedure. They asked urban White middle-class males between the ages of 21 and 35 and who were at least third-generation Americans to express with nonverbal actions 220 verbal messages. Then the researchers selected those nonverbal actions that were visually similar for at least 70% of the subjects. These actions were then presented on videotape to culturally similar decoders. If 70% of the decoders matched the action with the verbal message that had been given to the original subjects, the action was considered a verified emblem. There turned out to be 67 verified American emblems—a number far below that of many other cultures.

The preceding discussion has pointed to cultural dissimilarities in the use of simple gestures. Dissimilarities can also be seen in rituals such as greetings and farewells. Greetings that involve little or no physical contact between people are conveyed in many different ways across the world—by hat lifting, as on the European continent; by bowing, as in Japan; or even by shaking one's own hand, as in China (Brun, 1969). Salutation through contact, too, can take on a variety of forms cross-culturally. Hands may be kissed, as on the Continent; shoulders may be lightly buffeted, as among the Eskimos; or hugs may be combined with pats on the back, as in Latin America. The breadth of the forms of greeting becomes obvious when one adopts a global rather than a provincial perspective.

One of the most confusing nonverbal acts that a North American may encounter is the bow. It is seldom seen on this continent, and, on those rare occasions in which it does appear, it is likely to elicit confusion and embarrassment. In fact, if one is not directly involved in a bowing encounter, one can observe a comedy of manners. One of the protagonists is a good-intentioned but unsophisticated North American who, upon being bowed to, bows in return. His timing is off, however, and he cracks heads with his companion as they bow in unison. Or he begins to look like a rocking doll forever set in motion, as each of his bows elicits still another one in return.

In Japan, the bow is one of the most important nonverbal gestures, since it is used to start, maintain, as well as end interactions between people (Morsbach, 1973). And not only is it used frequently, but its use is a far more intricate procedure than many Westerners realize. Although most Americans

In the bowing ritual, it is important to know not only the movement but also the rhythm, duration, and contextual use.

in Japan learn to adapt to the bowing ritual, it is the exceptional American who can even begin to feel comfortable with it and to know the nuances of the sentiments that the bow conveys (Taylor, 1974).

Although there is considerable cross-cultural diversity in emblematic form and usage, Ekman (1976) reports cross-cultural similarities in the kinds of emblems that are used to convey insults, directions, greetings, replies, physical states (like sleep), and emotion. What this means is that, when a message describes a body activity, it tends to be performed in similar ways in different cultures for anatomical reasons.

It is important to note here that the use of emblems varies contextually. For example, several researchers have noted that emblems occur much more in informal than in formal communication (Brault, 1962; Sparhawk, 1976); also, when distance, secrecy, and an ongoing conversation preclude the use of words; and when children and lower-class people are communicating.

Illustrators

Illustrators (as you recall from our discussion in Chapter 10) are nonverbal movements that accompany verbal messages. They are conveyed primarily through the hands—for example, when a person points while saying "Hey, look over there"—but can also be done with the head, face, or even the whole body. Illustrators are the kinds of nonverbal behaviors that you are most likely to think of when describing cultural differences in nonverbal style. In fact, there is an oft-repeated story concerning the nonverbal illustrators displayed by a former mayor of New York, Fiorello La Guardia, during his political speeches. These speeches were delivered in three different languages—English, Italian, and Yiddish—depending on the constituents he was addressing. The story goes that, if one looks at the film records of these speeches, one can, without soundtrack, detect which language La Guardia was speaking just by referring to his accompanying distinctive nonverbal behaviors.

There is research support for the ethnic differences that exist in learned nonverbal styles. Almost 40 years ago, an anthropologist examined the gestures of two immigrant groups in the Lower East Side of New York and found distinctive gestural patterns (Efron, 1941/1972). Among first-generation immigrants, the Italians were found to use broad, full-arm gestures, while the Jewish immigrants tended to use gestures close to the body and that seemed to trace the flow of what was being said. It is interesting to note also that these same distinctive styles began to fade among the second-generation immigrants.

Many cultural groups share the use of the head nod, especially while listening. But there are considerable disparities when it comes to interpretation. The Japanese head nod means only continued attention and not the assent typically attributed to it by North Americans. Consequently, an American can suffer a rude awakening when, at the end of a long presentation, he finds that his Japanese listeners disagree with him wholeheartedly in spite of the countless nods they gave his presentation. A comparable confusion can arise when dealing with Bulgarians (Jakobson, 1972). The Bulgarian head movement for "no" consists of throwing the head back and then returning it to the upright position. When emphatically displayed, the return to the upright position can involve a slight bend of the head forward, thus appearing very much like the Western "yes."

Regulators

Many nonverbal cues, as we have noted, help conversations run smoothly. Through such cues as eye contact, paralanguage, and body movement, people signal their conversational intentions.

Nonverbal regulators often vary from culture to culture; at times, they also vary from group to group when, although sharing the same language, these groups don't share the same ethnic identity. For example, we have found that Black and White North Americans differ in their listening behavior (LaFrance & Mayo, 1976). In both a laboratory study and a field study, we found in Blacks a reversal of the gaze pattern described by Kendon (1967) for White listeners. As you may recall from Chapter 10, the listening pattern usually followed by Whites is to gaze steadily at the speaker. Not so for Black Americans. During a conversation, Blacks don't look nearly as much when listening. It is important to note here that the differences we found related to *timing* and not to *amount*. In our study, Blacks and Whites did not differ in their overall amount of looking; they differed in their choice of when to look. Such results have been corroborated by Hall (1974), who reported that a familiar complaint among Whites is that working-class Blacks won't look them in the eye. This may be a clear instance of miscueing, because it appears from our work that it is not that Blacks don't look at the other when engaged in conversation but that they don't look when Whites expect them to.

Not surprisingly, these differences between Blacks and Whites can cause havoc in interracial classrooms. White children are taught to look directly at the teacher when being spoken to. Many Black children are instead socialized into *not* looking when spoken to. For the Black child, to look is a sign of disrespect (Byers & Byers, 1972). Erickson (1976) has noted comparable problems in interracial counseling situations. With White clients, eye contact is always necessary during active listening, while, with Black clients, eye contact is optional. Also, White listeners usually accompany "accented" head nods with verbal responses like "mhm." Black listeners, instead, show attention by either an unaccented head nod *or* a vocal back channel (such as "m-hm").

The distribution of pauses, too, seems to differ for Blacks and Whites. A recent study of children's story telling found that, while White speakers paused at the beginning of clauses or before conjunctions, Black speakers were found to pause whenever there was a significant change in pitch, sometimes in the middle of a clause (French & von Raffler Engel, 1973). Since the pausing occurred where Whites didn't expect it, the pauses were perceived by Whites as ungrammatical.

As this study shows, differences often prove troublesome. Nonverbal styles that are similar to those of one's own group are generally perceived as pleasing, while dissimilar styles tend to elicit less positive responses. A recent study, for example, found that White subjects were much more favorable toward a Black when she spoke standard English than when she spoke in a Black dialect (Bishop, 1976). Similarly, another study, focusing on interactions between junior-college counselors and students, found that, the more alike counselors and students were in terms of social identity and communication style, the more smoothly the interaction proceeded (Erickson, 1975a). One way of coping with communicational-style differences is to use the other's style. Subcultural groups learn to communicate with the dominant culture by code switching, and this includes being "binonverbal" as well as bilingual. For example, Cuban Americans engage in one conversational style when they speak Spanish and switch to another style when they converse in English (Gallois & Markel, 1975). In teaching North Americans to speak French, Wylie (Wylie & Stafford, 1977) has experimented with having students imitate French nonverbal behavior prior to learning the language. He believes that this system facilitates the initial learning and also results in better long-term mastery of the language.

It is clear that reactions to nonverbal differences are complex. When you meet a foreigner, you expect differences. If the foreigner is dressed in "native" garb, speaks accented English, and looks or acts in unfamiliar ways, your expectation is reinforced. Some rejoice that the world community contains such variability; others become impatient and critical.

We have suggested throughout this chapter that nonverbal differences can lead to breakdown and misunderstanding. But they don't have to. We can, in fact, reach one another, no matter how great the differences. But, to do so, we need to know a good deal more about these differences and what makes intercultural variability a path to celebration and what makes it instead a path to boundaries and isolation (McDermott & Gospodinoff, 1976).

Summary

Humans are many-layered beings. At the core, we are perhaps all alike. Some might take this to mean that we should therefore dispense with all the rest. But "all the rest" is the essential stuff of interaction; to understand and be understood, especially by a "foreigner," you need it all. If you assume that you've caught the essence of an apple by eating the innermost core, you are unlikely to know what an apple is really like, simply because you've missed the best part.

At the core we all feel and express happiness, sadness, anger, disgust, and many other emotions. But the aspects of the environment that elicit these reactions and the display rules that are operating to shape their expression are culturally defined. Moreover, in intercultural encounters, it is as important to know how an emotional expression is to be taken as to know what the emotion is.

All people interact differently with friends than with strangers. For example, they all stand closer to friends than to strangers. But the closest distances for some might still be too far away for others.

The wonder of watching people converse in an unfamiliar tongue is that they seem to be conversing in an unfamiliar body, too. Growing up in a particular culture, people learn gesture and motion along with words and grammar. Some of these emblematic gestures may be recognizable worldwide, but, even so, there are cultural rules about who should use them, with whom, and under what circumstances. In the intercultural context, to understand the report without the accompanying command may be a more serious problem than not to understand the report at all.

Misunderstandings also arise between the subgroups within a culture. When the language is the same, interactants are less able to recognize nonverbal differences and, when they do recognize them, are less willing to acknowledge their base in culture. Verbal and nonverbal code switching by members of subcultures permits communication with the dominant culture.

Chapter 14

Moving On to Conclusions

Rules

Contexts

Reports and Commands

By now, you've been hunched over your microscope looking at this thing called nonverbal communication for quite a while. And, at times, you may have felt that it was yourself that you were seeing through that lens. It's really quite an experience to see so much movement and hear so much sound coming out of that body of yours. Through that lens, you've also seen other people, some of whom you knew and some who were new to you. Your reaction was probably like our own—a sense of surprise that, from the nonverbal aspect as well, people are all so different and yet so much alike.

When you turn your microscope to high power, you're more likely to see the differences, because then you're focusing on details. When you use, instead, the low power, you get a broader view, and so you see the commonalities, like the rules of age, gender, and culture. At the high power, you observe the manners of moving and standing that are particular and unique to each individual. At the low power, you begin to see similarity; you recognize the behavior on that slide because you've seen it before. And, a little at a time, your sense of recognition begins to include the knowledge of what is to follow. When you both recognize something as familiar and know what is likely to happen next, you have learned quite a bit about the plans and programs of human interaction. In other words, you have learned that nonverbal behavior at one point in time is as much a response to what has just preceded it as it is one step in a sequence whose pattern, progression, and outcome you know.

Rules

To say that nonverbal behavior follows rules is not to deny its kaleidoscopic and individual nature. No rule determines every detail of nonverbal behavior; rules constrain behavior without, at the same time, removing all options. Some situations allow more choice than others, of course. But even those that offer the greatest choice are governed by rules. If they weren't, understanding of others would be impossible.

Just as a musical score does not determine every aspect of a performance, so, too, do the rules of nonverbal communication not dictate every move. Think, for example, of the same piece of music—say, Beethoven's Fifth—being played by the Boston Symphony and by a beginner tapping out the first few notes at the piano. It's the same piece, but hardly recognizable as such. However, knowing the piece helps you understand at least what the beginner is *trying* to do.

Individual variation in nonverbal behavior is also not just a matter of skill. Variation in performance can come from other factors as well (Duncan & Fiske, 1977). Some rules, such as those for greetings, are pretty clearly defined, whereas others, such as those for getting to know someone better, are quite loose. Variations can come, too, from violation of the rules. The degree to which interactants violate or move beyond the expected baselines tells you not only about the existence of the baselines but also about the person doing the violating. Such "out-of-bounds" behavior focuses attention on the individual and probably has some effect on the partner's opinion of the violator.

Contexts

Rules for nonverbal behavior are applied according to the situations in which they are appropriately used. In other words, the environment or context in which interaction is taking place suggests the rules for the occasion. This highlights an important feature of nonverbal behavior—namely, that the mere display of nonverbal behavior is less crucial than the issue of when, where, and in what context it occurs.

But context is not any one thing. Context includes the physical environment, the purpose of the interaction, and the relationships and social characteristics—such as age, sex, and culture—of those involved. These latter two features point to a critical element in the understanding of nonverbal communication; people in interaction become environments for one another. You constitute a significant aspect of the environment for those with whom you're interacting, as they do for you. This means that, if you want to comprehend your interactant's nonverbal behavior, you should ask not just what is going on within that person's skin but also what is going on between the two of you. Your capacity to monitor the environment, of which you are often a part, is an essential feature of your social effectiveness.

Monitoring is a continuous process. It is necessarily so because nonverbal behavior is dynamic and constantly changing. Messages are to be interpreted moment to moment. You receive some help with this swift-flowing task from the multichanneled nature of communication, which helps people get the socially important messages of what is happening and what is changing. The messages recur and overlap in an ongoing stream of interaction.

Reports and Commands

The very fact that the nature of communication is multichanneled warns you about the pitfalls of looking only at one channel or even taking one channel at a time. Each of the channels provides a minienvironment for the others. Taken out of context, each channel does not contain by itself enough information for you to know what is happening interpersonally. In other words, to guess correctly, you need to use the various channels to cross-reference your guesses. Nonverbal behavior is not just a source of commands for interpreting verbal behavior; nonverbal cues can serve as reports to which the verbal adds the command. For example, as described in Chapter 6, a stare can be a report for which the context or verbal accompaniment provides the command concerning how the stare should be taken. The notion that communication consists of a primary verbal mode to which other modes contribute only secondary or supplementary information must be abandoned. Communication is multichanneled; all the channels combine and interact to create meaningful messages.

You have seen the ubiquitous and powerful nature of nonverbal communication. Good, as well as ill, can come from it. You can nonverbally communicate warmth and involvement, but you can also send hostility and rejection. Overall, we hope you've learned that, in one way or another, you are responsible for *all your* communication.

References

Addington, D. W. The relationship of selected vocal characteristics to personality perception. *Speech Monographs,* 1968, *35,* 492–503.

Aiello, J. R., & Cooper, R. E. Use of personal space as a function of social affect. *Proceedings of the 80th Annual Convention of the American Psychological Association,* 1972, *7* (Pt. 1), 207–208.

Aiello, J. R., & Jones, S. E. Field study of the proxemic behavior of young school children in the three subcultural groups. *Journal of Personality and Social Psychology,* 1971, *19,* 351–356.

Albert, S., & Dabbs, J. M., Jr. Physical distance and persuasion. *Journal of Personality and Social Psychology,* 1970, *15,* 265–270.

Allingham, M. *Mystery mile.* Harmondsworth, England: Penguin Books, 1950.

Allport, G. W., & Vernon, P. E. *Studies in expressive movement.* New York: Macmillan, 1933.

Argyle, M. *Bodily communication.* New York: International Universities Press, 1975.

Argyle, M., Alkema, F., & Gilmour, R. The communication of friendly and hostile attitudes by verbal and non-verbal signals. *European Journal of Social Psychology,* 1972, *1,* 385–402.

Argyle, M., & Cook, M. *Gaze and mutual gaze.* Cambridge, England: Cambridge University Press, 1976.

Argyle, M., & Dean, J. Eye contact, distance, and affiliation. *Sociometry,* 1965, *28,* 289–304.

Argyle, M., & Ingham, R. Gaze, mutual gaze, and proximity. *Semiotica,* 1972, *6,* 32–49.

Argyle, M., & Kendon, A. The experimental analysis of social performance. In L. Berkowitz (Ed.), *Advances in experimental social psychology* (Vol. 3). New York: Academic Press, 1967.

Argyle, M., Lalljee, M., & Cook, M. The effects of visibility on interaction in a dyad. *Human Relations,* 1968, *21,* 3–17.

Aronovitch, C. D. The voice of personality: Stereotyped judgments and their relation to voice quality and sex of speaker. *Journal of Social Psychology,* 1976, *99,* 207–220.

Bakan, D. *The duality of human existence.* Chicago: Rand McNally, 1966.

Bakken, D. *Intimacy regulation in social encounters.* Manuscript submitted for publication, 1977.

Bakken, D. Saying goodbye: An observational study of parting rituals. *Man-Environment Systems,* 1977, *7,* 95–100.

Barash, D. P. Human ethology: Personal space reiterated. *Environment and Behavior,* 1973, *5,* 67–72.

Barefoot, J. C., Hoople, H., & McClay, D. Avoidance of an act which would violate personal space. *Psychonomic Science,* 1972, *28,* 205–206.

Barnlund, D. C. Communicative styles in two cultures: Japan and the United States. In A. Kendon, R. M. Harris, & M. R. Key (Eds.), *Organization of behavior in face-to-face interaction.* The Hague: Mouton, 1975.

Bates, J. E. Effects of children's nonverbal behavior upon adults. *Child Development,* 1976, *47,* 1079–1088.

Bateson, M. C. Mother-infant exchanges: The epigenesis of conversational interaction. *Annals of the New York Academy of Sciences,* 1975, *263,* 101–113.

Baxter, J. C. Interpersonal spacing in natural settings. *Sociometry,* 1970, *33,* 444–456.

Baxter, J. C., & Rozelle, R. M. Nonverbal expression as a function of crowding during a simulated police-citizen encounter. *Journal of Personality and Social Psychology,* 1975, *32,* 40–54.

Bell, C., Cheney, J., & Mayo, C. Structural and subject variation in communication networks. *Human Relations,* 1972, *25,* 1–8.

Bem, S. L. The measurement of psychological androgyny. *Journal of Consulting and Clinical Psychology,* 1974, *42,* 155–162.

Bem, S. L. Sex role adaptability: One consequence of psychological androgyny. *Journal of Personality and Social Psychology,* 1975, *31,* 634–643.

Bernard, J. *The sex game.* New York: Atheneum, 1968.

Birdwhistell, R. L. *Communication without words.* Unpublished manuscript, 1965.

Birdwhistell, R. L. Some body motion elements accompanying spoken American English. In L. Thayer (Ed.), *Communication: Concepts and perspectives.* Washington, D. C.: Spartan, 1967.

Birdwhistell, R. L. Communication as a multi-channel system. In the *International Encyclopedia of the Social Sciences* (Vol. 3). New York: Macmillan, 1968.

Birdwhistell, R. L. *Kinesics and context.* Philadelphia: University of Pennsylvania Press, 1970.

Bishop, G. D. *Effects of belief similarity and dialect style on interracial interaction.* Paper presented at the meeting of the American Psychological Association, Washington, D. C., September 1976.

Bloom, K. Social elicitation of infant vocal behavior. *Journal of Experimental Child Psychology,* 1975, *20,* 51–58.

Blurton Jones, N. G. An ethological study of some aspects of social behavior of children in nursery school. In D. Morris (Ed.), *Primate ethology.* London: Weidenfeld & Nicholson, 1967.

Boderman, A., Freed, D. W., & Kinnucan, M. J. Touch me, like me: Testing an encounter group assumption. *Journal of Applied Behavioral Science,* 1972, *8,* 527–533.

Bond, M. H., & Komai, H. Targets of gazing and eye contact during interviews: Effects on Japanese nonverbal behavior. *Journal of Personality and Social Psychology,* 1976, *34,* 1276–1284.

Boomer, D. S. Hesitation and grammatical encoding. *Language and Speech,* 1965, *8,* 148–158.

Boomer, D. S., & Dittman, A. T. Hesitation pauses and juncture pauses in speech. *Language and Speech,* 1962, *5,* 215–220.

Boucher, M. L. Effect of seating distance on interpersonal attraction in an interview situation. *Journal of Consulting and Clinical Psychology,* 1972, *38,* 15–19.

Brannigan, C. R., & Humphries, D. A. Human non-verbal behavior, a means of communication. In N. Blurton Jones (Ed.), *Ethological studies of child behavior.* London: Cambridge University Press, 1972.

Brault, G. J. Kinesics and the classroom: Some typical French gestures. *French Review*, 1962, *36*, 374–382.

Brazelton, T. B., Tronick, E., Adamson, L., Als, H., & Wise, S. Early mother-infant reciprocity in parent-infant interaction. *CIBA Foundation Symposium 33*. Amsterdam: Elsevier, 1975.

Breed, G. The effect of intimacy: Reciprocity or retreat? *British Journal of Clinical and Social Psychology*, 1972, *11*, 135–142.

Breed, G., & Ricci, J. S. "Touch me, like me": Artifact. *Proceedings of the 81st Annual Convention of the American Psychological Association*, 1973, *8*, 153–154.

Brend, R. M. Male-female differences in American English intonation. In B. Thorne & N. Henley (Eds.), *Language and sex: Difference and dominance*. Rowley, Mass.: Newbury House, 1975.

Bridges, K. Emotional development in early infancy. *Child Development*, 1932, *3*, 324–341.

Broen, P. A. The verbal environment of the language learning child. *American Speech and Hearing Monographs*, 1972, No. 17.

Broverman, I. K., Vogel, S. R., Broverman, D. M., Clarkson, F. E., & Rosenkrantz, P. S. Sex-role stereotypes: A current appraisal. *Journal of Social Issues*, 1972, *28*, 59–78.

Brown, R. *Social psychology*. Glencoe, Ill.: Free Press, 1965.

Brun, T. *International dictionary of sign language*. London: Wolfe, 1969.

Buck, R. Nonverbal communication of affect in children. *Journal of Personality and Social Psychology*, 1975, *31*, 644–653.

Buck, R. Nonverbal communication of affect in preschool children: Relationships with personality and skin conductance. *Journal of Personality and Social Psychology*, 1977, *35*, 225–236.

Buck, R., Miller, R. E., & Caul, W. F. Sex, personality and physiological variables in the communication of emotion via facial expression. *Journal of Personality and Social Psychology*, 1974, *30*, 587–596.

Buckhart, B. R. Apprehension about evaluation, paralanguage cues and the experimenter-bias effect. *Psychological Reports*, 1976, *39*, 15–23.

Bugental, D. E. Interpretations of naturally occurring discrepancies between words and intonation: Modes of inconsistency resolution. *Journal of Personality and Social Psychology*, 1974, *30*, 125–133.

Bugental, D. E., Henker, B., & Whalen, C. K. Attributional antecedents of verbal and vocal assertiveness. *Journal of Personality and Social Psychology*, 1976, *34*, 405–411.

Bugental, D. E., Kaswan, J. W., & Love, L. R. Perception of contradictory meanings conveyed by verbal and nonverbal channels. *Journal of Personality and Social Psychology*, 1970, *16*, 647–655.

Bugental, D. E., Kaswan, J. W., Love, L. R., & Fox, M. N. Child versus adult perception of evaluative messages in verbal, vocal, and visual channels. *Developmental Psychology*, 1970, *2*, 367–375.

Bugental, D. E., Love, L. R., & Gianetto, R. M. Perfidious feminine faces. *Journal of Personality and Social Psychology*, 1971, *17*, 314–318.

Buhler, C., & Hetzer, H. *Testing children's development from birth to school age*. New York: Farrar & Rinehart, 1935.

Byers, P., & Byers, H. Nonverbal communication and the education of children. In C. B. Cazden, V. P. John, & D. Hymes (Eds.), *Functions of language in the classroom*. New York: Teachers College Press, 1972.

Byrne, D., Ervin, C. R., & Lamberth, J. Continuity between the experimental study of attraction and real-life computer dating. *Journal of Personality and Social Psychology,* 1970, *16,* 157–165.

Chance, M. R. A. Attention structure as the basis of primate rank order. *Man,* 1967, *2,* 503–518.

Charney, E. J. Postural configurations in psychotherapy. *Psychosomatic Medicine,* 1966, *28,* 305–315.

Cheyne, J. A. Development of forms and functions of smiling in preschoolers. *Child Development,* 1976, *47,* 820–823.

Cohen, A. A., & Harrison, R. P. Intentionality in the use of hand illustrators in face-to-face communication situations. *Journal of Personality and Social Psychology,* 1973, *28,* 276–279.

Colby, C. Z., Lanzetta, J. T., & Kleck, R. E. *Effects of the expression of pain on autonomic and pain tolerance responses to subject controlled pain.* Paper presented at the meeting of the Eastern Psychological Association, Boston, April 1977.

Collett, P. On training Englishmen in the non-verbal behavior of Arabs: An experiment in inter-cultural communication. *International Journal of Psychology,* 1971, *6,* 209–215.

Collis, G. M., & Schaffer, H. R. Synchronization of visual attention in mother-infant pairs. *Journal of Child Psychology and Psychiatry,* 1975, *16,* 315–320.

Comer, R. J., & Piliavin, J. A. The effects of physical deviance upon face-to-face interaction: The other side. *Journal of Personality and Social Psychology,* 1972, *23,* 33–39.

Condon, J. C., & Yousef, F. *An introduction to intercultural communication.* New York: Bobbs-Merrill, 1975.

Condon, W. S., & Brosin, H. W. Microlinguistic-kinesic events in schizophrenic behavior. In D. V. Siva Sankar (Ed.), *Schizophrenia: Current concepts and research.* Hicksville, N. Y.: PJD Publications, 1969, pp. 812–837.

Condon, W. S., & Ogston, W. D. Sound film analysis of normal and pathological behavior patterns. *Journal of Nervous and Mental Disease,* 1966, *143,* 338–346.

Condon, W. S., & Ogston, W. D. A segmentation of behavior. *Journal of Psychiatric Research,* 1967, *5,* 221–235.

Condon, W. S., & Sander, L. W. Synchrony demonstrated between movements of the neonate and adult speech. *Child Development,* 1974, *45,* 456–462.

Condry, J., & Condry, S. Sex differences: A study for the eye of the beholder. *Child Development,* 1976, *47,* 812–819.

Cook, M. Anxiety, speech disturbances, and speech rate. *British Journal of Social and Clinical Psychology,* 1969, *8,* 13–21.

Cook, M. Experiments on orientation and proxemics. *Human Relations,* 1970, *23,* 61–76.

Dabbs, J. M., Jr. Similarity of gestures and interpersonal influence. *Proceedings of the 77th Annual Convention of the American Psychological Association,* 1969, *4,* 337–338.

Darwin, C. *The expression of the emotions in man and animals.* London: John Murray, 1872.

Dashiell, J. F. A new method of measuring reaction to facial expression of emotion. *Psychological Bulletin,* 1927, *24,* 174–175.

D'Augelli, A. R. Nonverbal behavior of helpers in initial helping interactions. *Journal of Counseling Psychology,* 1974, *21,* 360–363.

Davitz, J. R. *The communication of emotional meaning.* New York: McGraw-Hill, 1964.

Davitz, J. R., & Davitz, L. The communication of feelings by content-free speech. *Journal of Communication,* 1959, *9,* 6-13.

Dean, L. M., Willis, F. N., & Hewitt, J. Initial interaction distance among individuals equal and unequal in military rank. *Journal of Personality and Social Psychology,* 1975, *32,* 294-299.

De Lannoy, J. D., & Leyn, G. Body movements and sociometric status in male adolescents. *Psychologica Belgica,* 1973, *13,* 239-245.

De Long, A. Yielding the floor: The kinesic signals. *Journal of Communication,* 1977, *27,* 98-103.

Dibner, A. S. Ambiguity and anxiety. *Journal of Abnormal and Social Psychology,* 1958, *56,* 158-174.

Dimitrovsky, L. The ability to identify the emotional meaning of vocal expressions at successive age levels. In J. R. Davitz (Ed.), *The communication of emotional meaning.* New York: McGraw-Hill, 1964.

Dittmann, A. T. Kinesic research and therapeutic processes: Further discussion. In P. H. Knapp (Ed.), *Expression of the emotions in man.* New York: International Universities Press, 1963.

Dittmann, A. T. Review of *Kinesics and Context* by R. L. Birdwhistell. *Psychiatry,* 1971, *34,* 334-342.

Dittmann, A. T. *Interpersonal messages of emotion.* New York: Springer, 1972. (a)

Dittmann, A. T. Developmental factors in conversational behavior. *Journal of Communication,* 1972, *22,* 404-423. (b)

Dittmann, A. T., & Llewellyn, L. G. The phonemic clause as a unit of speech decoding. *Journal of Personality and Social Psychology,* 1967, *6,* 341-349.

Dittmann, A. T., & Llewellyn, L. G. Relationship between vocalizations and head nods as listener responses. *Journal of Personality and Social Psychology,* 1968, *9,* 79-84.

Dittmann, A. T., & Llewellyn, L. G. Body movement and speech rhythm in social conversation. *Journal of Personality and Social Psychology,* 1969, *11,* 98-106.

Dittmann, A. T., Parloff, M. B., & Boomer, D. S. Facial and bodily expression: A study of receptivity to emotional cues. *Psychiatry,* 1965, *28,* 239-244.

Dougherty, F. E., Bartlett, E. S., & Izard, C. E. Responses of schizophrenics to expressions of the fundamental emotions. *Journal of Clinical Psychology,* 1974, *30,* 243-246.

Duncan, S., Jr. Some signals and rules for taking speaking turns in conversations. *Journal of Personality and Social Psychology,* 1972, *23,* 283-292.

Duncan, S., Jr. Toward a grammar for dyadic conversation. *Semiotica,* 1973, *9,* 29-46.

Duncan, S., Jr., & Fiske, D. W. *Face-to-face interaction: Research, methods, and theory.* Hillsdale, N. J.: Lawrence Erlbaum Associates, 1977.

Duncan, S., Jr., Rice, L., & Butler, J. M. Therapists' paralanguage in peak and poor psychotherapy hours. *Journal of Abnormal Psychology,* 1968, *73,* 566-570.

Duncan, S., Jr., Rosenberg, M. J., & Finkelstein, J. The paralanguage of experimenter bias. *Sociometry,* 1969, *32,* 207-219.

Duncan, S., Jr., & Rosenthal, R. Vocal emphasis in experimenters' instruction reading as unintended determinant of subjects' responses. *Language and Speech,* 1968, *11,* 20-26.

Dusenbury, D., & Knower, F. H. Experimental studies of the symbolism of action and voice. 2: A study of the specificity of meaning in abstract tonal symbols. *Quarterly Journal of Speech,* 1939, *25,* 67-75.

Efran, M. G., & Cheyne, J. A. Affective concomitants of the invasion of shared space:

Behavioral, physiological, and verbal indicators. *Journal of Personality and Social Psychology,* 1974, *29,* 219–226.

Efron, D. *Gesture and environment.* New York: King's Crown, 1941. Republished as *Gesture, race and culture.* The Hague: Mouton, 1972.

Eibl-Eibesfeldt, I. Similarities and differences between cultures in expressive movements. In R. A. Hinde (Ed.), *Non-verbal communication.* London: Cambridge University Press, 1972.

Eibl-Eibesfeldt, I. *Love and hate: The natural history of behavior patterns.* New York: Schocken Books, 1974.

Ekman, P. The differential communication of affect by head and body cues. *Journal of Personality and Social Psychology,* 1965, *2,* 726–735.

Ekman, P. Universals and cultural differences in facial expressions of emotion. In J. K. Cole (Ed.), *Nebraska Symposium on Motivation* (Vol. 19). Lincoln: University of Nebraska Press, 1972.

Ekman, P. Movements with precise meanings. *Journal of Communication,* 1976, *26,* 14–26.

Ekman, P. Personal communication, April 21, 1977.

Ekman, P., & Friesen, W. V. Head and body cues in the judgment of emotion: A reformulation. *Conceptual and Motor Skills,* 1967, *24,* 711–724.

Ekman, P., & Friesen, W. V. Nonverbal behavior in psychotherapy research. In J. Shlien (Ed.), *Research in psychotherapy* (Vol. 3). Washington: American Psychological Association, 1968.

Ekman, P., & Friesen, W. V. Nonverbal leakage and clues to deception. *Psychiatry,* 1969, *32,* 88–106. (a)

Ekman, P., & Friesen, W. V. The repertoire of non-verbal behavior: Categories, origins, usage and coding. *Semiotica,* 1969, *1,* 1–20. (b)

Ekman, P., & Friesen, W. V. Hand movements. *Journal of Communication,* 1972, *22,* 353–374.

Ekman, P., & Friesen, W. V. Detecting deception from body or face. *Journal of Personality and Social Psychology,* 1974, *29,* 288–298.

Ekman, P., & Friesen, W. V. *Unmasking the face.* Englewood Cliffs, N. J.: Prentice-Hall, 1975.

Ekman, P., Friesen, W. V., & Ellsworth, P. C. *Emotion in the human face.* New York: Pergamon, 1972.

Ekman, P., Friesen, W. V., & Scherer, K. Body movements and voice pitch in deceptive interaction. *Semiotica,* 1977, in press.

Ellis, D. S. Speech and social status in America. *Social Forces,* 1967, *45,* 431–451.

Ellsworth, P. C. Direct gaze as a social stimulus. In P. Pliner, L. Krames, & T. Alloway (Eds.), *Nonverbal communication of aggression.* New York: Plenum, 1975.

Ellsworth, P. C., & Carlsmith, J. M. Effects of eye contact and verbal content on affective response to a dyadic interaction. *Journal of Personality and Social Psychology,* 1968, *10,* 15–20.

Ellsworth, P. C., & Carlsmith, J. M. Eye contact and gaze aversion in an aggressive encounter. *Journal of Personality and Social Psychology,* 1973, *28,* 280–292.

Ellsworth, P. C., Carlsmith, J. M., & Henson, A. The stare as a stimulus to flight in human subjects: A series of field experiments. *Journal of Personality and Social Psychology,* 1972, *21,* 302–311.

Ellsworth, P. C., & Langer, E. J. Staring and approach: An interpretation of the stare as a nonspecific activator. *Journal of Personality and Social Psychology,* 1976, *33,* 117–122.

Engebretson, D. E. Human territorial behavior: The role of interaction distance in therapeutic interventions. *American Journal of Orthopsychiatry,* 1973, *43,* 108–116.

Engebretson, D. E., & Fullmer, D. Cross-cultural differences in territoriality: Interaction distances of native Japanese, Hawaii Japanese, and American Caucasians. *Journal of Cross-Cultural Psychology,* 1970, *1,* 261–269.

Erickson, F. Gatekeeping and the melting pot. *Harvard Educational Review,* 1975, *45,* 44–70. (a)

Erickson, F. One function of proxemic shifts in face-to-face interaction. In A. Kendon, R. Harris, & M. R. Key (Eds.), *Organization of behavior in face-to-face interaction.* The Hague: Mouton, 1975. (b)

Erickson, F. *Talking down and giving reasons: Hyper-explanation and listening behavior in inter-racial interviews.* Paper presented at the International Conference on Non-Verbal Behavior, Ontario Institute for Studies in Education, Toronto, Canada, May 1976.

Evans, G. W., & Howard, R. B. Personal space. *Psychological Bulletin,* 1973, *80,* 334–344.

Exline, R. V. Explorations in the process of person perception: Visual interaction in relation to competition, sex, and need for affiliation. *Journal of Personality,* 1963, *31,* 1–20.

Exline, R. V. Visual interaction: The glances of power and preference. In J. K. Cole (Ed.), *Nebraska Symposium on Motivation* (Vol. 19). Lincoln: University of Nebraska Press, 1972.

Exline, R. V., Ellyson, S. L., & Long, B. Visual behavior as an aspect of power role relationships. In P. Pliner, L. Krames, & T. Alloway (Eds.), *Nonverbal communication of aggression* (Vol. 2). New York: Plenum, 1975.

Exline, R. V., Gray, D., & Schuette, D. Visual behavior in a dyad as affected by interview content and sex of respondent. *Journal of Personality and Social Psychology,* 1965, *1,* 201–209.

Exline, R. V., & Messick, D. The effects of dependency and social reinforcement upon visual behavior during an interview. *British Journal of Social and Clinical Psychology,* 1967, *6,* 256–266.

Exline, R. V., & Winters, L. C. Affective relations and mutual glances in dyads. In S. S. Tomkins & C. W. Izard (Eds.), *Affect, cognition and personality.* New York: Springer, 1965.

Fairbanks, G., & Pronovost, W. An experimental study of the durational characteristics of the voice during the expression of emotion. *Speech Monographs,* 1939, *6,* 87–104.

Fanselow, M. S. *The effectiveness of positively and negatively affective non-verbal behavior in biasing eyewitness identification testing.* Paper presented at the meeting of the Eastern Psychological Association, New York, April 1976.

Fein, G. G. Children's sensitivity to social contexts at 18 months of age. *Developmental Psychology,* 1975, *11,* 853–854.

Felipe, N. J., & Sommer, R. Invasions of personal space. *Social Problems,* 1966, *14,* 206–214.

Fenster, A., & Goldstein, A. M. The emotional world of children vis-à-vis the emotional world of adults: An examination of vocal communication. *Journal of Communication,* 1971, *21,* 353–362.

Fisher, J. D., & Byrne, D. Too close for comfort: Sex differences in response to invasions of personal space. *Journal of Personality and Social Psychology,* 1975, *32,* 15–21.

Fisher, J. D., Rytting, M., & Heslin, R. Hands touching hands: Affective and evaluative effects of an interpersonal touch. *Sociometry,* 1976, *39,* 416–421.

Forston, R. F., & Larson, C. U. The dynamics of space: An experimental study of proxemic behavior among Latin Americans and North Americans. *Journal of Communication,* 1968, *18,* 109–116.

Frank, L. K. Tactile communication. *Genetic Psychology Monographs,* 1957, *56,* 204–255.

Freedman, J. L., Levey, A. S., Buchanan, R. W., & Price, J. Crowding and human aggressiveness. *Journal of Experimental Social Psychology,* 1972, *8,* 528–548.

Freedman, N., Blass, T., Rifkin, A., & Quitkin, F. Body movements and the verbal encoding of aggressive affect. *Journal of Personality and Social Psychology,* 1973, *26,* 72–85.

Freedman, N., O'Hanlon, J., Oltman, P., & Witkin, H. A. The imprint of psychological differentiation on kinetic behavior in varying communicative contexts. *Journal of Abnormal Psychology,* 1972, *79,* 239–258.

French, P., & von Raffler Engel, W. *The kinesics of bilingualism.* Unpublished manuscript, Vanderbilt University, 1973.

Freud, S. [*Fragment of an analysis of a case of hysteria*] (Joan Riviere, trans.). In *Collected Papers* (Vol. 3). New York: Basic Books, 1959. (Originally published, 1905.)

Fries, C. C. *The structure of English.* New York: Harcourt Brace, 1952.

Fromm-Reichman, F. *Psychoanalysis and psychotherapy.* Chicago: University of Chicago Press, 1950.

Fromme, D. K., & Beam, D. C. Dominance and sex differences in nonverbal responses to differential eye contact. *Journal of Research in Personality,* 1974, *8,* 76–87.

Fromme, D. K., & Schmidt, D. K. Affective role enactment and expressive behavior. *Journal of Personality and Social Psychology,* 1972, *24,* 413–419.

Fry, A. M., & Willis, F. N. Invasion of personal space as a function of the age of the invader. *Psychological Record,* 1971, *21,* 385–389.

Gallois, C., & Markel, N. M. Turn taking: Social personality and conversational style. *Journal of Personality and Social Psychology,* 1975, *31,* 1134–1140.

Galloway, C. M. *Teaching and non-verbal behavior.* Paper presented at the International Conference on Non-Verbal Behavior, Ontario Institute for Studies in Education, Toronto, Canada, May 1976.

Gardin, H., Kaplan, K. J., Firestone, I. J., & Cowan, G. A. Proxemic effects on cooperation, attitude, and approval-avoidance in a Prisoner's Dilemma game. *Journal of Personality and Social Psychology,* 1973, *27,* 13–18.

Gates, G. S. An experimental study of the growth of social perception. *Journal of Educational Psychology,* 1923, *14,* 449–461.

Giles, H. Communicative effectiveness as a function of accented speech. *Speech Monographs,* 1973, *40,* 330–331.

Ginsburg, H. J., Wauson, M. S., & Easley, M. *Omega children: A study of lowest ranking members of the children's play group hierarchy.* Paper presented at the meeting of the Society for Research in Child Development, New Orleans, March 1977.

Goffman, E. *The presentation of self in everyday life.* New York: Anchor Books, 1959.

Goffman, E. *Encounters.* Indianapolis: Bobbs-Merrill, 1961.

Goffman, E. *Stigma: Notes on the management of spoiled identity.* Englewood Cliffs, N. J.: Prentice-Hall, 1963.

Goffman, E. Discussion. In T. A. Sebeok, A. S. Hayes, & M. C. Bateson (Eds.), *Approaches to semiotics.* The Hague: Mouton, 1964.

Goffman, E. *Interaction ritual*. Garden City, N. Y.: Anchor, 1967.

Goffman, E. *Relations in public*. New York: Basic Books, 1971.

Goldberg, G. N., Kiesler, C. A., & Collins, B. E. Visual behavior and face-to-face distance during interaction. *Sociometry*, 1969, *32*, 43–53.

Goldberg, S., & Lewis, M. Play behavior in the year-old infant: Early sex differences. *Child Development*, 1969, *40*, 21–31.

Goldman-Eisler, F. A comparative study of two hesitation phenomena. *Language and Speech*, 1961, *4*, 18–26.

Goldman-Eisler, F. *Psycholinguistics: Experiments in spontaneous speech*. New York: Academic Press, 1968.

Grady, K. E., Miransky, L. J., & Mulvey, M. A. *A nonverbal measure of dominance*. Paper presented at the meeting of the American Psychological Association, Washington, D. C., August 1976.

Graham, J. A., & Heywood, S. The effects of elimination of hand gestures and of verbal codability on speech performance. *European Journal of Social Psychology*, 1975, *5*, 189–195.

Grant, E. C. Human facial expression. *Man*, 1969, *4*, 177–184.

Grant, E. C. Facial expressions and gesture. *Journal of Psychosomatic Research*, 1971, *15*, 391–394.

Graves, J. R., & Robinson, J. D., II. Proxemic behavior as a function of inconsistent verbal and nonverbal messages. *Journal of Counseling Psychology*, 1976, *23*, 333–338.

Greene, L. R. Effects of field dependence on affective reactions and compliance in dyadic interactions. *Journal of Personality and Social Psychology*, 1976, *34*, 569–577.

Guardo, C. J. Personal space in children. *Child Development*, 1969, *40*, 143–151.

Guardo, C. J. Personal space, sex differences, and interpersonal attraction. *Journal of Psychology*, 1976, *92*, 9–14.

Guardo, C. J., & Meisels, M. Child-parent spacial patterns under praise and reproof. *Developmental Psychology*, 1971, *2*, 365.

Haggard, E. A., & Isaacs, K. S. Micro-momentary facial expressions as indicators of ego mechanisms in psychotherapy. In L. A. Gottschalk & A. H. Auerbach (Eds.), *Methods of research in psychotherapy*. New York: Appleton-Century-Crofts, 1966.

Hall, E. T. *The silent language*. Garden City, N.Y.: Doubleday, 1959.

Hall, E. T. *The hidden dimension*. Garden City, N. Y.: Doubleday, 1966.

Hall, E. T. *Handbook for proxemic research*. Washington, D. C.: Society for the Anthropology of Visual Communication, 1974.

Hamelian, L. Communication by gesture in the Middle East. *ETC: A Review of General Semantics*, 1965, *22*, 43–49.

Hamilton, M. L. Imitation of facial expression of emotion. *Journal of Psychology*, 1972, *80*, 345–350.

Hamilton, M. L. Imitative behavior and expressive ability in facial expression of emotion. *Developmental Psychology*, 1973, *8*, 138.

Hare, A., & Bales, R. Seating position and small group interaction. *Sociometry*, 1963, *26*, 480–486.

Hargreaves, W. A., Starkweather, J. A., & Blacker, K. H. Voice quality in depression. *Journal of Abnormal and Social Psychology*, 1965, *70*, 218–220.

Harms, L. S. Listener judgments of status cues in speech. *Quarterly Journal of Speech*, 1961, *47*, 164–168.

Harrison, R. P. *Beyond words: An introduction to nonverbal communication*. Englewood Cliffs, N.J.: Prentice-Hall, 1974.

Harter, S., Schultz, T. R., & Blum, B. Smiling in children as a function of their sense of mastery. *Journal of Experimental Child Psychology*, 1971, *12*, 396–404.

Hartnett, J. J., Bailey, K. G., & Gibson, F. W., Jr. Personal space as influenced by sex and type of movement. *Journal of Psychology*, 1970, *76*, 139–144.

Hastorf, A. H., Schneider, D. J., & Polefka, J. *Person perception*. Reading, Mass.: Addison-Wesley, 1970.

Haviland, J. M. *Sex-related pragmatics in infants' nonverbal communication*. Paper presented at the meeting of the Eastern Psychological Association, New York, April 1976.

Hearn, G. Leadership and the spatial factor in small groups. *Journal of Abnormal and Social Psychology*, 1957, *54*, 269–272.

Heckel, R. V. Leadership and voluntary seating choice. *Psychological Reports*, 1973, *32*, 141–142.

Henderson, A., Goldman-Eisler, F., & Starbek, A. Temporal patterns of cognitive activity and breath control in speech. *Language and Speech*, 1965, *8*, 236–242.

Henley, N. M. Status and sex: Some touching observations. *Bulletin of the Psychonomic Society*, 1973, *2*, 91–93.

Henley, N. M. *Body politics: Power, sex, and nonverbal communication*. Englewood Cliffs, N. J.: Prentice-Hall, 1977.

Heshka, S., & Nelson, Y. Interpersonal speaking distance as a function of age, sex, and relationship. *Sociometry*, 1972, *35*, 491–498.

Heslin, R., & Boss, D. *Nonverbal intimacy in arrival and departure at an airport*. Unpublished manuscript, 1976. (Available from Richard Heslin, Department of Psychological Sciences, Purdue University, West Lafayette, Ind. 47907.)

Hess, E. H. *The tell-tale eye*. New York: Van Nostrand Reinhold, 1975.

Hinchcliffe, M. K., Lancashire, M., & Roberts, F. J. A study of eye contact changes in depressed and recovered psychiatric patients. *British Journal of Psychiatry*, 1971, *119*, 213–215.

Hinde, R. A. On describing relationships. *Journal of Child Psychology and Psychiatry*, 1976, *17*, 1–19.

Hoggart, R. *On culture and communication*. New York: Oxford University Press, 1972.

Holahan, C. Seating patterns and patient behavior in an experimental dayroom. *Journal of Abnormal Psychology*, 1972, *80*, 115–124.

Horowitz, M. J. Spatial behavior and psychopathology. *Journal of Nervous and Mental Disease*, 1968, *146*, 24–35.

Hutt, C., & Ounsted, C. The biological significance of gaze aversion with particular reference to the syndrome of infantile autism. *Behavioral Science*, 1966, *11*, 346–356.

Hymes, D. H. The ethnography of speaking. In T. Gladwin & W. C. Sturtevent (Eds.), *Anthropology and human behavior*. Washington, D. C.: Anthropological Society of Washington, 1962.

Izard, C. E. The emotions and emotion constructs in personality and culture research. In R. B. Cattell (Ed.), *Handbook of modern personality theory*. Chicago: Aldine, 1969.

Izard, C. E. Patterns of emotions and emotion communication in "hostility" and aggression. In P. Pliner, L. Krames, & T. Alloway (Eds.), *Nonverbal communication of aggression* (Vol. 2). New York: Plenum, 1975.

Jaffe, J. Computer analysis of verbal behavior in psychiatric interviews. In D. Rioch

(Ed.), *Disorders in communication: Proceedings of the Association for Research in Nervous and Mental Diseases* (Vol. 42). Baltimore: Williams & Wilkins, 1967.

Jakobson, R. Motor signs for "yes" and "no." *Language in Society,* 1972, *1,* 91–96.

Janis, I. *Groupthink.* Boston: Houghton-Mifflin, 1972.

Jenni, D. A., & Jenni, M. A. Carrying behavior in humans: Analysis of sex differences. *Science,* 1976, *194,* 859–860.

Johnson, H. G., Ekman, P., & Friesen, W. V. Communicative body movements: American emblems. *Semiotica,* 1975, *15,* 335–353.

Jorgenson, D. O. Field study of the relationship between status discrepancy and proxemic behavior. *Journal of Social Psychology,* 1975, *97,* 173–179.

Jourard, S. M. *The transparent self.* Princeton, N. J.: Van Nostrand, 1964.

Jourard, S. M. An exploratory study of body-accessibility. *British Journal of Social and Clinical Psychology,* 1966, *5,* 221–231.

Jourard, S. M., & Friedman, R. Experimenter-subject "distance" and self-disclosure. *Journal of Personality and Social Psychology,* 1970, *15,* 278–282.

Jourard, S. M., & Rubin, J. E. Self-disclosure and touching: A study of two modes of interpersonal encounter and their inter-relations. *Journal of Humanistic Psychology,* 1968, *8,* 39–48.

Kasl, S. V., & Mahl, G. F. The relationship of disturbances and hesitations in spontaneous speech to anxiety. *Journal of Personality and Social Psychology,* 1965 *1,* 425–433.

Kazdin, A. E., & Klock, J. The effect of nonverbal teacher approval on student attentive behavior. *Journal of Applied Behavioral Analysis,* 1973, *6,* 643–654.

Kelly, F. D. Communicational significance of therapist proxemic cues. *Journal of Consulting and Clinical Psychology,* 1972, *39,* 345.

Kendon, A. Some functions of gaze-direction in social interaction. *Acta Psychologica,* 1967, *26,* 22–63.

Kendon, A. Movement coordination in social interaction. Some examples described. *Acta Psychologica,* 1970, *32,* 101–125. (a)

Kendon, A. Some relationships between body motion and speech: An analysis of an example. In A. Siegman & B. Pope (Eds.), *Studies in dyadic communication.* New York: Pergamon, 1970. (b)

Kendon, A. Introduction. In A. Kendon, R. M. Harris, & M. R. Key (Eds.), *Organization of behavior in face-to-face interaction.* The Hague: Mouton, 1975.

Kendon, A. The F-formation system: The spatial organization of social encounters. *Man-Environment Systems,* 1976, *6,* 291–296.

Kendon, A., & Cook, M. The consistency of gaze patterns in social interaction. *British Journal of Psychology,* 1969, *69,* 481–494.

Kendon, A., & Ferber, A. A description of some human greetings. In R. P. Michael & J. H. Crook (Eds.), *Comparative ecology and behavior of primates.* New York: Academic Press, 1973.

Kidd, R. F. Pupil size, eye contact, and instrumental aggression. *Perceptual and Motor Skills,* 1975, *41,* 538.

Kimura, D. Manual activity during speaking. 1: Right-handers. *Neuropsychologia,* 1973, *11,* 45–50.

King, M. G. Interpersonal relations in preschool children and average approach distance. *Journal of Genetic Psychology,* 1966, *109,* 109–116.

Kleck, R. E., Buck, P. L., Goller, W. L., London, R. S., Pfeiffer, J. R., & Vukcevic, D. P. Effect of stigmatizing conditions on the use of personal space. *Psychological*

Reports, 1968, *23,* 111-118.

Kleck, R. E., Vaughan, R. C., Cartwright-Smith, J., Vaughan, K. B., Colby, C. Z., & Lanzetta, J. T. Effects of being observed on expressive, subjective, and physiological responses to painful stimuli. *Journal of Personality and Social Psychology,* 1976, *34,* 1211-1218.

Kleinfeld, J. S. Effects of nonverbally communicated personal warmth on the intelligence test performance of Indian and Eskimo adolescents. *Journal of Social Psychology,* 1973, *91,* 149-150.

Kleinke, C. L., Bustos, A. A., Meeker, F. B., & Staneski, R. A. Effects of self-attributed and other attributed gaze on interpersonal evaluations between males and females. *Journal of Experimental Social Psychology,* 1973, *9,* 154-163.

Kleinke, C. L., Meeker, F. B., & La Fong, C. Effects of gaze, touch, and use of name on evaluation of "engaged" couples. *Journal of Research in Personality,* 1974, *7,* 368-373.

Knapp, M. L., Hart, R. P., & Dennis, H. S. An exploration of deception as a communication construct. *Human Communication Research,* 1974, *1,* 15-29.

Knapp, M. L., Hart, R. P., Friedrich, G. W., & Shulman, G. M. The rhetoric of goodbye: Verbal and nonverbal correlates of human leave taking. *Speech Monographs,* 1973, *40,* 182-198.

Knowles, E. S. Boundaries around group interaction: The effect of group size and member status on boundary permeability. *Journal of Personality and Social Psychology,* 1973, *26,* 327-331.

Konstadt, N., & Forman, E. Field dependence and external directedness. *Journal of Personality and Social Psychology,* 1965, *1,* 490-493.

Kowal, S., O'Connell, D. C., & Sabin, E. J. Development of temporal patterning and vocal hesitations in spontaneous narratives. *Journal of Psycholinguistic Research,* 1975, *4,* 195-207.

Kramer, E. The judgment of personal characteristics and emotions from nonverbal properties of speech. *Psychological Bulletin,* 1963, *60,* 408-420.

Kramer, E. Personality stereotypes in voice: A reconsideration of the data. *Journal of Social Psychology,* 1964, *62,* 247-251.

Krause, M. S., & Pilisuk, M. Anxiety in verbal behavior: A validation study. *Journal of Consulting Psychology,* 1961, *25,* 414-419.

Krauss, R. M., Geller, V., & Olson, C. *Modalities and cues in the detection of deception.* Paper presented at the meeting of the American Psychological Association, Washington, D. C., September 1976.

Krout, M. H. The social and psychological significance of gestures: A differential analysis. *Journal of Genetic Psychology,* 1935, *47,* 385-412.

Krout, M. H. An experimental attempt to determine the significance of unconscious manual symbolic movements. *Journal of General Psychology,* 1954, *51,* 121-152.

Laban, R. *Principles of dance and movement notation.* London: Macdonald & Evans, 1956.

LaFrance, M., & Broadbent, M. Group rapport: Posture sharing as a nonverbal indicator. *Group and Organizational Studies,* 1976, *1,* 328-333.

LaFrance, M., & Broadbent, M. *Nonverbal synchrony and rapport: Analysis by the cross-lag panel technique.* Paper presented at the meeting of the American Psychological Association, San Francisco, August 1977.

LaFrance, M., & Mayo, C. Racial differences in gaze behavior during conversation. *Journal of Personality and Social Psychology,* 1976, *33,* 547-552.

Laird, J. D. Self-attribution of emotion: The effects of expressive behavior on the quality of emotional experience. *Journal of Personality and Social Psychology,* 1974, *29,* 475–486.

Lakoff, R. Language and woman's place. *Language in Society,* 1973, *2,* 45–79.

Lalljee, M., & Cook, M. Uncertainty in first encounters. *Journal of Personality and Social Psychology,* 1973, *26,* 137–141.

Lamb, M. E. *Infants, fathers, and mothers: Interaction at 8 months of age in the home and in the laboratory.* Paper presented at the meeting of the Eastern Psychological Association, New York, April 1975.

Lamb, W. *Posture and gesture: An introduction to the study of physical behavior.* London: Gerald Duckworth, 1965.

Langer, E. J., Fiske, S., Taylor, S. E., & Chanowitz, B. Stigma, staring, and discomfort: A novel-stimulus hypothesis. *Journal of Experimental Social Psychology,* 1976, *12,* 451–463.

Lassen, C. L. Effect of proximity on anxiety and communication in the initial psychiatric interview. *Journal of Abnormal Psychology,* 1973, *81,* 226–232.

Laver, J. Communicative functions of phatic communication. In A. Kendon, R. Harris, & M. R. Key (Eds.), *Organization of behavior in face-to-face interaction.* The Hague: Mouton, 1975.

Lefcourt, H. M., Rotenberg, F., Buckspan, B., & Steffy, R. A. Visual interaction and performance of process and reactive schizophrenics as a function of examiner's sex. *Journal of Personality,* 1967, *35,* 535–546.

Lefebvre, L. Encoding and decoding of ingratiation in modes of smiling and gaze. *British Journal of Social and Clinical Psychology,* 1975, *14,* 33–42.

Levin, H., Silverman, I., & Ford, B. L. Hesitations in children's speech during explanation and description. *Learning and Verbal Behavior,* 1967, *6,* 560–564.

Lewin, K. *Field theory in social science: Selected theoretical papers.* Edited by D. Cartwright. New York: Harper, 1951.

Lewis, D. K. *Convention.* Cambridge, Mass.: Harvard University Press, 1969.

Lewis, M. M. *Infant speech: A study of the beginnings of language.* New York: Harcourt Brace, 1936.

Libby, W. L., Jr., & Yaklevich, D. Personality determinants of eye contact and direction of gaze aversion. *Journal of Personality and Social Psychology,* 1973, *27,* 197–206.

Lieberman, P. *Intonation, perception and language.* Cambridge, Mass.: M.I.T. Press, 1966.

Ling, D., & Ling, A. H. Communication development in the first three years of life. *Journal of Speech and Hearing Research,* 1974, *17,* 146–159.

Lippa, R. The naive perception of masculinity-femininity on the basis of expressive cues. *Journal of Research in Personality,* in press.

Little, K. B. Cultural variations in social schemata. *Journal of Personality and Social Psychology,* 1968, *10,* 1–7.

Lomranz, J. Cultural variations in personal space. *Journal of Social Psychology,* 1976, *99,* 21–27.

Lomranz, J., & Shapira, A. Communicative patterns of self disclosure and touching behavior. *Journal of Psychology,* 1974, *88,* 223–227.

Lott, D. F., & Sommer, R. Seating arrangements and status. *Journal of Personality and Social Psychology,* 1967, *7,* 90–94.

Maccoby, E., & Jacklin, C. *The psychology of sex differences.* Stanford, Calif.: Stanford University Press, 1974.

Mackey, W. C. Parameters of the smile as a social signal. *Journal of Genetic Psychology*, 1976, *129*, 125–130.

Mahl, G. F. Some clinical observations on nonverbal behavior in interviews. *The Journal of Nervous and Mental Disease*, 1967, *144*, 492–505.

Malinowski, B. *A scientific theory of culture.* Chapel Hill: University of North Carolina Press, 1944.

Markel, N. N. Relationship between voice-quality profiles and MMPI profiles in psychiatric patients. *Journal of Abnormal Psychology*, 1969, *74*, 61–66.

Markel, N. N., Long, J. F., & Saine, T. J. Sex effects in conversational interaction: Another look at male dominance. *Human Communication Research*, 1976, *2*, 356–364.

Markel, N. N., Meisels, M., & Houck, J. E. Judging personality from voice quality. *Journal of Abnormal and Social Psychology*, 1964, *69*, 458–463.

Marsh, N. *Enter a murderer.* New York: Berkeley, 1963.

Matarazzo, J. D., Weitman, M., Saslow, G., & Wiens, A. N. Interviewer influence on duration of interviewee speech. *Journal of Verbal Learning and Verbal Behavior*, 1963, *1*, 451–458.

McClintock, C. C., & Hunt, R. C. Nonverbal indicators of affect and deception in an interview setting. *Journal of Applied Social Psychology*, 1975, *5*, 54–67.

McDermott, R. P., & Gospodinoff, K. *Social contexts for ethnic borders and school failure: A communicative analysis.* Paper presented at the International Conference on Non-Verbal Behavior, Ontario Institute for Studies in Education, Toronto, Canada, May 1976.

McGinley, H., LeFevre, R., & McGinley, P. The influence of a communicator's body position on opinion change in others. *Journal of Personality and Social Psychology*, 1975, *31*, 686–690.

McGrew, P. L., & McGrew, W. C. Changes in children's spacing behavior with nursery school experience. *Human Development*, 1972, *15*, 359–372.

McGrew, P. L., & McGrew, W. C. Interpersonal spacing behavior in preschool children during group formation. *Man-Environment Systems*, 1975, *5*, 43–48.

Mehrabian, A. Inference of attitude from the posture, orientation, and distance of a communicator. *Journal of Consulting and Clinical Psychology*, 1968, *32*, 296–308. (a)

Mehrabian, A. Relationship of attitude to seated posture, orientation, and distance. *Journal of Personality and Social Psychology*, 1968, *10*, 26–30. (b)

Mehrabian, A. Significance of posture and position in the communication of attitude and status relationships. *Psychological Bulletin*, 1969, *71*, 359–372.

Mehrabian, A. When are feelings communicated inconsistently? *Journal of Experimental Research in Personality*, 1970, *4*, 198–212.

Mehrabian, A. Nonverbal betrayal of feeling. *Journal of Experimental Research in Personality*, 1971, *5*, 64–73. (a)

Mehrabian, A. Verbal and nonverbal interaction of strangers in a waiting situation. *Journal of Experimental Research in Personality*, 1971, *5*, 127–138. (b)

Mehrabian, A. *Nonverbal communication.* Chicago: Aldine-Atherton, 1972.

Mehrabian, A., & Diamond, S. G. Effects of furniture arrangements, props, and personality on social interaction. *Journal of Personality and Social Psychology*, 1971, *20*, 18–30.

Mehrabian, A., & Ferris, S. R. Inference of attitudes from nonverbal communication in two channels. *Journal of Consulting Psychology*, 1967, *31*, 248–252.

Mehrabian, A., & Wiener, M. Decoding of inconsistent communications. *Journal of*

Personality and Social Psychology, 1967, *6,* 109–114.

Mehrabian, A., & Williams, M. Nonverbal concomitants of perceived and intended persuasiveness. *Journal of Personality and Social Psychology,* 1969, *13,* 37–58.

Meisels, M., & Canter, F. M. Personal space and personality characteristics: A non-confirmation. *Psychological Reports,* 1970, *27,* 287–290.

Meisels, M., & Guardo, C. J. Development of personal space schemata. *Child Development,* 1969, *40,* 1167–1178.

Middlemist, R. D., Knowles, E.S., & Matter, C. F. Personal space invasions in the lavatory: Suggestive evidence for arousal. *Journal of Personality and Social Psychology,* 1976, *33,* 541–546.

Miller, N., Maruyama, G., Beaber, R. J., & Valone, K. Speed of speech and persuasion. *Journal of Personality and Social Psychology,* 1976, *34,* 615–624.

Mishler, E. G., & Waxler, N. E. Functions of hesitations in the speech of normal families and families of schizophrenic patients. *Language and Speech,* 1970, *13,* 102–117.

Mobbs, N. A. Eye contact in relation to social introversion-extraversion. *British Journal of Social and Clinical Psychology,* 1968, *7,* 305–306.

Montagu, A. *Touching: The human significance of the skin.* New York: Columbia University Press, 1971.

Morley, I. E., & Stephenson, G. M. Interpersonal and interparty exchange: A laboratory simulation of an industrial negotiation at the plant level. *British Journal of Psychology,* 1969, *60,* 543–545.

Morsbach, H. Aspects of nonverbal communication in Japan. *Journal of Nervous and Mental Disease,* 1973, *157,* 262–277.

Mueller, E., & Lucas, T. A developmental analysis of peer interaction among toddlers. In M. Lewis & L. A. Rosenblum (Eds.), *Friendship and peer relations.* New York: Wiley, 1975.

Mueller, E., & Rich, A. Clustering and socially directed behavior in a playgroup of one-year-olds. *Journal of Child Psychology and Psychiatry,* 1976, *17,* 315–322.

Nash, H. Perception of vocal expression of emotion by hospital staff and patients. *Genetic Psychology Monographs,* 1974, *89,* 25–87.

Natale, M. Convergence of mean vocal intensity in dyadic communication as a function of social desirability. *Journal of Personality and Social Psychology,* 1975, *32,* 790–804.

Nesbitt, P. D., & Steven, G. Personal space and stimulus intensity at a Southern California amusement park. *Sociometry,* 1974, *37,* 105–115.

Nevill, D. Experimental manipulation of dependency motivation and its effects on eye contact and measures of field dependency. *Journal of Personality and Social Psychology,* 1974, *29,* 72–79.

Newman, S. S., & Mather, V. G. Analyses of spoken language of patients with affective disorders. *American Journal of Psychiatry,* 1938, *94,* 913–942.

Newtson, D. Foundations of attribution: The perception of ongoing behavior. In J. Harvey, W. Ickes, & R. Kidd (Eds.), *New directions in attribution research.* Hillsdale, N.J.: Lawrence Erlbaum Associates, 1976.

Nguyen, T., Heslin, R., & Nguyen, M. The meanings of touch: Sex differences. *Journal of Communication,* 1975, *25,* 92–103.

Nielsen, G. *Studies in self confrontation.* Copenhagen: Munksgaard, 1964.

Norum, G. A., Russo, N. J., & Sommer, R. Seating patterns and group task. *Psychology in the Schools,* 1967, *4,* 276–280.

Odom, R. D., & Lemond, C. M. Developmental differences in the perception and production of facial expressions. *Child Development,* 1972, *43,* 359-369.

Osmond, H. Function as the basis of psychiatric ward design. *Mental Hospitals,* 1957, *8,* 23-30.

Patterson, M. L. Compensation in nonverbal immediacy behaviors: A review. *Sociometry,* 1973, *36,* 237-252.

Patterson, M. L. An arousal model of interpersonal intimacy. *Psychological Review,* 1976, *83,* 235-245.

Patterson, M. L., & Sechrest, L. B. Interpersonal distance and impression formation. *Journal of Personality,* 1970, *38,* 161-166.

Pattison, J. E. Effects of touch on self-exploration and the therapeutic relationship. *Journal of Consulting and Clinical Psychology,* 1973, *40,* 170-175.

Peery, J. C., & Stern, D. N. Mother-infant gazing during play, bottle feeding, and spoon feeding. *Journal of Psychology,* 1975, *91,* 207-213.

Pellegrini, R. J., & Empey, J. Interpersonal spatial orientation in dyads. *Journal of Psychology,* 1970, *76,* 67-70.

Peterson, C. L., Danner, F. W., & Flavell, J. H. Developmental changes in children's response to three indications of communicative failure. *Child Development,* 1972, *43,* 1463-1468.

Piaget, J. *The origins of intelligence in children.* New York: Norton, 1963.

Pleck, J. H., & Sawyer, J. (Eds.). *Men and masculinity.* Englewood Cliffs, N.J.: Prentice-Hall, 1974.

Polit, D., & LaFrance, M. Sex differences in reaction to spatial invasion. *Journal of Social Psychology,* 1977, *102,* 59-60.

Pope, B., Blass, T., Siegman, A. W., & Raher, J. Anxiety and depression in speech. *Journal of Consulting and Clinical Psychology,* 1970, *35,* 128-133.

Pope, B., & Siegman, A. W. The effect of therapist verbal activity and specificity on patient productivity and speech disturbance in the initial interview. *Journal of Consulting Psychology,* 1962, *26,* 489.

Post, B., & Hetherington, E. M. Sex differences in the use of proximity and eye contact in judgments of affiliation in preschool children. *Developmental Psychology,* 1974, *10,* 881-889.

Reece, M., & Whitman, R. Expressive movements, warmth and verbal reinforcement. *Journal of Abnormal and Social Psychology,* 1962, *64,* 234-236.

Reich, W. *Character analysis* (3rd ed.). New York: Farrar, Strauss & Giroux, 1949.

Riemer, M. D. Abnormalities of the gaze—A classification. *Psychiatric Quarterly,* 1955, *29,* 659-672.

Robson, K. S. The role of eye-to-eye contact in maternal-infant attachment. *Journal of Child Psychology and Psychiatry,* 1967, *8,* 13-25.

Rohner, R. P. Proxemics and stress: An empirical study of the relationship between living space and roommate turnover. *Human Relations,* 1974, *27,* 697-702.

Rosenfeld, H. M. Effect of approval-seeking induction on interpersonal proximity. *Psychological Reports,* 1965, *17,* 120-122.

Rosenfeld, H. M. Approval-seeking and approval-inducing functions of verbal and nonverbal responses in the dyad. *Journal of Personality and Social Psychology,* 1966, *4,* 597-605.

Rosenfeld, H. M. Conversational control functions of nonverbal behavior. In A. Siegman & S. Feldstein (Eds.), *Nonverbal behavior and communication.* Hillsdale, N.J.: Lawrence Erlbaum Associates, in press.

Rosenthal, R. *Experimenter effects in behavioral research.* New York: Appleton-Century-Crofts, 1966.

Rosenthal, R., Hall, J. A., DiMatteo, R., Rogers, P. L., & Archer, D. *Sensitivity to non-verbal communication: The PONS test.* Unpublished monograph, Harvard University, 1977.

Rubin, Z. Measurement of romantic love. *Journal of Personality and Social Psychology,* 1970, *16,* 265–273.

Ruesch, J., & Bateson, G. *Communication: The social matrix of psychiatry* (Rev. ed.). New York: Norton, 1968.

Ruesch, J., & Kees, W. *Nonverbal communication.* Berkeley: University of California Press, 1956.

Russo, N. F. Eye contact, interpersonal distance, and the equilibrium theory. *Journal of Personality and Social Psychology,* 1975, *31,* 497–502.

Rutter, D. R. Visual interaction in recently admitted and chronic long-stay schizophrenic patients. *British Journal of Social and Clinical Psychology,* 1976, *15,* 295–303.

Rutter, D. R., & Stephenson, G. M. Visual interaction in a group of schizophrenic and depressive patients. *British Journal of Social and Clinical Psychology,* 1972, *11,* 57–65.

Ryen, A. H., & Kahn, A. Effects of intergroup orientation on group attitudes and proxemic behavior. *Journal of Personality and Social Psychology,* 1975, *31,* 302–310.

Sachs, J., Lieberman, P., & Erickson, D. Anatomical and cultural determinants of male and female speech. In R. W. Shuy & R. W. Fasold (Eds.), *Language attitudes: Current trends and prospects.* Washington, D. C.: Georgetown University Press, 1973.

Sainsbury, P. Gestural movement during psychiatric interview. *Psychosomatic Medicine,* 1955, *17,* 458–469.

Saitz, R. L., & Cervenka, E. J. *Handbook of gestures: Colombia and the United States.* The Hague: Mouton, 1972.

Savitsky, J. C., Izard, C. E., Kotsch, W. E., & Christy, L. Aggressor's response to the victim's facial expression of emotion. *Journal of Research in Personality,* 1974, *7,* 346–357.

Scaife, M., & Bruner, J. S. The capacity for joint visual attention in the infant. *Nature,* 1975, *253,* 265–266.

Schaffer, H. R., & Emerson, P. E. Patterns of response to physical contact in early human development. *Journal of Child Psychology and Psychiatry,* 1964, *5,* 1–13.

Scheflen, A. E. The significance of posture in communication systems. *Psychiatry,* 1964, *27,* 316–331.

Scheflen, A. E. Natural history method in psychotherapy: Communication research. In L. A. Gottschalk & A. H. Auerbach (Eds.), *Methods of research in psychotherapy.* New York: Appleton-Century-Crofts, 1966.

Scheflen, A. E. Human communication: Behavioral programs and their integration in interaction. *Behavioral Science,* 1968, *13,* 44–55.

Scheier, M. F., Fenigstein, A., & Buss, A. H. Self-awareness and physical aggression. *Journal of Experimental Social Psychology,* 1974, *10,* 264–273.

Scherer, K. R. Acoustic concomitants of emotional dimensions: Judging affect from synthesized tone sequences. In S. Weitz (Ed.), *Nonverbal communication.* New York: Oxford University Press, 1974.

Scherer, K. R., London, H., & Wolf, J. J. The voice of confidence: Paralinguistic cues and audience evaluation. *Journal of Research in Personality,* 1973, *7,* 31–44.

Scherer, S. E. Proxemic behavior of primary school children as a function of their socioeconomic class and subculture. *Journal of Personality and Social Psychology*, 1974, *29*, 800–805.

Scherwitz, L., & Helmreich, R. Interactive effects of eye contact and verbal content on interpersonal attraction in dyads. *Journal of Personality and Social Psychology*, 1973, *25*, 6–14.

Schiffenbauer, A. When will people use facial information to attribute emotion? The effect of judge's emotional state and intensity of facial expression on attribution of emotion. *Representative Research in Social Psychology*, 1974, *5*, 47–53.

Schiffenbauer, A., & Schiavo, R. S. Physical distance and attraction: An intensification effect. *Journal of Experimental Social Psychology*, 1976, *12*, 274–282.

Schulman, D., & Shontz, F. C. Body posture and thinking. *Perceptual and Motor Skills*, 1971, *32*, 27–33.

Schutz, W. C. *The interpersonal underworld.* Palo Alto, Calif.: Science and Behavior Books, 1966.

Schwartz, G. E., Fair, P. L., Salt, P., Mandel, M. R., & Klerman, G. L. Facial muscle patterning to affective imagery in depressed and non-depressed subjects. *Science*, 1976, *192*, 489–491.

Seaford, H. W., Jr. Facial expression dialect: An example. In A. Kendon, R. M. Harris, & M. R. Key (Eds.), *Organization of behavior in face-to-face interaction.* The Hague: Mouton, 1975.

Sechrest, L. Nonreactive assessment of attitudes. In E. P. Willems & H. L. Rausch (Eds.), *Naturalistic viewpoints in psychological research.* New York: Holt, Rinehart & Winston, 1969.

Seta, J. J., Paulus, P. B., & Schkade, J. K. Effects of group size and proximity under cooperative and competitive conditions. *Journal of Personality and Social Psychology*, 1976, *34*, 47–53.

Sherif, M. *The psychology of social norms.* New York: Harper, 1936.

Silveira, J. Thoughts on the politics of touch. Eugene, Oreg.: *Women's Press,* 1972. *1*, 13.

Smith, W. J., Chase, J., & Lieblich, A. K. Tongue showing: A facial display of humans and other primate species. *Semiotica,* 1974, *11*, 201–246.

Sommer, R. Studies in personal space. *Sociometry,* 1959, *22*, 247–260.

Sommer, R. *Personal space.* Englewood Cliffs, N. J.: Prentice-Hall, 1969.

Sommer, R., & Becker, F. D. Territorial defense and the good neighbor. *Journal of Personality and Social Psychology,* 1969, *11*, 85–92.

Soskin, W. F., & John, V. P. The study of spontaneous talk. In R. Barker (Ed.,) *The stream of behavior.* New York: Appleton-Century-Crofts, 1963.

Sparhawk, C. M. P. *Linguistics and gesture: An application of linguistic theory to the study of Persian emblems.* Unpublished doctoral dissertation, University of Michigan, 1976.

Spiegel, J. P., & Machotka, P. *Messages of the body.* New York: Free Press, 1974.

Spitz, R., & Wolf, K. The smiling response: A contribution to the ontogenesis of social relations. *Genetic Psychology Monographs,* 1946, *34*, 57–125.

Stang, D. J. Effect of interaction rate on ratings of leadership and liking. *Journal of Personality and Social Psychology,* 1973, *27*, 405–408.

Stephan, F. F. The relative rate of communication between members of small groups. *American Sociological Review,* 1952, *17*, 482–486.

Stephenson, G. M., Ayling, K., & Rutter, D. R. The role of visual communication in social exchange. *British Journal of Social and Clinical Psychology,* 1976, *15,* 113–120.

Stern, D. N. Mother and infant at play: The dyadic interaction involving facial, vocal and gaze behavior. In M. Lewis & L. A. Rosenblum (Eds.), *The effect of the infant on its caregiver.* New York: Wiley, 1974.

Stern, D. N., Jaffe, J., Beebe, B., & Bennett, S. L. Vocalizing in unison and in alternation: Two modes of communication within the mother-infant dyad. *Annals of the New York Academy of Sciences,* 1975, *263,* 89–100.

Strodtbeck, F. L. Husband-wife interaction over revealed differences. *American Sociological Review,* 1951, *16,* 468–473.

Strodtbeck, F. L., & Hook, L. H. The social dimensions of a twelve-man jury table. *Sociometry,* 1961, *24,* 297–315.

Strodtbeck, F. L., & Mann, R. D. Sex role differentiation in jury deliberations. *Sociometry,* 1956, *19,* 3–11.

Strongman, K. T., & Chapness, B. G. Dominance hierarchies and conflict in eye contact. *Acta Psychologica,* 1968, *28,* 376–386.

Suci, G. J. The validity of pause as an index of units in language. *Journal of Verbal Learning and Verbal Behavior,* 1967, *6,* 26–32.

Sundstrom, E., & Altman, I. Field study of territorial behavior and dominance. *Journal of Personality and Social Psychology,* 1974, *30,* 115–124.

Sundstrom, E., & Altman, I. Personal space and interpersonal relationships: Research review and theoretical model. *Human Ecology,* 1976, *4,* 47–67.

Swacker, M. The sex of the speaker as a sociolinguistic variable. In B. Thorne & N. Henley (Eds.), *Language and sex: Difference and dominance.* Rowley, Mass.: Newbury House, 1975.

Taylor, H. M. American and Japanese nonverbal communication. In J. V. Neustupny (Ed.), *Papers in Japanese Linguistics 3.* Melbourne: Monash University, 1974.

Tesch, F. E., Huston, T. L., & Indenbaum, E. A. Attitude similarity, attraction, and physical proximity in a dynamic space. *Journal of Applied Social Psychology,* 1973, *3,* 63–72.

Thigpen, C. H., & Cleckley, H. *The three faces of Eve.* Kingsport, Tenn.: Kingsport Press, 1957.

Thorne, B., & Henley, N. (Eds.). *Language and sex: Difference and dominance.* Rowley, Mass.: Newbury House, 1975.

Touhey, J. C. Effects of dominance and competence on heterosexual attraction. *British Journal of Social and Clinical Psychology,* 1974, *13,* 22–26.

Tronick, E. D., Als, H., & Brazelton, T. B. Mutuality in mother-infant interaction. *Journal of Communication,* 1977, *27,* 74–79.

Turner, J. le B. Schizophrenics as judges of vocal expressions of emotional meaning. In J. Davitz (Ed.), *The communication of emotional meaning.* New York: McGraw-Hill, 1964.

van Hooff, J. A. R. A. M. A comparative approach to the phylogeny of laughter and smiling. In R. A. Hinde (Ed.), *Non-verbal communication.* Cambridge, England: Cambridge University Press, 1972.

Ward, C. D. Seating arrangement and leadership emergence in small discussion groups. *Journal of Social Psychology,* 1968, *74,* 83–90.

Washburn, P. V., & Hakel, M. D. Visual cues and verbal content as influences on impressions formed after simulated employment interviews. *Journal of Applied Psychology,* 1973, *58,* 137–141.

Waters, E., Matas, L., & Sroufe, L. A. Infants' reactions to an approaching stranger:

Description, validation and functional significance of wariness. *Child Development,* 1975, *46,* 348-356.

Watson, O. M., & Graves, T. D. Quantitative research in proxemic behavior. *American Anthropologist,* 1966, *68,* 971-985.

Watzlawick, P., Beavin, J. H., & Jackson, D. D. *Pragmatics of human communication.* New York: Norton, 1967.

Waxer, P. Nonverbal cues for depression. *Journal of Abnormal Psychology,* 1974, *83,* 319-322.

Webb, J. T. Interview synchrony: An investigation of two speech rate measures in an automated standardized interview. In A. W. Siegman & B. Pope (Eds.), *Studies in dyadic communication: Proceedings of a research conference on the interview.* New York: Pergamon, 1970.

Weeks, T. E. Speech registers in young children. *Child Development,* 1971, *42,* 1119-1131.

Weitz, S. Attitude, voice and behavior: A repressed affect model of interracial interaction. *Journal of Personality and Social Psychology,* 1972, *24,* 14-21.

Weitz, S. Sex differences in nonverbal communication. *Sex Roles,* 1976, *2,* 175-184.

Welkowitz, J., Cariffe, G., & Feldstein, S. *Conversational congruence as a criterion of socialization in children.* Paper presented at the meeting of the American Psychological Association, New Orleans, August 1974.

Werner, H., & Kaplan, B. *Symbolic formation.* New York: Wiley, 1963.

Wexley, K. N., Fugita, S. S., & Malone, M. P. An applicant's nonverbal behavior and student-evaluators' judgments in a structured interview setting. *Psychological Reports,* 1975, *36,* 391-394.

Whalen, C. K., Flowers, J. V., Fuller, M. J., & Jernigan, T. Behavioral studies of personal space during early adolescence. *Man-Environment Systems,* 1975, *5,* 289-297.

Whiting, B., & Edwards, C. A cross-cultural analysis of sex differences in the behavior of children aged 3 through 11. *Journal of Psychology,* 1973, *91,* 171-188.

Wiener, M., Devoe, S., Rubinow, S., & Geller, J. Nonverbal behavior and nonverbal communication. *Psychological Review,* 1972, *79,* 185-214.

Wiens, A. N., Saslow, G., & Matarazzo, J. D. Speech interruption behavior during interviews. *Psychotherapy: Theory, Research, and Practice,* 1966, *3,* 153-158.

Williams, E. An analysis of gaze in schizophrenics. *British Journal of Social and Clinical Psychology,* 1974, *13,* 1-8.

Williams, J. L. Personal space and its relation to extraversion-introversion. *Canadian Journal of Behavioral Science,* 1971, *3,* 156-160.

Willis, F. N., Jr. Initial speaking distance as a function of the speakers' relationship. *Psychonomic Science,* 1966, *5,* 221-222.

Witkin, H. A., Dyk, R. B., Faterson, H. F., Goodenough, D. R., & Karp, S. A. *Psychological differentiation: Studies of development.* New York: Wiley, 1962.

Wolff, P., & Gutstein, J. Effects of induced motor gestures on vocal output. *Journal of Communication,* 1972, *22,* 277-288.

Word, C. O., Zanna, M. P., & Cooper, J. The nonverbal mediation of self-fulfilling prophecies in interracial interaction. *Journal of Experimental Social Psychology,* 1974, *10,* 109-120.

Wylie, L., & Stafford, R. *Beaux gestes: A guide to French body talk,* Cambridge, Mass.: Undergraduate Press, 1977.

Yogman, M. W., Dixon, S., Tronick, E., Adamson, L., Als, H., & Brazelton, T. B. *Development of infant social interaction with fathers.* Paper presented at the meeting of the Eastern Psychological Association, New York, April 1976.

Zaidel, S. F., & Mehrabian, A. The ability to communicate and infer positive and negative attitudes facially and vocally. *Journal of Experimental Research in Personality,* 1969, *3,* 233–241.

Zimmerman, D. H., & West, C. Sex roles, interruptions and silences in conversation. In B. Thorne & N. Henley (Eds.), *Language and sex: Difference and dominance,* Rowley, Mass.: Newbury House, 1975.

Zuckerman, M., Lipets, M. S., Koivumaki, J. H., & Rosenthal, R. Encoding and decoding nonverbal cues of emotion. *Journal of Personality and Social Psychology,* 1975, *32,* 1068–1076.

Author Index

216

Subject Index